Wang Shiwei
and
"Wild Lilies"

The painting on the cover of this book was specially prepared
and dedicated to Ms. Dai Qing by Huang Yong yu, the
world-renowned Chinese artist. The poem in the painting reads:

Perhaps in a hundred years
all sorrow shall be diminished,
but at present, I am
embedded in great sorrow.

Wang Shiwei
and
"Wild Lilies"

Rectification and Purges
in the
Chinese Communist Party
1942-1944

Dai Qing

Edited by David E. Apter and Timothy Cheek
Translated by Nancy Liu and Lawrence R. Sullivan
Documents compiled by Song Jinshou

An East Gate Book

M. E. Sharpe INC.
ARMONK, NEW YORK
LONDON, ENGLAND

An East Gate Book

Copyright © 1994 by M. E. Sharpe, Inc.

An earlier version of this study appeared in *Chinese Studies in History*,
Vol. 26, No. 2 (winter 1992–93), and Vol. 26, No. 3 (spring 1993).

Library of Congress Cataloging-in-Publication Data

Tai, Ch'ing, 1941–
[Wang Shih-wei yü "Yeh pai ho hua". English]
Wang Shiwei and "Wild lilies": rectification and purges in the
Chinese Communist Party, 1942–1944 / Dai Qing; edited by David E.
Apter and Timothy Cheek; translated by Nancy Liu and
Lawrence R. Sullivan; documents compiled by Song Jinshou.
p. cm.
Translation of: Wang Shih-wei yü "Yeh pai ho hua."
"East gate book."
Includes bibliographical references and index.
ISBN 1–56324–256–7 (pbk.)
1. Wang, Shih-wei, 1906–1947. 2. Chung-kuo kung ch'an tang—Discipline.
I. Apter, David Ernest, 1924–
II. Cheek, Timothy.
III. Sung, Chin-shou. IV. Title.
JQ1519.A5T16213 1993
324.251'075—dc20
93–34022
CIP

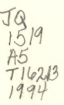

FOR LIU YING

AND THE SPOUSES OF ALL PERSECUTED PERSONS IN CHINA

"Don't cry. Don't laugh. But please do understand."

—Spinoza

"I don't agree with what you say, but I'll fight to death to protect your right to say it."

— Voltaire

"The faults of a gentleman are just like the eclipses of the sun or the moon. If he has faltered, everyone sees it. When he corrects his ways, all will respect him."

— The Analects

Contents

Translators' Note

In translating Dai Qing's *Wang Shiwei and "Wild Lilies"* we have tried through minimal editing to retain Dai Qing's original, if somewhat disjointed, style. Thus there is considerable overlap between the book and the documents she frequently quotes. Ms. Dai's quixotic style of sudden asides on related issues with quick returns to the main narrative may also occasionally confuse the reader. Finally, we have followed Dai Qing in offering few explanatory notes, generally avoiding elaborations on the many subtleties of the text. This is a style generally appreciated by Chinese readers, which led us to offer as literal a translation as possible.

It is unfortunate that much of Dai Qing's biting sarcasm may be lost on those not intimately acquainted with China's current political and journalistic culture, a problem exacerbated by the usual difficulties of rendering political Chinese into English. The word *comrade* (*tongzhi*) in Dai's use seems innocent enough, but when applied to Wang Shiwei's accusers, like Kang Sheng and Hu Qiaomu, the intent is quite sarcastic and scornful.

Other examples abound throughout the text.

The endnotes, bibliography, supplement, and appendixes (A and B) to the book are Dai Qing's. The translators and editors have added only the explanatory footnotes indicated in the text by asterisks (*). Thanks to Professor Timothy Cheek for his assistance in this translation; to Professor David E. Apter for acquiring this most valuable manuscript while in China and for organizing a colloquium "On Revolutionary Intellectuals: The Case of Wang Shiwei," Whitney Center for the Humanities, Yale University, November 13–14, 1992; to Professor Anthony Saich for permission to use, with slight modifications, his translation of Wen Jize's "Diary of a Struggle"; and to Mr. Song Jinshou of the CCP Organization Department who compiled many of the documents and composed the introductions in Part Two. The translators also wish to thank Professor Harriet C. Mills, University of Michigan, for her generous assistance in translating and editing critical parts of the manuscript. Finally, we are all indebted to Ms. Dai Qing, whose tenacity and search for the truth has made this a most enriching, though often sobering, enterprise.

Nancy (Yang) Liu, Columbia University
Lawrence R. Sullivan, Adelphi University and
the East Asian Institute, Columbia University

Preface

After hurrying day and night to Shiyan City,* Hubei Province, two cadres from the People's Republic Public Security Department announced to the elderly woman that they had been looking for the "Decision on Rehabilitation" which restored the word *comrade* (*tongzhi*) to her long-dead husband.

Hearing the appellation *tongzhi,* Liu Ying, now eighty-five years old, could not hold back her tears. That was 1991.

It had been forty-nine years since "comrade" had been struck from her husband's name, and it had been forty-three years since her husband's head had been removed as a result of losing that appellation.

A sum of money—ten thousand yuan—came along with the rehabilitation. Liu Ying was at a loss trying to figure out what the money was for and how the authorities had decided on this amount.

Liu Ying did not ask any questions and refused the money.

Her son suggested, however, that it be donated to the technology library of the city where he was teaching, under the condition that the flyleaf of all the books purchased with the funds be inscribed "In Commemoration of Wang Shiwei's Rehabilitation."

Liu Ying and the two Public Security Department agents agreed, but the "relevant organization of the city" found the wording inappropriate and objected.

A local cadre in the Writer's Union then suggested putting the money into a literary and artistic fund that he administered. Each year when the money was awarded, the words *Wang Shiwei Fund* could be mentioned in passing.

Both parties agreed.

The famous Wang Shiwei case had now finally come to an end, and the connection with future generations is this paltry sum of money. . . .

---

*The medium-sized city known for its automobile industry where Liu Ying (Wang Shiwei's widow) resides.

Probably, on some day in the future a little girl in Shiyan will be honored for her outstanding performance in dancing or singing. Upon receiving a certificate of merit, she will come across the name of a man whose life and death and the struggle after his death will be unknown to her. In actuality, that was the ugliest nightmare in human history—the smothering of dignity and freedom of thought in the name of revolution. The nightmare started when Wang Shiwei, the stranger, was persecuted; the announcement of his wrongful persecution could be the beginning of the end of this nightmare.

Dai Qing
Harvard University, Spring 1992

Introduction: "The Trial"

DAVID E. APTER AND TIMOTHY CHEEK

Imagine a Marxist militant holed up in the caves in Yan'an during the most difficult days of the period, beginning a devastating critical analysis of the situation with a prose poem to the woman he loves: "As I walked alone on the river bank, seeing the old fashioned cotton shoes of a female comrade in front of me reminded me of one who used to wear this type of shoes, comrade Li Fen—the oldest most beloved friend in my life. Whenever I think of her, my heart pounds and my blood quickens." So begins "Wild Lilies" with a personal lament for a revolutionary martyr. In the best Lu Xun tradition, it is a cry from the heart. It personalizes the world of stylized public experience. It punctures the language of political illusion. It breaks through the conspiracy of personal silences and by so doing deliberately challenges the official position on virtually every aspect of social and political life in Yan'an, not least of all the role of literature and art, and the critical responsibilities of the revolutionary intellectual.

Yan'an made extravagant claims to egalitarianism, between officers and men, and men and women. In 1942, Wang Shiwei punctured such claims and exposed the differences between those in and out of power, particularly the habitual and unequal access to (and use of) women, food, uniforms, and shelter. Wang asserted that in a society in which equality is a chief moral claim, the principle on which the nature of truth itself is to be re-rendered, transformed, and redeemed, cannot—indeed must not—be compromised by such hypocrisies. Extending his critique further, to the heartland of socialism—the Soviet Union—he cast doubt on the validity of the Moscow trials. He flatly said that the Kirov murder was a frame-up, Radek innocent, Zinoviev not guilty, and Stalin a highly dubious character. In so doing he exposed the Stalinist aspects of Maoism, despite Mao's separation from Stalin's views about China.

Finally, Wang Shiwei claimed moral and ideological autonomy within the communist movement to criticize abuses of power and to offer, publicly, alternative policies. Wang claimed this authority on the basis of the romantic and pure motivations of the artist. He compared the qualities of the artist to the limitations of the politician in his 1942 essay, "Politicians, Artists." In this and other writings, Wang claimed, and by most reports attracted, the support of idealistic youth. Wang confronted the party with its own ideals and its hypocrisy.

Wang Shiwei was to pay for this with his life. His was one of the four celebrated "cases" that box the compass of Mao's monopoly of power (the others being Zhang Guotao, Liu Zhidan, and Wang Ming). Wang Shiwei embodied the Lu Xun tradition by representing a radical critical view of daily life at odds with a radical conformism. Wang also embodied the fundamental cosmopolitanism and international worldview of the New Culture Movement.

Yet at the beginning, rectification was not targeted at such a relatively insignificant person as Wang Shiwei. According to Dai Qing, the real targets were Mao's major political competitors, the Russian Returned Students (Internationalists)—Wang Ming, Zhang Wentian, and Qin Bangxian, whose political theories and organizational ideas directly challenged Mao's growing personal autocracy. "Wang Shiwei and his lot had nothing whatsoever to do with this campaign: they were neither its target nor its chief supporters. Their task was simple: all they had to do was listen to the relevant reports, applaud on cue, and write an ideological report or two on demand. That was all."[1] But once Wang Shiwei took the CCP's call for speaking out seriously and provoked popular reaction in Yan'an with his cutting "critical essay" (*zawen*), the party, Mao stated, now had a "target" for its "ideological struggle." This translator of Trotsky's works, a cultural worker at the Academy for Marxist-Leninist Studies (the very place where the documents and procedures for the campaign were being prepared) had gone far beyond the role of gadfly to argue that so great were the discrepancies between theory and practice in Yan'an that the entire revolutionary enterprise was becoming (especially for the young) an exercise in illusion. It was not accidental that Wang Shiwei began his critique in a personalized, intimate, and individualized way (indeed, the way of liberalism) just at the moment when the party leadership had decided to enforce a radically depersonalized system, substituting discipline for intimacy and collective self-sacrifice for individual choice, within the tutelary environment of rectification. Like the student standing up against the tank in Tiananmen Square so many years later, Wang Shiwei in his time stood—stubbornly, and almost alone—against the apotheosis of the collective spirit and in principled terms.

Wang Shiwei was undoubtedly an irritating man. Those who knew him describe him as abrasive. He was one of the "four eccentrics" who, like the "five olds" and the "nine beauties," had already become distinctive in their differences. Moreover, he was stubborn, and when friendly colleagues pointed out the error of minding the flaws of other people's ways, he refused to listen. In the end he tried to resign from the party, but this would have been such a slap in the face that it was not allowed. Instead he was made to stand trial. The trial itself was a foretaste of things to come—not once but many times, in the People's Republic.

It was said that Mao had considerable respect for Wang Shiwei and personally read Wang's essays (even though he was infuriated by Wang), and that he ordered that Wang not be killed. During his imprisonment Wang was, from time to time, allowed to be interviewed by reporters. It was not until 1947 that he was executed (probably on orders from Kang Sheng, who could hardly have acted on his own initiative) either by Li Kenong as Guilhem Fabre would have it or, as Dai Qing and Wen Jize suggest, by Xu Haidong or He Long.[2]

Dai Qing's book, in effect, memorializes Wang Shiwei in several ways. First, it makes him into a symbol for the sacrifice of China's intellectuals to Mao's version of the truth. There is a sense in which the trial of Wang Shiwei was the first attempt to orchestrate the ideas laid down in the Yan'an Forum on Literature and Art in May 1942 and other of Mao's crucial texts, elevating them into a form of truth that could tolerate no others. Wang Shiwei's resistance became the focal point for an attack so carefully orchestrated that it created its own terminology, discourse, and demonology. Wang became the stylized foil to the party's final solution for outspoken intellectuals—democratic centralism.

What did he do wrong? Well, nothing and everything. He was candid in his belief about what a good communist was, a subject of great moment and discussion during this period. All who defined the good communist mentioned a certain stalwart integrity. But also required was a certain kind of discipline, so that part of what it meant to be a good communist was keeping your mouth shut against your own judgment in the interests of the higher truth. It was that second aspect that did not stick with Wang.

Wang Shiwei was outraged by false pieties. He saw inequalities and took them personally: sexual inequality, the differential access of senior leaders to younger women, social inequality, the differential access to food, uniforms, sleeping quarters.[3] He wrote about these things elegantly and passionately. Even the title of his polemic "Wild Lilies," which caused such a furor, was carefully chosen, for the wild lily is both beautiful and also bitter, a medicine.

On one level, the case of Wang Shiwei is an example of one of the few genuine intellectuals in Yan'an (best known as a translator) who became a symbol of resistance to Mao's definition of how the intellectual's role should be subordinated to the revolution as laid down in Mao's Yan'an Forum. Wang Shiwei, stalwartly rejecting subordination, became something of a hero. The putative representative of the Lu Xun intellectuals (one of the few such intellectuals who went to Yan'an rather than to Chungking or Kunming, Yunnan), his activities coincided with a preliminary phase of ideological purification, from 1939 to 1941, extending as well into the first phase of the rectification campaign.

The latter began on February 1, 1942, with a speech by Mao ("Reform in Learning, the Party, and Literature") and culminated in June 1942 with a series of anti-Wang Shiwei meetings.[4] This period became known as the "expose one's thoughts" period, or "the exposure phase." Emphasizing openness, encouraging wall posters and bold speaking, this period (like that of the "hundred flowers" a decade and a half later) eventually led to a crackdown. For Kang Sheng, head of the secret police, "half-heartedness" and "two-heartedness" (i.e., a lack of genuine revolutionary fervor and antirevolutionary feelings, respectively) were suddenly revealed and he moved against both kinds of backsliders as well as spies, enemies, and "Trotskyites." Where such enemies were, in fact, lacking, Kang created them. Wang Shiwei, and his purported "Five Member Anti-Party Gang" revealed in Dai Qing's book were among the first to be pressed into such "service" for the sake of the revolution.

Wang had joined the party in 1926, working mainly in Shanghai. He became involved with some of the Trotskyist opposition, translated some of Trotsky's writing, and thus gave some substance to the later charge that he was a "Trotskyite" (a charge now recognized as an "error" by the Central Committee).[5] He went to Yan'an in 1936 to become a research officer in the Academy for Marxist-Leninist Studies (which subsequently became the Central Research Institute), and worked mainly as a translator.

Wang became embroiled in a dispute with Chen Boda (later to become one of Mao's personal secretaries) over the nature and content of revolutionary literature. This debate followed the publication of Mao's revolutionary blueprint, "On New Democracy," in January 1940. In view of the importance attached by Mao in this essay to literary texts, this touched an extremely sensitive nerve. Moreover, it evoked an early conflict over the same issue between the party and China's greatest modern writer, Lu Xun.

Lu Xun, by far the most outstanding among the radical intellectuals representative of the New Culture Movement and also a source of inspiration to "real" intellectuals, had never taken kindly to the "discipline" the party wanted to impose on intellectuals. In Shanghai where he lived he ran afoul of the local party cultural czar in the CCP, Zhou Yang. Indeed, in an article Lu Xun wrote in Shanghai he characterized Zhou Yang as a dandy, a fop, and a vain man who liked fast cars and was ignorant of culture and literature. Zhou attacked Lu (who by this time was very ill), removing him from the Left-Wing Writers Association which Lu himself had founded. Shortly afterward Lu Xun died and Zhou Yang repaired to Yan'an. When Mao established an academy for artists and writers, he named it after Lu Xun and made Zhou Yang the director. It was a gesture not lost on Wang Shiwei.

Wang was a dissenter from the start. He associated himself with Ding Ling and Liu Xuewei, both editors of the Literature and Art Column in *Liberation Daily*.[6] Liu Xuewei wrote an article on "Revolutionary Literature," published in June 1941, in which he criticized revolutionary literature as coarse, dull, direct, and inferior and urging a higher artistic level. This article was followed up by another on June 7, calling for freedom of thought as the basis of the New Democracy. On September 22 another article argued that too much emphasis on politics lowered the development of the arts.

In October 1941, Ding Ling called for the revival of *zawen* in Yan'an. In a *Liberation Daily* article entitled "We Need Critical Essays" she said: "I think it would do us the most good if we emulate his [Lu Xun's] steadfastness in facing the truth, his courage to speak out for the sake of truth, and his fearlessness. This age of ours still needs critical essays, a weapon that we should never lay down."[7]

Shortly after the rectification campaign began in February 1942, Ding Ling published her famous article "Thoughts on March 8" (International Women's Day), that attacked the party for its treatment of women. Mao was quite upset by the article. A few days later Ding Ling was dismissed as an editor of the Literature and Art Column, and a few days after that Wang Shiwei took up her call and published "Wild Lilies."

It proved to be a bombshell. Published in two parts on March 13 and 23 in *Liberation Daily*, it was (according to Cheek) modeled after Lu Xun's 1926 satirical essay "A Rose Without Blooms."[8] Attacking Mao's taste for beautiful women, it offered as an alternative to Jiang Qing (Mao's controversial new young wife) an exemplary model of a woman revolutionary executed in 1928. Wang attacked dancing and the parties that the leadership became noted for, while soldiers died at the front. He parodied Mao's style. He implied that the three classes of clothing and five classes of food, which differentiated people at different levels of rank, represented unjustified privilege, indeed class, a charge that struck Mao's rawest nerve.

Coming as it did in the context of other criticisms of party policy in Yan'an, "Wild Lilies" represented the rebellion of the intellectuals, a subversion of rectification away from Mao's planned attack on rival Wang Ming. It invoked the spirit of Lu Xun, arousing great concern on the part of the senior party cadres. All the more because Wang had already become something of a local hero by having already been thrust into the rectification campaign in its first phase, i.e., during the time when many people put up dissenting wall posters. So alarmed was the party at the time that it proposed to establish a Rectification Campaign Examination Committee to monitor wall posters.

Wang, at that time thirty-six years old, vigorously opposed such a committee. When it became clear that one would be established he insisted that its members be chosen by a vote, and the directors of all departments and the president of the Central Research Institute as well. He also proposed that the writers of wall posters remain anonymous to protect the rights of the writer. Wang's proposals were overwhelmingly supported. Elections were carried out, and while those elected were not favored by Wang Shiwei and his group, the latter were jubilant at this "triumph of democracy." Wang continued to write articles attacking Luo Mai (Li Weihan), the director of the Institute. He began a wall poster newspaper series called *Arrow and Target*. When some of its articles were posted outside the southern gate of Yan'an City, "so many people reading made it like a temple fair." Wang Shiwei became a star in Yan'an.[9]

It did not take long for the party to react. On May 27, 1942, the "struggle session" with Wang Shiwei began. This amazing show trial is recorded in the pages of the *Liberation Daily* in late June 1942 as "Diary of a Struggle" (Document 2.1). Among the charges were that Wang had associations with "Trotskyites," that he claimed Stalin's nature was not "praiseworthy," and that Karl Radek (accused of complicity in the Kirov assassination) was a good person. More astounding, he charged that the Comintern itself must be held accountable for the failure of the Chinese revolution of 1927 (a charge also brought by Trotsky); that the trial of Zinoviev and the accusation that he was a traitor needed to be taken with a grain of salt; and that parts of Trotsky's theory were correct. He was also accused of slandering party leaders by calling them corrupt, that he disrupted party unity, and that he used the term "hardbones" (strong willed) in reference to his friends and "softbones" (weak willed) to other comrades. Finally, it was said that Wang's articles slandered the party, and that, describing himself as a modern Lu Xun, he had called upon the youth to shake hands with him.

The results of the attack were mixed. A good many sided wih Wang Shiwei. To correct the confusion, everyone was instructed by the CCP Politburo Standing Committee to read Lenin's "Party Organization and Literature," Lu Xun's speech at the Founding Congress of the Left-Wing Writers' Association, Mao's conclusion to the Yan'an Forum on Literature and Art, the first section of chapter ten in Stalin's *History of the CPSU (Bolsheviks), Short Course*, and selections from the second volume of *Selected Works of Stalin* (about crushing opposition cliques).

Wang attempted to resign from the party. His request was refused. In his subsequent testimony he withdrew his request. Most importantly, Wang refused to admit mistakes. Without confession he was denied redemption. Others, such as Ding Ling, recanted, did penance in the countryside, and were forgiven by the party. Wang Shiwei, on the other hand, was vilified by Kang Sheng, Chen Boda, and others as a filthy character. Invectives, filthy puns, and animal names—linguistic dehumanization—showered upon the unrepentant Wang. He was no longer human, but he was still useful—Wang had become a negative model, a key (if highly undesirable) role in all CCP rectification campaigns.[10] Finally, all the members of the Central Research Institute demanded that Wang Shiwei be expelled from the party. On June 11, the last day of the proceedings, Ding Ling recanted her "Thoughts on March 8" and also attacked Wang Shiwei for insulting "the literature and arts circle."

Wang Shiwei was put in prison. Mao did not want him killed. He wanted to use Wang Shiwei as the negative model during the rectification campaign while he was building up the "Yan'an Way" as the obverse. Despite explicit orders that he not be killed (Wang was weak and sick in prison), when Yan'an was attacked by the Nationalist Forces in 1947, he was evacuated to a rear area and summarily executed.

There is a secret history of Wang's demise between the summer of 1942 and his execution five years later. Dai Qing's narrative and the documents and interviews she collects reveal that the literary rectification of spring 1942 is directly and inextricably linked to the now notorious "rescue campaign" spy purges of fall 1942 and 1943. Wang Shiwei became the first "leader of an antiparty clique" to be used in an inner-party purge. Dai Qing uncovers the "Five Member Anti-Party Gang" around Wang Shiwei that Kang Sheng and Yang Shangkun concocted in order to push forward the brutal cadre investigation campaign. This purge campaign quickly got out of hand, degenerating into a vicious witch hunt in which thousands of party cadres joined Wang Shiwei's fate without his heresy. The spy campaign was, in the opinion of Frederick Teiwes, the only immediate failure of Mao's Yan'an policies and one from which Mao quickly distanced himself (leaving the blame on an appropriate target, secret police chief Kang Sheng).[11]

What this "Five Member Anti-Party Gang" ruse demonstrates is a troubling link between the idealism of rectification (enshrined in Mark Selden's *The Yenan Way*) and the ugliness of the later purges. Despite its harsh treatment of intellectuals, the Yan'an Rectification Movement is broadly acknowledged as a key source of the CCP's ultimate victory.[12] Regardless of our values today, many patriotic Chinese, including intellectuals and writers, felt the Yan'an rectification was at least necessary under the circumstances (not to mention those who thought it was a great idea!).[13] But no one liked the spy campaign, and the party went to pains to hide it from public view. Dai Qing's work, particularly the documents she presents us, brings to historical consciousness the "shadow self" of the Yan'an "hero"—showing that the *salvation* of rectification is inseparably linked to the *inquisition* of Mao's and Kang Sheng's spy campaign. This is not only of historical significance in our understanding of Yan'an and the communist movement. It is systemic. The abuses of the Cultural Revolution—the "mass criticism," the fabricated "antiparty cliques," the witch hunts—as well as the ludicrous but tragic purges of writers and journalists in the 1980s (e.g., "anti-Spiritual Pollution" and "anti-bourgeois liberalization") are not examples of the violation of the Yan'an Way; they are the expression of Yan'an's dark side, as authentic a part of Yan'an's inner "symbolic capital" as the outer manifestations of frugality, self-sacrifice, and national salvation. But for that symbolic capital to work, to give the party legitimacy, the shadow self must be politically subconscious. Dai Qing is an unwelcome political psychiatrist, revealing Yan'an as a Dr. Jekyll and Mr. Hyde Janus-faced god. Thus, with the insight Dai Qing provides, the narrative of Chinese communism's decline is less a story of betrayal or lost idealism than tragedy playing out its initial flaws.

Wang's 1942 trial is, of course, Kafkaesque. Moreover, it throws into relief something that was of concern to Walter Benjamin, the political importance of the art of the interpreter, the one who probes the inner meanings of language. Wang's crime was not simply translating Trotsky, or even being a "Trotskyite." It was the role of critic as such that was at fault. He refused complicity in converting the communist intellectual pedigree into a Chinese mold. He knew what Mao was doing to the original texts that became the required reading of rectification. He saw how Mao was using the intellectuals, in effect violating them by attacking the principal function of intellectual understanding: free inquiry. Wang's major crime was that as a principled and radical intellectual he judged Mao, something the latter could not tolerate.

The trial also tells us a good deal about the uses Mao made in Yan'an of educational structures. These became the building blocks of social structure in the PRC, serving two purposes, first, to indoctrinate in such a way as to make each individual fulfilled. Education was an overcoming process, mind taking possession, especially for the dispossessed at the hands of imperialists, the Japanese, and the Nationalists as well. One learned what one believed as fundamental truths. Second, these institutions served to separate and reallocate those whose affiliations had been to other communist leaders, Wang Ming, Zhang

Guotao, and to other regiments and armies, especially the Fourth Front Army. Under the rubric of education, both institutions and the curriculum provided for an exceptional form of teaching, a kind of exegetical bonding aimed at producing a new discourse community, mythic in what it retrieved, utopic in what it claimed. Westerners will have to think of Franklin Roosevelt, Winston Churchill, or Charles De Gaulle to imagine how powerful this bond was.

The Wang Shiwei affair marked a kind of turning point in Chinese communist history. It continues to represent the guilty knowledge of the present leadership even though the present regime, which finally rehabilitated Wang Shiwei in 1991, has admitted that Wang was not a Trotskyite, one of the principal charges against him.[14] But they are not likely to dwell on the implications of their persecution of Wang since now, more than ever, Wang Shiwei raises up the specter of the revolutionary critic as the symbol of man's fate in communist China. By daring to attack the redeemers on the grounds that to realize the promise of Marxism requires that everyone, high and low, follow the same rules it was not only the substance of Wang's critique that Mao found objectionable, it was Wang's presumptuousness. He not only dared to judge those in power who claimed a monopoly of truth, he found them morally wanting. Two generations later so would the students in Tiananmen Square.

The case has been exhumed lately in China largely through the efforts of the remarkable woman journalist Dai Qing. But it had already aroused considerable interest among American and French specialists on China.[15] Those who have written extensively on the case include such scholars as Kyna Rubin, Timothy Cheek, Merle Goldman, Geremie Barmé, and Guilhem Fabre, whose book *Genèse du pouvoir et de l'opposition en Chine: Le printemps de Yan'an* contains the fullest discussion of this tragedy. Each has added something to our knowledge of Wang, his writings, and the role he played. All show very well how, in a country where size and numbers are numbing, individuals can still count as individuals. Fabre indeed, evaluating him in terms of subsequent events, shows just how right Wang Shiwei was on almost all counts, and how wrong the authorities.

No outsider, however, could possibly have Dai Qing's intimate knowledge of the case. Persisting in her inquiry despite the resistance of the authorities, she eventually gains access to and acquaintance with people and documents dealing with the critical events of the time. Indeed, at some considerable personal risk, she probes deeply into the case through the prism of what might be called the utopia moment of the Chinese revolution, and there she finds fatal flaws.

Her discussion avoids the too easy kind of posthistorical judgment with which succeeding generations rewrite history according to their own hindsight, preferring instead to go back to the source to show the deliberate fabrications, the distortions of the truth that occurred, and not least the acquiescence of those who represented themselves as heroes.

Through the documents in the second part of this book, one watches the inevitable as individual after individual is mobilized, and the charges against Wang Shiwei intensify and accumulate. The language changes, and the tone. From opinion it goes to accusation, to anger, to fury, to execration, and to execution. We watch everyone get caught up in the frenzy, including those who should have known better. Mao took exceptional care to undermine and destroy the support that Wang Shiwei originally had on his side. One after the other, Wang's friends turn against him, even Wen Jize, who in the end despite initial support for Wang comes to believe that he was wrong, and worse, that he was behaving badly.[16] By the time Wang's "trial" finishes, everyone has given evidence against him, even his compatriot Ding Ling.

Reading this book is like having a peek into a forbidden archive. History is returned to itself but not on a flat plane. One can distinguish the many and complex "levels" of events—the relationship between symbol, discourse, and the exercise of sheer manipulative power. Mao does not interfere directly. But his presence looms over the proceedings, a kind of intimate distancing that was his style during the Yan'an years.

In fact, Dai Qing has given us two books: a powerful post-Mao reportage of the Wang Shiwei case and a collection of important documents on dissent and purges in the CCP during one of its formative stages. Her narration has been published in China and in Hong Kong, but the second part, the documents (compiled by Song Jinshou), appears for the first time in print in this English translation.[17]

Dai Qing's style of narration and documentation is a well-known genre in state socialist societies; it is the classic rectification format that was applied originally to Wang Shiwei. Cheek calls it "textual analysis," in which full or lengthy excerpts of offending writing is provided along with a harsh analysis which, to us at least, appears illogical and forced. For example, at the Central Research Institute meetings recounted in "Diary of a Struggle" in 1942, cadres were provided with full texts of Wang's writings and later, cadres across North China were given a similar opportunity in Fan Wenlan's 1944 compilation of the anti-Wang essays from *Liberation Daily* (Wang's "Wild Lilies" was appended, in full, at the end of the book).[18] This same genre was used over and over again in the PRC—against Hu Feng in 1955, in the antirightist campaign of 1957 (against Li Xiling, for example), in the Cultural Revolution (Red Guard "reference copies" of *Three Family Village* essays by Wu Han, Deng Tuo, and Liao Mosha), and in the post-Mao period (the public collection of *Three Family Village*, exonerating the authors, denouncing their Cultural Revolution critics, and including, "for reference," a copy of Yao Wenyuan's Cultural Revolution denunciation of *Three Family Village*). The genre need not support radical views; it can support the victims of purges when they are later rehabilitated. The genre has, however, been controlled by the state since 1942.

Dai Qing's *Wang Shiwei and "Wild Lilies"* is but another example of this genre, but with an important exception. It is now in *private* hands. Its "textual analysis" (and it is up to the reader to judge how convincing her logic is on various points) is a civil society version of the old Maoist government cudgel. In a supreme and justly ironic sense it is the gun that shot Wang Shiwei blasting back at the people who cut him down. It is sweet revenge in form as well as content.

It is also extremely popular writing today in China. Dai Qing is one of the most influential of what Geremie Barmé calls the new "mass media historians." Hers is a "parallel history" to the official party version, one that restores "intellectually independent people" to China's revolutionary history.[19] In this sense, Dai Qing provides Wang Shiwei the ultimate service. She continues his agenda of personalizing public life and puncturing the language of political illusion.

Dai Qing's book provides us with a sense of how past and present continue to intertwine in Chinese politics. Dai is one of a small number of exceptionally courageous journalists who believe that China must rectify its own past if it is to liberate itself, and for her the Wang Shiwei affair symbolizes the "guilty knowledge" still obtaining within the Chinese Communist Party that needs to be exorcised. The documents enable us to understand "rectification" as a pattern, as antihistory, including as an essential part the Stalinist methods used by Kang

Sheng and others in mobilizing the campaign against Wang. It is a pattern that will repeat itself both in Yan'an and again during the Cultural Revolution and after.

Perhaps we should say a few words about how this book came to be published in the United States. David Apter interviewed Dai Qing on numerous occasions in 1988 and 1989 in China, the last time the day before the military crackdown in Beijing and Tiananmen Square. In 1988, during the course of these initial discussions, Dai Qing let David Apter have a look at the manuscript. Apter told her he thought it ought to be published in English and rather reluctantly she agreed to let him take a copy back to the United States. He then discussed the matter with Timothy Cheek. We came to the conclusion that the material was very important, too important to ignore. We made plans to publish it when we were overtaken by events in Tiananmen, after which Dai Qing was imprisoned. We tried but were unable to get in touch with her in China until after she came to Harvard as a Nieman Fellow in 1992. In the end we had decided to go ahead and publish a translation of the manuscript, happily locating a pair of excellent translators, Ms. Nancy (Yang) Liu (Columbia University) and Professor Lawrence R. Sullivan (Adelphi University). We are delighted that Dai Qing has contributed a preface to the English edition of her book.

Notes

1. See book text, pp. 14–15. Zhang Wentian's advocacy of less authoritarian leadership in the party and his support for accepting Trotskyists back into CCP ranks during the Second United Front, were obviously antithetical to Mao's political goals. It was probably no accident that the Rectification Movement began when Zhang, the head of the Central Research Institute, was away from Yan'an.

2. Guilhem Fabre, *Genèse du pouvoir et de l'opposition en Chine: Le printemps de Yan'an* (Paris: Editions l'Harmattan, 1990). Xu Haidong (1900–1970) was commander of the Fifteenth Battalion of the Eighth Route Army and was promoted to the rank of "Great Marshal" in 1955. Hounded by Red Guards during the Cultural Revolution, he died in 1970.

3. Harrison Salisbury's recent revelations regarding the sexual exploits and attraction for young women of the top leadership—especially Mao Zedong—undoubtedly made this a very sensitive topic in ostensibly "puritanical" Yan'an. See, *The New Emperors: China in the Era of Mao and Deng* (Boston: Little, Brown, 1992), p. 218.

4. Mao's kickoff speech for the Rectification Movement is translated along with all the other major "study documents" of the movement in Boyd Compton's excellent collection, *Mao's China: Party Reform Documents, 1942–44* (Seattle: University of Washington Press, 1952).

5. Notice of Wang Shiwei's "rehabilitation" (*pingfan*) is reproduced in the afterword.

6. "Eight specialized columns" were produced in *Liberation Daily* between September 1941 and March 31, 1942, at which time Mao Zedong issued personal orders to transform the newspaper's layout and to publish articles more obedient to the party line. Lu Dingyi and other party members more obedient to Mao were installed at the newspaper to maintain control. Ding Ling was dismissed as literary editor and replaced by Shu Qun, with Ai Siqi maintaining overall responsibility for page four, the miscellany section (science, medicine, agriculture, literature, and art). Sent to the countryside, Ding Ling returned two years later to write literature bereft of the individualism and anxiety that had characterized her earlier work. See, Patricia Stranahan, *Molding the Medium: The Chinese Communist Party and the Liberation Daily* (Armonk, NY: M.E. Sharpe, 1990), pp. 26–39, and Chen Xuezhao *Surviving the Storm: A Memoir*, edited with an introduction by Jeffrey C. Kinkley (Armonk, NY: M.E. Sharpe, 1990), p. xxi.

7. *Liberation Daily* (Jiefang ribao), October 23, 1941, p. 4. Sadly, Ding Ling did lay her weapon down the following June and even turned against Wang Shiwei. For an excellent analysis of the role of *Liberation Daily* in the Rectification Movement and an extended guide to its articles, see Stranahan, ibid. An indispensable research guide for readers of Chinese is *Personal Name Index to the Liberation Daily* (Jiefang ribao ren ming suoyin), May 1941–March 1947 (Beijing: Shumu wenxian chubanshe, 1983).

8. Timothy Cheek, "The Fading of Wild Lilies: Wang Shiwei and Mao Zedong's *Yan'an Talks* in the First CPC Rectification Movement" in *The Australian Journal of Chinese Affairs*, no. 11 (January 1984), pp. 25–58.

9. We are indebted to Wen Jize and Dai Qing for interviews and materials on the Wang Shiwei affair. Further details on Wang's wall newspaper articles are given by Wang Ruowang, who published *Arrow and Target* in Yan'an. See Kyna Rubin, "An Interview with Mr. Wang Ruowang," *The China Quarterly*, no. 87 (September 1981), p. 509.

10. The stages of Wang's decline in the literary rectification are, according to Cheek (1984, p. 38), the archetypic first instance of the persuasive-coercive continuum described for rectification campaigns by Frederick C. Teiwes. See *Politics and Purges In China: Rectification and the Decline of Party Norms 1950–65*, second edition (Armonk, NY: M.E. Sharpe, 1993), pp. 25–40.

11. Frederick C. Teiwes with Warren Sun, "The Formation of the Maoist Leadership: From the Return of Wang Ming to the Seventh Party Congress," in Anthony Saich and Hans Van de ven, eds., "New Perspectives on the Chinese Communist Revolution," unpublished manuscript. Teiwes demonstrates that Mao was intimately involved in the "rescue campaign." Peter Seybolt also sees the purge as linked to rectification, but lacked the sources Dai Qing provides. See Seybolt, "Terror and Conformity: Counterespionage Campaigns, Rectification and Mass Movements, 1942–43," *Modern China* (January 1986), pp. 39–73.

12. Mark Selden, *The Yenan Way in Revolutionary China* (Cambridge: Harvard University Press, 1971); Teiwes, *Politics and Purges* and "Formation of the Maoist Leadership"; Raymond F. Wylie, *The Emergence of Maoism: Mao Tsetung, Ch'en Po-ta and the Search for Chinese Theory 1935–45* (Stanford: Stanford University Press, 1980).

13. An example of the "silent majority" of party intellectuals who found they could live with the public version of rectification is explored by Timothy Cheek in *Broken Jade: Deng Tuo and Intellectual Service in Mao's China* (forthcoming). Also see Chen Xuezhao, *Surviving the Storm*, p. xxi, where Jeffrey Kinkley describes Chen—an accomplished writer on romantic themes and a journalist strongly attracted to French culture—as one who "quite willingly underwent the great rectification campaign, yearning to rein in her 'immature' idealism and to learn to write for a different audience: workers, peasants, and soldiers, as specified by Mao Zedong."

14. See the last page of volume two of *Mao Zedong Reader* (Mao Zedong xuandu) (Beijing: Renmin chubanshe, 1986).

15. See, for example, Merle Goldman, *China's Intellectuals* (Cambridge: Harvard University Press, 1981), p. 21; Cheek, "The Fading of Wild Lilies" and *Broken Jade*; Geremie Barmé, "Using the Past to Save the Present: Dai Qing's Historiographical Dissent," in *East Asian History*, no. 1 (June 1991), pp. 141–81; and Kyna Rubin, "Writers' Discontent and Party Response in Yan'an Before 'Wild Lilies': the Manchurian Writers and Zhou Yang" in *Modern Chinese Literature*, vol. 1 (September 1984), pp. 79–102.

16. Wen Jize was the official recorder of the proceedings in "Diary of a Struggle" (Document 2.1). His reportage is interrupted by carefully inserted, salutary, and admonishing remarks that make this clear, even as a certain sadness is evident in his notes on the testimony translated in this volume.

17. Versions of *Wang Shiwei and "Wild Lilies"* were published in May 1988 in the PRC in *Wenhui yuekan* (which made a number of cuts, such as material relating to Wang Zhen) and, in full length, in Hong Kong's *Mingbao yuehkan* (issues five and six), May and June, 1988. The full version was finally published in the PRC as part of Dai Qing's *Liang Shuming, Wang Shiwei, Chu Anping* (Nanjing: Jiangsu wenyi chubanshe, June 1989), pp. 41–110, which is the text on which the current translation is based. The Chinese texts of the documents and interviews translated in part two of this book are on file at the Fairbank Center Library, Harvard University, and will be published by the Center for Chinese Research Materials. We have not been able to locate printed versions for all the documents that Dai collects here, but those we have located confirm the accuracy of her versions.

18. Fan Wenlan, ed., *On the Ideological Consciousness of Wang Shiwei* (Lun Wang Shiwei sixiang yishi) (np.: Qi-Lu-Yu shudian, 1944) on reel three of *Materials on the Chinese Communist Party* (Youguan Zhongguo gongchandang cailiao) (Tokyo: Yushodo Microfilms, 1970). So much of Wang's "Politicians, Artists" was cited in the critical articles in Yan'an that for decades they provided the only public record of Wang's essay. When "Politicians, Artists" was finally published in the late 1970s, the critical extracts proved to be accurate.

19. See the extensive treatment of Dai Qing's writings by Geremie Barmé, "Using the Past."

PART I
TEXT

Chapter One

Spring 1947, Shanxi

Whistling through the mountain chains, the wind blows the thick dust into every tight seam of one's clothing. *Qing ming* [April 5, Chinese Lunar Calendar] is over, yet the landscape is devoid of any greenness.

Xing County, a small dilapidated town. The only indications that it's the capital of the Jin-Sui revolutionary base are the small flags occasionally poking out of the windows of the cavelike, one-story huts here and there.

A few hundred miles away in Hexi, a battle is raging. But here in Xing county everything is tranquil at dusk.

Caijiayao is the location of the General Police Bureau of the Jin-Sui Administrative Office.

A young man with cadre airs and armed with a hatchet goes into one of the huts and yanks out a middle-aged man with cadre airs, dragging him all the way to a desolate and remote valley in the mountains.

The hand rises and the hatchet falls . . .

Globs of red blood spatter over the dry, hard yellow dirt.

Deceased: Wang Shiwei. *Crime*: Trotskyite faction member, KMT spy, and head of an anti-party gang. Neither a final judgment nor court decision, nor an appeal is allowed. The sentence is based solely on an approved report.

In Wang's forty-one years of life, his most outstanding act and the earliest thing to bring misfortune upon him was to write that essay (four parts) published in two installments in the Literature and Art Column of *Liberation Daily* in Yan'an. These were the same essays later mentioned by Mao Zedong at the high-level (*zuigaoceng*) meeting among senior leaders in 1962.

"Wild Lilies" [Part One]*

WANG SHIWEI

Preface

As I walked alone on the river bank, seeing the old fashioned cotton shoes of a female comrade in front of me reminded me of one who used to wear this type of shoes, comrade Li Fen—the oldest most beloved friend in my life. Whenever I think of her, my heart pounds and my blood quickens.

Li Fen was a student in the humanities preparatory course at Beida [Peking University] in 1926. In the same year she entered the communist party. In the spring of 1928 she sacrificed her life in her native town—Baoqing, Hunan Province. She died not as a result of being captured, but because her maternal uncle tied her up and delivered her to the local army garrison. This reveals how cruel these representatives of old China were. Before going to her death, Li Fen had put on all three sets of her underclothes and closely sewn them together. She did this because when young female communists were arrested and shot in Baoqing, vagrants would rape the corpse, often with the army's encouragement! This further shows how bloodthirsty and evil and filthy and dark old China was! Ever since I heard such disgusting reports, my veins have burned with uncontrollable love and venomous hatred. Whenever I think of her, images float before my eyes of that pure and noble martyr wearing her three sets of closely sewn underwear, being bound and turned over by her maternal uncle to face a martyr's death with

---

*This translation of Wang Shiwei's "Wild Lilies" was prepared by Timothy Cheek with the assistance of Professor Harriet C. Mills. For another translation, see Gregor Benton, "The Yenan [Yan'an] Opposition," *New Left Review* 92 (July–August 1975), pp. 93–102.

dignity! Every time I think of her my heart pounds and my blood roars through my veins! (At a time when a song of peaceful enchantment and the rhythms of the golden lotus dance abound,* it may seem out of harmony to bring up such an old story. But consider the present reality—close your eyes and think for a moment of all our beloved comrades who have fallen in pools of blood—this, too, is not in harmony with the season!)

For the nation's sake, we do not want to go over again the old scores of class hatred. We are truly impartial and magnanimous, so much so that we are using all of our strength to recruit representatives of old China to walk with us on the same road to brightness. But in the process of recruitment, old China's dirt and filth contaminate us, spreading germs and infecting us with disease.

Over and over again I have drawn strength from the image of Li Fen—strength for life, strength for struggle. When thinking of her this time, I made up my mind to write a few "critical essays" (*zawen*). "Wild Lilies" is my general title. This has two implied meanings: In the mountains of Yan'an this lily is the most beautiful of all the lilies. I use it as an offering to Li Fen's pure and noble image. Next, it is said that this type of lily has a scaly bulb, tastes slightly bitter and unlike the other lilies is not sweet to the pallet. Yet it has great medicinal value—I don't know if this is true or not.

February 26, 1942

One: What's missing in our lives?

Recently, the youth of Yan'an seem dispirited and are apparently harboring some troubling discomfort.

Why? What is missing in our lives? Some say: "We are badly nourished, we lack VITAMINS, therefore etc., etc." Others say: "The ratio of men to women in Yan'an is eighteen to one, many young people cannot find a lover, so . . ." Still others say: "Life in Yan'an is too monotonous, too 'dry,' we lack amusement, so . . ."

None of these responses are totally unfounded; we want to eat a bit better, have the opposite sex to marry, and need some fun in our lives.

---

*Two five-character phrases poetically describing a time of peace, hence used as sarcastic contrast to the bitter conditions in Yan'an in 1942. The song cited in the text, *Spring in the Jade Hall* (Yu tang chun), is a Peking opera aria.

All this goes without saying. But everyone has to admit: Yan'an's youth all bring a spirit of sacrifice to their revolutionary tasks. They did not come here to seek the satisfactions of food and sex or the pleasures of life. When it's said that their lack of enthusiasm and even their harboring of some troubling resentment is because these questions cannot be completely satisfactorily resolved, I cannot easily agree.

So deep down what is missing in our lives? The following short conversation might be revealing.

During the New Year Holiday, as I was returning from a friend's home one evening, there were two young female comrades walking in the dark ahead of me chatting animatedly in a low voice. We were some ten feet apart. I walked lightly and listened attentively.

"[A]t the drop of a hat, he'll talk about other peoples' petty bourgeois egalitarianism; yet he himself has his own doctrine of privilege (*teshuzhuyi*). No matter what the occasion he makes sure of his special privilege. He is constantly taking care of his special interests. But with lower level comrades he could care less whether they're healthy or frail, sick or dead!

"Hmmh! Crows are black wherever you see them.* Our comrade XX is like that too!

"They talk a good line: class friendship. Ha! Shit! They don't even have normal human sympathy; when they meet people they put on the smiles, but it's all superficial—not from the heart. You never really know what they're thinking. If something offends them slightly, they glare at you, adopt the grandiose air of a department head and lecture you!

"High or low, leaders are all alike. Our section chief, so-and-so, is all respect and honor to the higher ups, but he's haughty towards us. Often when comrades are sick, he doesn't even bother to call. *But* once, when an eagle snatched a small chicken of his, you should have seen the big fuss he made over that weighty matter! Since then every time the eagle shows up, he screams and yells, throwing clods of dirt at the bird—that selfish, self-seeking jerk!"

Silence fell for a moment. On the one hand, I admired these young female comrades' eloquence, on the other, I felt in a daze as if I had lost something.

---

*This idiom *tianxia wuya yiban hei*, was evidently intended by Wang as a parody of Mao Zedong's literary style.

"There are too many comrades who get sick; it makes people very sad. But in fact, if you're sick, you wouldn't want that sort of man visiting you. He would only make you feel worse. Nothing in his voice, facial expression, or attitude would inspire any confidence that he had the slightest concern or affection for you.

"In the last two years I have changed jobs three or four times. From department heads to section chiefs to unit heads, there are just too damn few cadres who really care about us.

"Yeah, you're not wrong! He hasn't a bit of affection for others, so naturally no one feels affection for him. If they want to do mass work, they're bound to fail."

The female comrades continued their animated whispers, but as I had come to turn off the path I could hear no more. This conversation may perhaps be biased and exaggerated and its "image" may not be universally accepted; but we cannot deny that it can serve as a mirror.

Deep down, what is missing in our lives? Look in the mirror.*

Two: Confronting "Running into Difficulties"

On the "Youth Page" number twenty of this paper [*Liberation Daily*] an article by a certain comrade appeared entitled "Running into Difficulties."†Reading it made me ponder.

First, here let's copy a few lines from the text: "A middle aged friend recently returned from the [Kuomintang] rear areas (*da houfang*) and noticed that the youth of Yan'an were unable to endure some minor unpleasantness; they grumbled and complained about everything. Resenting this he said: 'What do they think this is! People outside Yan'an have encountered innumerable difficulties and have taken much bullying.'

"What he says is true. Although many aspects of life in Yan'an make people angry and some realities cannot please everyone, from

---

*Deng Liqun later attacked Wang's proposal in the article "Looking in the mirror" (Wo lai zhaozhaojing), *Liberation Daily*, June 20, 1942.

†"Running into Difficulties" (Peng pi) appeared in *Liberation Daily,* February 22, 1942, on page 4, and was written by Liu Xibo. In the next two paragraphs of this text, Wang Shiwei quotes half the article. The rest, which is not reproduced here, maintains that since "difficulties" are part of heaven's plan people will always encounter problems and be rebuffed. So we shouldn't complain, but rather brave the tasks ahead. This reflected the view of many Long March veterans.

the perspective of a man who has encountered many difficulties and tasted the vagaries of life, they are totally insignificant. But with inexperienced youth, especially those from a student background, it's totally different. Their families and schools have suckled them into adulthood, love and warmth have nurtured their views on life and taught them to reach for naïve and beautiful fantasies. The ugliness and bleakness of the present reality are strange to them. It's not surprising that when they encounter some minor upset they cry out moved by the anguish of something they have never experienced."

I don't know what kind of person the author's "middle-aged friend" is, but I think his know-how-to-be-content-with-what-you-have philosophy of life is not only "wrong" but is also harmful. The potential value of youth lies in its purity, sensitivity, fervor, and love of life. When others haven't felt the darkness, they sense it first. When others are reluctant to utter the unmentionable, they speak out courageously. Because of this they criticize a lot, which is not the same thing as "grumbling." Perhaps what they say is not sufficiently balanced, but it is not necessarily "bawling." From their so-called "grumbling," "bawling," and "uneasiness" we should search for the essential nature of the problems behind these phenomena and eliminate them in a reasonable way (take note: reasonable! Young people are not necessarily all "blindly screaming"). To say Yan'an is far superior to the "outside world," to tell young people not to "grumble," and simply to describe Yan'an's dark side as some "slight disappointment" and "nothing worth worrying about" will not solve problems. True, Yan'an is superior to the "outside world," but Yan'an can and must become even better.

Of course, young people are often passionate and impatient. This seems to be the main point of "Running into Difficulties." But if the youth all became "youthful sages" what a lonely world this would be! In reality, Yan'an youth have already matured enough. The "grumbling" of the two female comrades, quoted above, was very appropriately uttered in the dark in low and heavy tones. Instead of despising such "grumbling," we should use it as a mirror and examine ourselves.

To say that youth of "student background were suckled by family and school into adulthood, that love and warmth nurtured their views of life . . ." is, I think, somewhat subjective. Although generally of "student background," "inexperienced in the world" and "inexperienced in the ups and downs of life," the great majority of Yan'an youth have already experienced many bitter struggles. They did not experience much "love and warmth" in the past. On the contrary, only after coming to know the meaning of "hatred and callousness" have they entered our revolutionary camp to seek "love and warmth." From what the writer of "Running into Difficulties" says, it would seem that all Yan'an youth have lived sheltered lives and "grumble" only when lacking their sweets. But "hatred and callousness" are not "unfamiliar" to them. Actually it was because of "hatred and callousness" that they have come to Yan'an seeking "beauty and warmth." When they see such "intolerable hatred and callousness" in Yan'an, they "grumble" hoping to arouse popular interest in minimizing both as much as possible.

In the winter of 1938 during our party's first great internal examination, the Central Committee called upon us to "discuss everything" and said that "no matter what opinion, right or wrong, all should be raised without reservation." I hope that kind of internal examination will come again.* Listen to the "grumbling" of the lower ranking youth. It certainly has great value for our work.

This essay was published in the Literature and Art Column of [*Liberation Daily*] on March 23, 1942. Although Ding Ling was no longer literary editor of the paper, she helped get Wang's essay published. Her own essay, "Thoughts on March 8,"† was published shortly before (note by Dai Qing).

---

*Here Wang is challenging the party center to abide by the democratic purposes of rectification as originally announced by the party leadership.

†Translated in Benton, *New Left Review*, pp. 102–105.

Chapter Two

Yan'an, 1942

The Pacific War broke out engulfing the entire world in conflict.

While carrying out an unprecedented assault on the battlefield of north China, the Japanese Army was confronted by the incomparable resistance of the [Communist Eighth Route] army and ordinary people from the base areas.

The third anticommunist campaign was already being prepared while the ashes of the second campaign were still hovering in the air.

Most of the countryside at the battle front was in the hands of the Japanese: "Defeated [KMT] officials were as numerous as ox hair; defeated generals were rising like the tide." Young people searching for a way to rescue the nation had broken through the lines of the KMT and Japanese blockade and had arrived at or were on their way to Yan'an—the barren yellow dirt plateau that in the young people's passionate aspirations was a holy place without exploitation and suppression, where equality, freedom, and democracy reigned. Then as now, it was viewed as the backbone of the resistance struggle and the hope of the nation. . . .

Yan'an, 1942

At that time it had already been five years since Kang Sheng and Wang Ming had returned to China from the Comintern [in Moscow]. Wang Ming's policy of concession toward the power-holding KMT had been completely demolished three years earlier by the cruel reality of war. But the ideological weapons the two men had borrowed directly from Stalin to carry out inner party "purges" (*qingxi*), especially when combined with the extreme terror brought about by the mere mention of "Trotsky"—a terror comparable to electric shock from too close proximity to a six hundred thousand volt electric grid—was like a dark cloud gradually moving over the heads of communists and noncommunists alike gathered in Yan'an or scattered along the various fronts of the anti-Japanese war. Of course, similar things had already taken place in the Chinese Communist Party. People still shuddered at the mention of the 1930 Futian massacre in the Central Soviet regions in which batches of "students" were tried together and sentenced to death. Even the term used for the "students" crime was Russian: "Anti-Bolshevik" (member of the AB group). If it is said that such actions of that time had elements of the immature and the blind, of cockiness and primordial cruelty and indifference, by this time in Yan'an because of the reverence for the magic shining sword (*shangfang baojian*) of the Comintern, together with constant invocation of the rich and powerful USSR, their arrogance suddenly increased a hundred fold. Even more so did the infallibility and supreme authority assumed by the purgers and the obedience and compliance demanded by the purged fit so perfectly with the traditional character of the Chinese people. . . . The "Buddha halo" (*fuoguang*) has hovered over our heads for nearly half a century and almost no one has been able to escape it. It is said that there is a way to break the spell through the fresh blood of the innocent, the martyred, and the fighters for democracy.

Yan'an, 1942

On March 18, the forum on examining rectification and mobilization work was held at the highest institute in Yan'an: the Central Research Institute—the forerunner to the Chinese Academy of Social Sciences [CASS].

This Research Institute had been established the previous year out of a reorganization of the Academy for Marxist-Leninist Studies (*Ma-Lie xueyuan*). Aside from the fact that newcomers to Yan'an had dramatically changed, one has only to note the conversion of the "academy" to a "research institute" to see Mao Zedong's basic change in attitude toward Marxism. Especially after Wang Ming returned to "capture the emperor to control the officials,"* Mao was no longer satisfied with

---

*That is, after losing out to Mao in the leadership struggle at the 1938 Sixth Plenum, Wang Ming was now trying to use his ideological expertise to influence Mao and gain control over cadres.

merely mouthing words from Marxist texts. He now emphasized study of its theoretical system and its application to the domestic situation in China.

Membership in the Central Research Institute was restricted to Yan'an's academic elite. Luo Fu (Zhang Wentian) was the president, and Fan Wenlan vice-president. Luo Mai (Li Weihan) was deputy director of the Propaganda Department and was responsible for "managing" the Institute when Luo Fu was away. Xu Jiansheng was chief secretary. Li Yan, who today is the director of the Law Research Institute of CASS, was the party secretary. The leading character of this book, Wang Shiwei, had already been transferred from the translation section of Luo Fu's Academy for Marxist-Leninist Studies to Ouyang Shan's Art Research Office and was also appointed "special research fellow" (*tebie yanjiuyuan*) at the Institute (the rank of "research fellow" was slightly lower). Below research fellow was the rank of graduate student to which Ye Qun [Lin Biao's wife] was appointed. After the Rectification Movement began she was temporarily transferred to the Institute's Party Committee as secretary of the organization. Special research fellows wore the same clothes as Mao Zedong, woven out of black refined cloth imported from KMT-controlled regions. They were also issued four and one half kuai of "legal script" (*fabi*). Mao Zedong himself was only issued five bills. Lin Boqu, who was the former financial minister and then chairman of the border areas government, received only four.

The Institute's mobilization meeting was held on March 18. Since Luo Fu was in a village with an investigation team, Fan Wenlan, the forty-nine year old historian, gave the report on mobilization. Fan had joined the CCP in the 1920s but had terminated his involvement when the KMT thoroughly destroyed the party organization in his area. He rejoined the CCP in 1939 and then traveled to Yan'an. At the time of the March 18 meeting he was entrusted with compiling a *Brief History of China* (Zhongguo tongshi jianbian) which, in the 1960s, was in the hands of virtually every Chinese student.

By 1939, Mao had long since completed his report on "Reform Our Study," while his lectures, "Rectify the Party's Style of Work" and "Oppose Stereotyped Party Writing," had just been delivered. The targets, substance, methods, and results of the rectification would from our perspective today probably seem: "[ambivalent] to the [ambivalent],* and intelligent to the intelligent."

Once Mao Zedong had gained control of the military after the 1935 Zunyi Conference and political power after the 1938 Sixth Plenary Session, he obviously intended to settle accounts with Wang Ming and his supporters over their dogmatism. Mao would later emphasize at the 1945 Seventh Party Congress that "the party ought to have unified thought," and he also blamed Wang Shiwei for "taking command in Yan'an and causing our failures." But during February and March 1942, Mao obviously did not expect so many young people to utilize such publications as the Youth Committee's *Light Cavalry* (Qing qibing), the Central Research Institute's *Arrow and Target* (Shi yu di), the Northwest Bureau's *Northwest Wind* (Xibei feng), the Three Frontiers' (San bian), *Camel Bells* (Tuo ling), and the *New Malan* (Xin malan)† of Guanzhong [central Shaanxi], plus other arenas, including even a letter sent to Mao himself, to proclaim with great emotion that "rectification should focus on ourselves and our camp."

Kang Sheng, according to available sources, came across at this time as someone obsessed with power but totally lacking in beliefs. After being an assistant to Wang Ming at the Comintern [in Moscow] and then witnessing Wang's collapse, Kang Sheng found it somewhat difficult to switch in just a few months from proclaiming "long live Wang Ming" and supporting Wang Ming's "fight to further Bolshevize the CCP," to shouting "down with Wang Ming" and "down with his fight to further Menshevize the CCP." It was quite a feat for Kang Sheng to clear himself so completely of his organizational entanglements with Wang Ming that within three years he became director of the Central Social Department (*zhongyang shehui bu*) and the Intelligence Department (*qingbao bu*), and also a director of the Committee to Examine Party and non-Party Members, as well as the deputy director of the Central General Study Committee (*zhongyang zongxuewei*) of the Rectification Movement (with Mao as the director) and, additionally, the director of the General Study Committee of Units Directly Subordinate to the Central Committee. Within three years Kang Sheng ended up control-

---

*Literally, "benevolent to the benevolent."

†The *malan* is a flower from this region symbolizing persistence.

ling the fate of thousands of cadres in Yan'an.* Jiang Qing, a fellow provincial of Kang Sheng, may have backed this effort, but this is merely a guess. But one must keep in mind the Chinese people's tendency to accept such unfounded rumors as true. Even though it sounds reasonable, this interpretation of Jiang Qing's role [in the Rectification Movement] has not been verified by serious historians.

Kang Sheng appeared to have an innate defect, namely he enjoyed using politics to control people. From the following speech [Document 2.5] one can see that what he did during 1942–43 was merely an initial test of his "ox knife." The real life and death struggle would come twenty-five years later [during the Cultural Revolution].

Now Luo Mai had in the past "committed mistakes,"† but at this time he was determined to correct himself and, indeed, was actually reforming himself heart and soul. Although he had not completely understood Wang Shiwei's radicalism and stubbornness, it should be said that he essentially understood the ideological problems that rectification should solve and how the movement should proceed. It should also be mentioned that what Luo Mai knew was about to occur was almost totally consistent with the various "historical resolutions" that were first passed three years later and then again twenty to thirty years later.‡ Luo's predictions were also borne out when Wang Ming succumbed completely and Ding Ling thoroughly remolded herself. In contrast, Wang Shiwei and his lot had nothing whatsoever to do with this campaign: they were neither its targets nor its chief supporters. Their task was simple: all they had to do was listen to the relevant reports, applaud on cue, and write an ideological report or two on demand. That was all. Luo Mai in line with this "spirit" of not having to speak out consulted with the leaders of the Central Research Institute before the mobilization meeting that established the Committee to Examine Rectification Work. Naturally, the Institute leaders and directors of the various departments became members. Luo also established

---

*Stalin also recruited individuals previously associated with his past political enemies, especially Leon Trotsky, to serve his regime and carry out purges. Roy Medvedev, *Nikolai Bukharin: The Last Years*, trans. A. D. P. Briggs (New York: W.W. Norton, 1980), p. 132.

†Luo had supported the Internationalists.

‡Dai Qing is intimating that Luo Mai sensed that major political persecutions were about to occur that were later justified in the 1945 and 1982 "Historical Resolutions" issued by the party leadership.

a wall newspaper to coordinate the entire movement. These manifestations of "movement spirit" (*yundong jing*) are probably for forty-five year old readers and those less than forty-five as familiar as their hands and feet, for not only have they not had the slightest concern about the correctness of ethics, human rights, leaders and such areas, but they have become skilled practitioners of chess, knitting, and napping to let political movements flow over them like water off a duck's back [literally, "coping with a thousand changes by not making one change" (*yi bubian ying wanbian*)]. But young and middle-aged people in Yan'an in 1942—Wang Shiwei was thirty-six that year—had not yet enjoyed the rich experience gained from the repeated political movements of the 1950s, 1960s, and 1970s when political ideas were "melted into the soul and absorbed into the blood." Instead, these inexperienced young and middle-aged intellectuals directly challenged Fan Wenlan's arrangements that had been based on Luo Mai's ideas.

According to many memoirs published years later, Wang Shiwei voiced the sharpest words. His criticisms were actually quite common, merely to propose that the Examination Committee be elected by ordinary people in a democratic manner—to say nothing of the masses also having the right to determine whether the chairmen of the various departments or even the research institute could join the committee. Wang also proposed that pseudonymous or anonymous articles on wall newspapers be accepted so as to protect the democratic rights of the authors.

Fan Wenlan did not object to these proposals. But Luo Mai heatedly opposed them and outlined to Wang Shiwei the following six demands regarding: (1) the overall importance of the movement; (2) the need to separate discussion and examination; (3) the prime focus on examining both the work style of leaders and their personal ideology; (4) the cultivation of a self-dissecting (*ziwo jiepao*) character; (5) requiring that the president, party general secretary, and directors of the various departments be members of the Examination Committee; and (6) accepting only wall newspapers that conform to party organizational principles [i.e., reporting the author's name to the party]. Party members should not use anonymous names within the party.* These six points,

---

*A supporter of Bo Gu and the Internationalists, Luo evidently joined the denunciations of Wang Shiwei to save his own political skin. Stranahan, *Molding the Medium*, p. 51.

especially the last two, were vehemently rejected by an overwhelming majority. The mobilization meeting was in an uproar. Luo Mai got a headache and left before it was over. Fan Wenlan presided over the voting: the election procedure was voted upon first; Wang's proposal passed by an eighty-four to twenty-eight vote. However, it was merely a victory of the spirit since the actual election results almost followed Luo Mai's original proposal as only two people among the Institute and department leaders failed to be elected. One of them was Zhang Ruxin, the director of the Political Research Office.[1] Zhang later became a member of the four-member core group that actually led the Rectification Movement at the Institute organized by Luo Mai. Of course, hindsight is twenty-twenty. At that moment, Wang Shiwei was pleased and excited, and declared a victory for "democracy."

Then, on February 23, Wang reached the peak of his career by publishing the second part of "Wild Lilies" in the Literature and Art Column of the 106th issue of *Liberation Daily*.

Note: Dai Qing's notes to the text are located on pages 73–76.

"Wild Lilies" [Part Two]

WANG SHIWEI

Three: "Inevitability," "The Sky Is Not Falling," and "Triviality"

"Our camp exists in the midst of the dark old society and thus there will be darkness around us, that is inevitable." Correct! That's "Marxism." But, this is only one-half of Marxism; there is still the more important half that the "great masters of subjectivism and sectarianism" (*zhuguanzhuyi zongpaizhuyi de dashi*)* have forgotten. It is said that after realizing the inevitability of such darkness, we should use the Bolshevik fighting spirit to stop its rise, diminish its growth, and to the greatest possible extent stimulate the counterforce of its ideology on present reality. We cannot hope to eliminate darkness completely in our camp today. Yet, to lessen the darkness a little is not only possible, but necessary. Still, not only have the "great masters" never stressed this point, they rarely even mention it. They simply point to the "inevitability" and go to sleep.

In fact, they don't just sleep. The "great masters" take "inevitability" as an excuse for being very lenient with themselves. In their dreams they tell themselves confidently: "Comrade, you're from the old society. Your soul has some tiny, tiny speck of darkness in it. That's inevitable. Don't be embarrassed by it."

And so we indirectly encourage darkness, and even manufacture it directly.

---

*Apparently quotes from Mao Zedong used by Wang to question the attitudes of high-level cadres, including the Internationalist faction of Wang Ming et al., who tolerated old-style politics and social attitudes in Yan'an.

After the "inevitability theory" there is a "national form* theory" called "the sky won't fall." True. The sky indeed cannot fall. But just because "the sky won't fall," are our work and activities immune from losses? On this level the "great masters" think so little as to not think at all. If we let this "inevitable" "inevitableness" go on, then the sky—the sky of revolutionary work—will "inevitably" fall. Don't feel so self-secure!

Related to this is a "theory" called "trivia." You criticize him and he tells you not to pay attention to "trivialities." Some "great masters" even go so far as to say: "Screw you! It's bad enough that female comrades dwell on trivial matters, now male comrades are also focusing on trivialities!" True, it's very unlikely that an anti-party or anti-national rebellion will occur in Yan'an, but in the "trivia" of each person's code of deportment there are small points that help either the bright side or the dark side. And when these "trivial incidents" are the work of "august personages," they are more than sufficient to arouse in the minds of ordinary folks either warmth or isolation.

Four: "Egalitarianism and Hierarchy"

I've heard that a certain comrade has already used the same topic in an essay for his organization's wall newspaper.† The result was that he was criticized and attacked by that organization's "department head" ultimately becoming partially demented. I hope this is just baseless hearsay. But even unseasoned youngsters have really gone mad, and so, I'm afraid, it's not completely impossible that an adult could go mad as well. Although I don't feel my nerves are as "healthy" as some other men, I feel I still have enough vitality to not sink into madness under any circumstances. Therefore I will dare to follow that certain comrade and speak on egalitarianism and hierarchy.

That communism is not egalitarianism (moreover we are not today promoting a communist revolution) does not need me to elucidate in an

---

*Promoted by Wang Shiwei's major nemeses, Chen Boda and Zhou Yang, the idea of "national form" demanded literature and art more in tune with Chinese traditions than with the Western forms preferred by Wang and others.

†Wall newspapers (*chuangbao*, also called *pibao*, or *dazi bao*) are still a popular form of public writing in China, especially on political issues. Wang Shiwei himself wrote several wall newspaper articles around this time. See Kyna Rubin, "An Interview with Mr. Wang Ruowang," *The China Quarterly*, p. 509.

eight-legged essay. Because, I assure you there is not one cook who would dream of sharing the life style of a "department head." (I would not dare to write "culinary orderly" since I feel that such a term has a satirical flavor.* But when I do talk to them, my "innate human nature" and "heaven-sent good conscience" invariably makes me address them in a warm and gentle tone as "comrade culinary officer"—such a pitiful bit of warmth!†). As for the system of hierarchical ranks, this problem is a little more complicated.

One man says: "Our Yan'an has no hierarchy." But this is not true, because it exists. Another says: "True, we have a system of ranks, but they are reasonable." This requires that we all do some thinking.

Those who say the system of hierarchical ranks is reasonable, for the most part give the following justifications: (1) Under the principle of "From each according to his ability, to each according to his value," those who bear greater responsibility should be indulged a bit; (2) Under the three-thirds system of government we will soon put into practice a salary system, under which compensation and perks will naturally differ; (3) The Soviet Union has hierarchical ranks. These reasons I think all need further discussion.

As to the first, today we are in the midst of a bitter and harsh revolution with great hardships and continuous difficulties for everyone. Many people have lost their priceless health and so we should not speak in terms of "according to one's value" and "indulging." On the contrary, men with a heavier responsibility ought to share the life-style of lower level comrades (a national virtue that truly ought to be fostered) and by doing so, the lower levels will feel heartfelt affection for them. Only this can weld an ironclad unity. Of course, for those with important responsibilities and special health needs, it's entirely reasonable and necessary to give them special treatment. Those with moderate responsibilities should also get some special treatment. As to the second argument, the pay discrepancies under the three-thirds system need not be too great. Non-party members [in the government] could be given somewhat better treatment, while party members should still carry on

---

*That is, satirical bureaucratic titles, such as one may dub garbagemen "sanitary engineers."

†Satiric use of the pompous Confucian philosophical terms, *li xing* and *liang xin*. Here they denote an old fashioned sentimentality and politeness that Wang sees as a pitiful excuse for egalitarianism.

the fine tradition of austere struggle so as to move the hearts of more people outside the party to come and work with us. On the third point, forgive my rashness, but I ask that those "great masters" who can't open their mouths without talking about "Ancient Greece" to shut up.

I am not an egalitarian, but the three classes of clothing and five grades of food are not necessarily reasonable and needed—this is especially true with clothes (I myself am of the so-called cadre uniform and small pot (*ganbufu xiao chufang*) rank, so I'm not merely engaging in sour grapes). These should all be allocated according to need.* If, on the one hand, the ill can't get a bowl of noodles and the young eat only two bowls of congee a day (party members when asked if they really had enough to eat must still set a good example and say "I'm full!"), while, on the other hand, there are some rather healthy "big shots" who receive unnecessary and unreasonable perks, such a situation makes subordinates see their superiors as belonging to another species; not only do they not feel affection for them, but . . . if one is forced to think about it, this cannot but result in trouble. . . .

Could it be perhaps that always talking about "love" and "warmth" is an effect of "petty bourgeois sentimentality"? I await your criticism.

March 17 [1942]

[Dai Qing continues]:

On this same day [March 17], *Arrow and Target*, the rectification wall newspaper of the Central Research Institute, began publication. Fan Wenlan composed the forward where he proposed to "shoot the arrow of democracy into the evil wind," "thoroughly carry out democracy" [and] "absolute democracy," and also proclaimed that "whoever hinders democracy will surely shed blood after colliding with the wall of democ-

---

*Mark Selden, *The Yenan Way*, notes that salary differences in the Shaan-Gan-Ning border area from 1937 onward were pegged to subsistence needs but without total uniformity. Regional department heads got five yuan per month, and district magistrates two and one-half yuan per month.

"Small Pot" refers to better food served to high-level cadres in small pots. The "cadre uniform" was of better material and tailoring than the clothing issued to lower ranks. The tradition of personal perks for top leaders continues to the present day as agricultural fields in Yuquanshan near the Summer Palace just outside Beijing are used to grow special foods for central leaders.

racy." Wang Shiwei published two articles on his own aimed directly at his immediate superior—the Institute leader Luo Mai. The first was titled "My Criticisms of Comrade Luo Mai's Speech at the Mobilization Meeting for Rectification and Examination of Work" [Document 1.3]. The second was "Two Random Thoughts" (Lingsui liangze) [Document 1.4]. Neither was anonymous.

In addition to these articles, the wall newspaper also carried a cartoon with the caption "take off the pants to cut off the tail" (*tuo kuzi ge weiba*) [i.e., to expose and criticize people's faults in public] in which a large tail surrounded by four or five other people was pictured as a satirical reference to, but without mentioning any names, the deputy director of the Institute's propaganda department who was at that time substituting for the Institute president [Zhang Wentian]; also pictured was a small, cocked tail that alluded to Zhang Ruxin who had "approved" his own membership on the committee.

In the second and third issues of the paper, Luo Mai restated his views and made a self-criticism regarding his attitude toward Wang Shiwei. Some comrades refuted Wang and he responded with his own refutation in the article titled "Response to Comrades Li Yuchao and Mei Luo" [Document 1.5]. At that time the general situation, according to Li Yan, was one in which "those comrades abiding by party principles were satirized and suppressed. Suddenly, Yan'an was hit by an evil wind with a vicious impact."[2]

The wall newspaper was posted inside the two one-story apartments used as reception rooms near the Institute gate. Although there was an editor-in-chief (Chen Dao), everyone was free to put up an article. As for the popular response, let's consider Luo Mai's comment: "People came to read *Arrow and Target* in an endless stream. As soon as some of the papers were attached to a piece of cloth hung on the south gate of Yan'an, so many people reading made it like a temple fair."

Wang Shiwei suddenly became a star in Yan'an.

What kind of person was he? And how did he come to Yan'an?

Chapter Three

Beijing, 1926

In the Literature Institute of Beida was a party branch operating under the Municipal Party Committee system of the Beijing underground party. Lacking full-time cadres all the positions were filled by students; the party Secretary was a man named Duan Chun from Hunan Province. (Duan withdrew from the party a year later and joined the KMT where he became a county official or something). Among the branch party committee members there was also a beloved "older brother" named Chen Qingchen from Henan. He was a fellow provincial of Wang Shiwei who had sponsored Wang in joining the party, but was later dismissed from the CCP after he became a Trotskyite. He once used the pen name Chen Zhongshan to write a letter to Lu Xun and received in reply Lu Xun's famous letter titled "A Letter in Response to the Trotskyites." Chen was later brutally murdered by Japanese soldiers.

Also, there was Zhang Guangren (Hu Feng) who had attended the same preparatory school attached to Beida as Wang Shiwei and who was Wang Shiwei's classmate in 1925, but who had not yet joined the party. Another was Wang Fanxi of the *October Magazine* published by the Chinese Trotskyites. Today, Wang Fanxi still publishes articles in overseas magazines.*

In the autumn of 1926, two women students joined the party branch. Both were from Hunan and would have great influence on Wang Shiwei. One was the martyr Li Fen whom we have come to know through "Wild Lilies." She was Wang's first love and remained so for his whole life. The other was Wang's [future] wife, Liu Ying, who

---

*See Wang Fan-hsi [Fanxi], *Chinese Revolutionary: Memoirs 1919–1949*, trans. Gregor Benton (New York: Oxford University Press, 1980).

would undertake all kinds of hardship with Wang Shiwei and bear his children. Today, she is in her eighties and is fighting hard to have her husband's name cleared, though the chances of success seem remote [see afterword]. The composed and resolute Li Fen had already joined the party when she was a student at a teacher's school in Hunan. The gentle and quiet Liu Ying came from a fairly wealthy family and was an intimate friend of Li Fen, who recommended her to join the party when Liu Ying entered Beida.

At that time, the "March 18" incident [i.e., the shooting of students in Tiananmen square in Beijing] had occurred six months earlier, while the "April 12" massacre [of communist party members in Shanghai] would occur half a year later. Underground party work had become increasingly dangerous. Wang Shiwei was twenty years old and had fallen in love with Li Fen. Like any young man, he started to write love letters to Li and asked to see her.

Li Fen was fond of Wang mainly because of his good writing skills, his honesty, and his commitment to revolutionary work. She was also aware of his biggest defect, his extreme cynicism. She was at a loss as to how to react after receiving his letter. This was not because of the Puritan style that was currently so popular among revolutionary youth in Beijing. Rather, Li Fen had her own reasons for being reticent.

Li Fen told Liu Ying that when she was only eighteen years old, her father, fearful that his daughter might be kidnapped and raped by roving bandits, had arranged for her to marry her cousin. The two were very intimate. The young husband had insisted that she continue her studies supported by his family. One summer Li Fen, then pregnant, was returning home from school in a sedan chair accompanied by her husband. After arriving home the young husband suddenly died of heat stroke apparently because they had run so fast to avoid being robbed or kidnapped. On the verge of giving birth, Li Fen almost died of grief. She received no sympathy from her parents-in-law; on the contrary, they blamed her for causing their son's death. Her father had no alternative but to take her back in. Li Fen indicated to Liu Ying that after such an experience, she didn't want to get emotionally involved again and was determined not to remarry, and would, instead, devote herself completely to the revolution.

This experience encouraged caution in Li Fen when dealing with male comrades and thus she never replied to Wang Shiwei. But with Wang so deeply in love, he was deeply anxious and became easily irritable as he wrote Li many sincere and heartfelt letters. Li Fen's only alternative was to go with Liu Ying to call on Duan Chun—the party branch secretary and Li's fellow provincial—and inform him about the love affair and about her secret reticence. She hoped Duan would tell Wang to put an end to the whole affair.

Hardly before Li Fen and Liu Ying had finished talking, Duan asked somebody to "go fetch Wang Shiwei!" Wanting to avoid any embarrassment, Li and Liu quickly ran away. Later they were told that Wang and Duan had argued after Duan ordered Wang "to leave Li Fen alone."

Spring, 1927. Li Dazhao was under arrest but had not yet been executed. In the midst of the white terror blanketing Beijing, Duan Chun decided to hold a joint meeting of Beijing's West District and Beida branches at the Hunan Association House so as to resolve the Wang Shiwei business. The meeting lasted for a whole day and involved more than ten people.

According to Wang Fanxi's memoir published in 1985: Duan Chun "emphasized at the meeting that Wang Shiwei had joined the party to chase after Li Fen rather than to participate in the revolution. Duan also accused Wang of reneging on his duty as a party member when in the midst of the harsh struggle with the white terror he ignored the danger to party leader Li Dazhao. It was most absurd for Wang Shiwei to chase after a female comrade and do shameful things. Duan proposed to the meeting that they pass a resolution to subject Wang to severe punishment, determine if his membership should be maintained, and put him under surveillance. Everyone joined in the criticism led by Chen Qingchen who used the harsh tones of an 'older brother' to blame a 'younger brother' for getting involved in such a silly affair. But nobody supported secretary Duan's 'theory of the shameful motive' nor his proposal to dismiss Wang Shiwei from the party or seriously punish him. My [Wang Fanxi's] speech went like this:

> There's nothing wrong with a male comrade dating a female comrade. But it's harmful if one partner is reluctant while the other keeps up the chase. If Wang would agree not to write any more letters to Li Fen, the case can be closed. I don't agree with the idea of confusing private, personal affairs with such serious matters as the party and revolution.

> Secretary Duan did not agree with our 'liberal' views, but since he was in the minority he went along. Wang Shiwei was issued a formal criticism and was ordered not to write anymore letters to Li Fen.[3]"

Wang's behavior throughout this entire meeting anticipated his later reaction to the [rectification] meeting in Yan'an on June 23, 1942. According to Wang Fanxi: "Wang sat in his seat and remained silent from beginning to end, listening intently to everyone's criticisms (as I remember it, Li Fen did not attend the meeting). As soon as he received the conclusion of the criticisms, the 'case' was over." Wang Fanxi also said: "That evening Wang Shiwei came over to my place and told me with great excitement that he could not stop loving Li Fen. But he would try to control himself and not write her anymore letters. At the same time, he was extremely agitated by Secretary Duan's highly bureaucratic work style in handling the case and his attitude toward love that Wang saw as feudal."[4]

It is hard to say whether or not at this time Wang Shiwei restrained himself. Although he stopped seeing Li Fen, he couldn't avoid searching out and shouting at Duan Chun. Duan was so irritated that he accused Wang of being an ill-disciplined anarchist unwilling to accept party criticism. If Wang continued with such behavior, Duan also threatened to kick him out of the party to which Wang Shiwei replied: "You are the party branch secretary. Of course you have the power! But don't think that by kicking me out of the party you can rid me of my communist ideals."

With no one around to mediate, Wang kept arguing with Duan. Afterwards, Wang finally dropped out of the CCP when he was twenty-one years old.

Wang Shiwei came from Hengchuan, Henan Province. His father led a hard life as a former provincial-level scholar-official in the Qing dynasty who later ran a school. Wang was the third son and his real name was Shu Han (叔翰). Starting about 1930, he began to write articles using the pen-name "Shiwei" (實味). He also used "Shiwei" (詩薇) and "Shiwei" (石巍), and so forth.

After graduating from middle school in 1923, Wang attended a preparatory school for study in the United States in Henan where he acquired his basic knowledge of English. A year later, however, when the school closed down, Wang worked in the post office to support himself and continued with his schooling. His innermost feelings, personal experiences, and various hardships during that period were depicted in his novel *Rest* (Xiuxi).*

Wang managed to save money and went to study at Beida, but two years later due to persistent poverty he was unable to continue. He returned to his hometown and with the help of one of his father's students he became a low-level staff member at KMT party headquarters in Nanjing.

If Wang Shiwei had changed his temper from that point onward, we wouldn't have the opportunity to tell the present story. Although he now confronted real privation, Wang Shiwei still maintained a tough and intolerant character. He could have maintained his "rice bowl" if he had just kept quiet. But during that period, he started to write short stories and kept in close contact with his former classmates at Beida, Cao Mengjun and Zhang Tianyi. He stayed with Cao in the spring of 1928 where once again he met Liu Ying.

Due to the shortage of cadres in the party, Liu Ying was sent to work as a secretary at the Northern Bureau of the Beijing Youth League even before she had graduated from school. Soon afterwards, the enemy destroyed the entire Beijing party and youth organizations. Trying to rescue comrades who had been arrested, Liu returned home to ask her father for the one thousand yuan money left to her by her grandfather to use as tuition, but unfortunately failed to get it. The party organization then asked her to go to Shanghai to reestablish connections between the party organization and its members.

Just then both Wang and Liu heard of Li Fen's death. Wang Shiwei was very agitated and was now obsessed with finding the communist party organization in order to take revenge for the martyr against the KMT. Since Liu Ying hadn't yet contacted the organization, she was unable to introduce Wang into the party. But even after she later married Wang and formally renewed her own involvement in party activities, she did not intend to provide Wang with an introduction into the CCP. Not because she doubted his loyalty; she merely thought that his political consciousness was too low. Anxiety-ridden, Wang had already told Liu that, before rejoining the party, he wanted to make money to give to his father to spend in his later years. This way Wang

---

*Published by Zhonghu shuchu in Shanghai in 1930, Wang's short and somewhat unspectacular novel depicted how economic distress and disgust with the "filth" and "darkness" of Chinese society led a classmate to seek "rest" in suicide.

would then be able to involve himself in the struggle and follow the party wholeheartedly, which is exactly what he would end up doing. At the time, however, Liu Ying thought that in putting support for his father before revolutionary work Wang demonstrated a lack of commitment expected of a party member.

Wang Shiwei and Liu Ying were married in January 1930 in Shanghai and afterwards lived in a small apartment on Caishi Road. At that time Xu Zhimo was compiling a collection titled *New Culture Books* for the China Book Bureau. This collection, recent research has shown, was composed of fourteen articles and seventeen translated works, including Wang Shiwei's *Rest* and five of his translations: [Gerhart] Hauptmann's *The Heretic of Soana* (German),* [Eugene] O'Neill's *Strange Interlude* (American), [John] Galsworthy's *A Man of Property* (British), and [Thomas] Hardy's *Return of the Native* (British). Wang Shiwei was also involved in translating *Sapho* by the French writer [Alphonse] Daudet.† Today, Liu Ying couldn't recall any of these works, even though she had studied literature at Beida. It's enough to just imagine the situation back then when Wang busied himself at the table translating, while Liu Ying took on all kinds of household chores. Wang Shiwei was very frank in describing the situation to his readers: "I started to translate these books from the English language versions published in the previous year by the Modern Library [spelled out in Roman letters]. Like many other translators, English is the only foreign language I know. I have to translate in order to make a living, there is no other way." Under such trying conditions, he would lose his temper frequently, suddenly bursting out in front of those rich and powerful people who controlled his fate. Wang Fanxi gave a description of Wang Shiwei's relationship with Xu Zhimuo in an article written in 1985:

---

*Published in German in 1918, the novella *The Heretic of Soana* portrays in the relationship between a man and woman who merge to produce a perfect love, a turning away from Christianity to the sensory world of Greek mythology and mysticism.

†*Sapho* (1884) depicts the world of students, artists, and *bohéme* through the story of a young student, who wants to stop an affair with an older women and yet does not have the courage to do it, leading the two to tear each other apart—a process described by Daudet as "oriental torture." Thanks to Professor Marie Louise Pesselier Vazquez, Department of Languages, Adelphi University.

Having made an appointment with Xu Zhimuo, Wang arrived at his home on time to find Xu unavailable. The next day Wang went there again and arrived a little earlier only this time to be informed by the house maid that: "The elder young master of the house is still in bed." Asked to wait, Wang got very angry and stomped out without saying a word. Back home, he wrote a long letter lambasting Xu who, after reading it, felt guilty and went to see Wang right away to apologize. They came to an agreement whereby Wang would "help" translate Thomas Hardy's *Return of the Native*.

However, Wang Shiwei was so poor that he couldn't afford the original copy [in English] and so Wang Fanxi had to buy the book for him. In spring 1932, Wang Fanxi was incarcerated as a political prisoner in the Caohejing prison in Shanghai:

One afternoon, the guard handed me a package of food and two books saying it was left by a visitor who wasn't allowed to see me. Both books were in English. One was the *Return of the Native* that I had bought for him. The other was *Salambo* by the French writer [Gustave] Flaubert. I figured it out that after Wang had finished his translations, he sent me the books to help an old friend kill some time while in prison.[5]

Wang had gone to the prison just after he and Liu Ying had returned from the Northeast where they had taught for one semester. Since Wang had also earned some royalties from translating, he took the small amount of money and returned to Hengchuan and told his father: "Use this money to start a business. From now on don't rely on me and don't worry about me. I'm on my way to join the revolution." He then returned to Shanghai possessed by an air of excitement.

Wang immediately decided that he should join the Shanghai Left-Wing Writers Association (*zuolian*). The Song-Hu Agreement that followed upon the "January 18 Incident" [the 1932 Japanese attack on Shanghai] merely strengthened his resolve. He kept telling Liu Ying: "Let's join the *zuolian* as quickly as possible so that we can expose the enemy!" He immediately started writing an article condemning the [CCP] traitor Gu Shunzhang whose conduct Wang had read about in the newspaper.* Convinced that publication of such an article was

---

*Captured by the KMT in Wuhan, Gu Shunzhang became a turncoat, leading to the arrest and execution of many communist party members.

impossible, Wang exploded in anger: "I can't stand this. Let's quickly join the party so we can take revenge!" According to documents now available, Wang met with two "CCP members" who immediately informed him that their involvement with the Anti-Leftist [anti-Li Lisan] faction had led to their expulsion from the [CCP] Central Committee. Although Liu Ying had succeeded in contacting the party, she was too frightened to follow orders to participate in Li Lisan's "flying gatherings" (feixing jihui). Liu did not fear death, having prepared for it as early as 1926 when she first joined the party. But she was afraid of being physically humiliated especially when three of her female classmates—Xiong Zongying, Liu Min, and Liu Zhongyi—were arrested after one of these meetings, and were then raped and turned into concubines of KMT police officials. Liu Ying thought that it was perfectly acceptable to leave the party and rejoin once its strategy had been altered. She never expected that she would be separated from party activities for half a century, never again to reenter. Although uninvolved in the party, Liu Ying still followed its serious warnings: Never have any relationship with the Trotskyites. After repeated persuasion by Liu Ying, Wang Shiwei decided to change their residence and break off contact with all of their old acquaintances. He would translate another book and then search out the zuolian. Thus Wang Fanxi was unaware that Wang Shiwei had meant to say goodbye when he went to see him in prison. Wang Shiwei also blew the whole plan to translate another book by arguing with the editor after discovering alterations had been made in his original translation. He angrily returned home and started to spit up blood a few days later [indicating he had contracted tuberculosis—Eds.].

Once again the couple faced severe hardship. Wang Shiwei's illness hampered his ability to support his wife and child and even more so prevented him from joining the revolution wholeheartedly. His father-in-law took Liu Ying and her child back home while Wang spent one year in Hangzhou recovering from his tuberculosis and afterwards he returned to Henan where he started teaching again.

During the Spring Festival [New Year] of 1936, Wang Shiwei, who was never appreciated by his father-in-law, returned to Changsha to see Liu Ying and his family. The first comment he made after seeing Liu Ying with the two children—age one and four—was: "Now it's time to fight the Japanese. Come out to work." Worshipped by Liu's younger brothers, he explained to them the reasons behind the resistance struggle and taught them to sing the "Internationale." Meanwhile he warned: "No one can join the pro-KMT Sanqing League. Otherwise, I won't consider you my little brothers!"[6]

The [1937] Xi'an Incident led Wang to consult Liu about heading north: "Why don't we go together to Yan'an and join the revolution?" He arranged to wait for Liu Ying in the city of Kaifeng, but she arrived two months late after she had gone to Wuhan to help her neurotic sister give birth. Wang exclaimed unhappily: "Now how is it that you can give up important resistance work to take care of your sister?" At the same time, Liu Ying was surprised to discover that she was pregnant. They found a doctor in Kaifeng who performed an abortion, though it failed after several attempts. She then decided to have another abortion in Changsha. Wang Shiwei couldn't wait any longer and along with six female students left for Yan'an. The couple planned to have their reunion in Yan'an a short time later. It was October 1937.

The two did not correspond for the first few months as Wang, with his party membership now restored, was teaching at the Lu Xun Arts College. He had apparently not yet developed the cynical feelings later expressed in "Wild Lilies." His first letters described the excitement stirred up in him by opposition to the Japanese and devotion to rescuing the country in Yan'an. It's a pity that Liu Ying didn't keep any of the letters, but then she was afraid that they might be discovered by KMT spies.

Both Wuhan and Changsha were soon occupied by the Japanese. Liu Ying escaped with her two children to western Hunan and broke off contact with the [party's] underground mail system. In Wang's last letter to Liu Ying, which was never delivered and returned to Yan'an, he implored his wife: "I worry about you. Why don't you write back?" Wang Shiwei must have thought that Liu Ying and the children had been killed in the war and so he no longer wrote them letters. His very last letter was addressed to his father. Contrary to his usual tone, his words were quite sad and miserable: "I have made some mistakes, but I'll surely correct them. Please tell the family to be at ease." It was written in the winter of 1943 without a return address. Below the signature was written: "Please ask the *Liberation Daily* to forward it."

Chapter Four

Few people in Yan'an knew Wang Shiwei, remember him, or had a personal relationship with him. Those who did know him and are still alive, such as Chen Boda, who is now in prison, and Zhou Yang, now in hospital,* cannot answer my question: "What is your view of the Wang Shiwei case today?" The following is a list of the articles and the authors that appeared in *Liberation Daily* two and one-half months after the publication of "Wild Lilies"†:

June 9 [1942]:

"On Comrade Wang Shiwei's Ideological Consciousness" (Lun Wang Shiwei tongzhi de sixiang yizhi) by Fan Wenlan.

"The 'Artist's' 'Wild Lilies'" ("Yishujia" de "yebaihehua") by Chen Dao

"Additional Thoughts on 'Some Feelings After Reading *Wild Lilies*'" (Ji "du 'yebaihehua' yougan" zhihou) by [Li] Bozhao

June 10:

"Politicians, Artists" (Zhengzhi jia yu yishujia) by Cai Tianxin

June 15:

"Concerning Wang Shiwei" (Guanyu Wang Shiwei) by Chen Boda

June 16:

"From Lu Xun's Critical Essays to a Discussion of Wang Shiwei" (Zong Lu Xun de zawen tan dao Wang Shiwei) by Zhou Wen

"The Literary and Artists Circle's Correct Attitude and Their Self-Examination Regarding Wang Shiwei" (Wenyijie dui Wang Shiwei ying you de taidu ji fanxing) by Ding Ling

---

*Both Chen Boda and Zhou Yang are now deceased.

†Comparing the following list to Stranahan's complete list in *Molding the Medium*, pp. 74–81, some of Dai Qing's titles for these articles are apparently incomplete.

June 17:

"Thoroughly Smash Wang Shiwei's Trotskyite Theories and Anti-Party Activities" (Chedi fenzui Wang Shiwei Tuopai lilun ji fan dang huodong) by Zhang Ruxin

Over the course of the eight days when these articles were published, the tone of the commentators changed as is evident from Zhang Ruxin's highly charged [June 17] article that differed fundamentally from Fan Wenlan's [June 9]. This change followed a three-day meeting in Yan'an of literary and artistic circles that was reported in *Liberation Daily* on June 19:

"Literature and Artistic Circle in Yan'an Holds Forum That Angrily Condemns Wang Shiwei's Reactionary Thoughts and Recommends That the Literary Resistance Association Revoke His Association Membership."

> (Special report from this newspaper): Literary and artistic circles in Yan'an held an unprecedented forum attended by more than forty people at the Literature Resistance Association. Ding Ling, Zhou Yang, and Sai Ke were elected to the Association's presidium. At the meeting, writers and artists unanimously expressed their anger towards the Trotskyite Wang Shiwei. They also discussed Wang's articles "Wild Lilies" and "Politicians, Artists," exposed Wang Shiwei's political conspiracy, and listed a series of political conspiratorial incidents conducted by the international Trotskyite bandits. Everybody agreed that the Trotskyite Wang Shiwei was both a political enemy and an enemy of literature and artistic circles. The writers especially rebuked Wang Shiwei's vicious thoughts as espoused in "Politicians, Artists": he had not only caused progressive politicians to be polarized from progressive artists, but his provocative conduct had also produced conflict that was detested by literary and artistic circles. The writers made their own self-examination regarding the incident and also agreed that petty bourgeois ideological thoughts must be completely eradicated. There was also another discussion at the forum on the issue of maintaining close contact with the masses. Altogether, the enthusiastic and successful discussion lasted for three days—from the fifteenth to noon on the eighteenth.

March 18 to June 18 was exactly three months. By the latter date, questions had already arisen concerning Wang Shiwei's activities as a writer and translator. What was waiting for Wang Shiwei was a change in label from a Trotskyite and a KMT spy, to the head of the Five

Member Anti-Party Gang. More than two hundred party members and non-party members, including Wang Shiwei, were arrested in one night to prevent these "internal traitors" from making contact with Hu Zongnan [a KMT general] who would soon arrive in Yan'an as the head of a delegation on April 1, 1943.*

Wang's four-year life as a prisoner thus began. Wang probably wrote his last letter [cited above] to his father during this period. How did Wang adapt to the change from being a special research fellow to becoming a prisoner?

Within his small circle of friends, Wang Shiwei was famous for his eccentricities. He was the third person recruited to work at the Translation Department of the Academy for Marxist-Leninist Studies along with He Xilin and Ke Bainian and was appointed to that position by Luo Fu [Zhang Wentian], director of the Propaganda Department. Wang was very industrious translating over four years one to two million words despite friction with his boss, Chen Boda. Wang's translations of works by Marx and Lenin were not only published in Yan'an and the anti-Japanese base areas, but also in Chongqing [KMT headquarters] and in the "isolated island" of the KMT occupied areas. The proofreader, Wang Xuewen, says: "I took Wang Shiwei's share of royalties totalling two hundred sixty four thousand from the republication in 1950 of *Value, Price, and Profit*, translated by Wang and published by the Sanlian Publishing House, and gave it to the party committee of the Academy for Marxist-Leninist Studies (it was in the old currency and in three separate payments. I still have the receipt in my pocket)."[7] Many people recalled Wang's contribution in helping to spread Marxism in China as was recently noted in the 1983 book *Dissemination of Marx-Engels Works in China*. At that time, Wang Shiwei prohibited anyone from altering his translations, which is exactly how he had dealt with the China Book Bureau. Ke Bainian, who was responsible for checking and proofreading manuscripts, was frequently involved in arguments with Wang Shiwei, for whenever Wang found that Ke had changed his version, Wang became furious. Once Wang got so angry that he kicked over a jar in the cave. According to Wang's Beida schoolmate, He Xilin, there were only three people with whom Wang never argued: Wang Xuewen, who was serious and honest and had

---

*Hu Zongnan would later surround and capture Yan'an in 1947.

once studied in Japan; Fan Wenlan, who only cared about his own work and did not care much . . . about other things; and Luo Fu, who was versatile but modest. He Xilin said that the reason why Wang Shiwei argued with Ke was because Ke claimed the correct translation [in the title] should be "price" while in Wang's version it was rendered as "money."

He Xilin has also commented that: "This man was not loveable. Most people didn't like him. We all ate the mid-size pot meals (including Wang Ruofei. Only members of the CCP Central Committee were allowed to eat small-pot meals).* The meals were sent over by the young soldiers and were of good quality. Wang Shiwei was totally immoral, picking out only the lean meat slices in the pot when he had already contracted tuberculosis."

Wang Shiwei's deadly foe was Chen Boda. The hatred between them can be traced back to 1940 when Wang wrote articles opposing Chen Boda on some literary issues. Chen suppressed Wang by attaching a political label to him (using the heroic tone of the Second Communist International). Later on, Chen Boda, who didn't know any foreign language, was appointed director of the Translation Department where Wang Shiwei was working. (The former director of the department was Luo Fu, who had held the post concurrently and had won Wang Shiwei's respect.) That was something else that agitated Wang. However, to consider this merely a matter of a vanity competition is an over-simplification. According to a memoir by Chen Jusun (Chen Jie), a temporary worker at the Translation Department, Wang and Chen were polar opposites. The easily irritable and cynical Wang Shiwei enjoyed "offending authority," while Chen Boda was just the opposite. This was evident as Chen passed on his "wily skills" to Chen Jusun whom he took as a fellow provincial: "The most important thing in life," Chen Boda instructed him, "is to follow the right person and stay with him. The second important thing is to organize your own followers." Chen Boda was so pleased when he heard that Chairman Mao had read his article attacking Wang Shiwei that Chen rubbed his hands and kept saying: "I've followed the right person! I've followed the right person!" Thus Chen Boda fulfilled his first important point. The

---

*Above Wang Shiwei claimed he had access to "small-pot" meals. See "Egalitarianism and Hierarchy."

second point was also fulfilled. But here I don't think I'll publish the list of bodies that Chen Boda gathered around himself and were then later revealed by Chen Jusun, even though Chen Jusun passed away in 1987.*

Together with Xi Xinghai, Xiao Jun, and Sai Ke, Wang Shiwei was considered one of "the four eccentric people in Yan'an" (*Yan'an sida guairen*). Sai Ke wore long hair down to his shoulders; Xiao [the Manchurian writer] was arrogant, egocentric, and wild, so wild that he once pulled a dagger on Ai Siqi; Xi Xinghai was famous for his pledge: "Make sure I have access to a plenty of chickens; otherwise, I won't produce one single line of musical notes." Wang Shiwei was most famous for his severity and harshness. He was eager to spread his own views. Once, after he had finished writing "Politicians, Artists," Wang visited his next door neighbor Pan Fang, who would also be accused of being a member of the Anti-Party Gang together with Wang, and read the article aloud. A gentle and graceful scholar who had studied in Germany, Pan Fang was generally unwilling to follow dissenting views, preferring, instead, to conform with the dominant view. Wang was so irritated by Pan's emotionless response that he shouted: "Forget it! I'll go talk with [Liu] Xuewei!" And so he left.

Wang spent more time arguing than talking with Xuewei. Liu was also a special research fellow, involved in compiling the *History of New Literature in China* (Zhongguo xin wenxue shi). Soon after he was appointed to work at the Central Research Institute, Luo Fu told him:

There's one person who has many ideas you can listen to and help yourself.

"Who is he?" Xuewei asked.

"Wang Shiwei," answered Luo.

There was less than ten meters between Xuewei's and Wang's caves, and naturally they talked frequently about everything from literary history, politics, and popular artistic views to personal experiences. Generally speaking, Wang Shiwei did most of the talking while Xuewei was mostly content to remain silent except when he felt that Wang had strayed too far from the topic.

---

*This group reportedly included the hard-line ideologue Deng Liqun. See Barmé, "Using the Past," p. 173.

As described above, the garments worn by the special research fellows were the same as Mao's. Wang Shiwei claimed that he himself was at the level of "wearing cadre garments and eating small-pot meals" and so he was not engaging in sour grapes when he attacked the idea of the "division of three colors in garments and the five categories of food." However, in the winter of 1941 Wang Shiwei was not given the cotton coat that the rules specified he should have been provided. "Wang Shiwei protested so loudly that, finally, Fan Wenlan offered his own coat to Wang to stop his complaining. Later I was told that Wang only took Fan's hat but not his coat."[8]

[Liu] Xuewei can hardly remember this incident. In fact, Xuewei also did not receive a coat, but, not caring about such petty matters, he kept it quiet. However, Xuewei does not agree with Rong Mengyuan's view that Wang Shiwei was advocating "absolute egalitarianism" (*pingjunzhuyi*). Xuewei, a specialist in literature, thinks that the egalitarian ideal in Yan'an coexisted with the acceptance of social ranks that had appeared ever since the Xi'an incident. What Wang Shiwei opposed was the social rank system. Having seen that it would be impossible to alter, Wang started to blame the administrative people for making concessions to this hierarchical order.

Life in Yan'an was very boring. But Wang Shiwei did not feel that way at all; for in his whole life "he neither smoked, drank, nor went to any movies. His only pastime was to take a walk" (according to Liu Ying). Many people think that Wang irritated Mao Zedong by purposely alluding to Jiang Qing in his criticism of the operatic lines "enchanting *Spring in the Jade Hall* and the rhythms of golden lotus dance." This provided Kang Sheng with an opportunity to flatter Mao and scold Wang. But this explanation is probably not true since after she married Mao in 1939 Jiang Qing seldom appeared in public. Moreover, Mao did not really appreciate *Spring in the Jade Hall* since he generally favored artistic works about workers, soldiers, and peasants, such as the realistic dramas *October Revolution Festival, Conquering Mount Liang by Force,* etc.

Jin Ziguang, one of the four busiest people in Yan'an, was responsible for arranging recreational activities. Jin had mixed feelings about Wang Shiwei for he disliked Wang's solemnity and inconsideration, though he respected Wang's knowledge and intelligence. Once Jin happened to be passing Wang's cave while Wang was outside sunbathing on a canvas chair. As soon as Wang spotted the lively and open-hearted club director Jin, Wang jumped up, grabbed the young man by the coat, and pointed his finger toward the auditorium located below the mountain from which music was blaring and said angrily: "If you people continue dancing and playing around, I'll drop a bomb on that place!" Wang also satirized the twenty-year-old Yin Bai who had not completed much school, but solely through his own efforts had managed to be appointed a writer-in-residence at the writers' association in Yan'an. Wang commented: "Zhang Jingqiu (Yin Bai's real name), whenever I see you, I can't help but think of Lu Xun's literary description of your smiling face." In Wang Shiwei's opinion, people in Yan'an were happy and gay while corruption went unnoticed. He simply couldn't stand it. Thank god that the above words uttered by Wang were only heard by a few people who kept it to themselves until they recalled them several years later. None of these people had revealed these lines at meetings in Yan'an criticizing Wang; otherwise he would have been accused of much more serious crimes.

Returning to the main point of discussion:

Around March 25, young intellectuals in the Central Research Institute attached pages from *Arrow and Target* onto a piece of red cloth and hung them on to the South Gate—a busy area in Yan'an similar to Wangfujing [the biggest shopping district in present-day Beijing]. Subsequent events were beyond the expectation of both those young people and even older individuals such as Fan Wenlan, Luo Mai, Li Yan, and Zhou Yang, though the degree of unexpectedness varied.

> In late March, Comrade Wang Zhen made a comment after reading Wang's articles at the Central Research Institute: "Our comrades at the front are shedding blood and sacrificing their lives for the party and the people of the whole nation, while you people after feeding yourselves in the rear areas are condemning the party!" It was indeed right to the point.
>
> One night holding a lamp Mao went to the Institute to read *Arrow and Target* and said immediately: "Our ideological struggle now has a target."* [9]

It seems that Mao made that comment sometime between March 23 and the end of March, as the tone of his speech at a meeting held to

---

*Immediately after reading "Wild Lilies," Mao demanded tighter party control over the press that led to a Central Committee decision a few days later (Stranahan, *Molding the Medium*, p. 30).

discuss reorganizing *Liberation Daily* on March 31 became much harsher: "Some people do not take the correct standpoint. This refers to the conduct of carrying out the absolute egalitarian concept through cold satire and innuendo. Recently, quite a few people have demanded egalitarianism. This is an unrealistic illusion."[10] Although some people were mentioned and the issue of "standpoint" was raised, it did not yet eliminate all opportunities to exclude oneself from it. Ding Ling, the author of "Thoughts on March 8," had problems with her "standpoint" but she was forgiven after admitting her faults and determining to correct them.[11]

Of course, the "recriticism" of Ding Ling in 1957 [the Anti-Rightist Campaign] was another story.

Hu Qiaomu, Mao's secretary in Yan'an, "had two talks with Wang Shiwei" and wrote him two letters. Here is an excerpt from one of them: "The mistake of 'Wild Lilies' is, first of all, in its standpoint that has already been criticized. Second, there are some more concrete criticisms. Last, are its writing techniques. What Chairman Mao wishes you to correct is your incorrect standpoint. The article is full of unfriendly feelings towards the leaders and is provocative in winning ordinary people's support to attack them. Such conduct is definitely not allowed among party members, no matter whether you are a politician or an artist. The more this kind of criticism draws some comrades together into opposition, the more dangerous it becomes to the party. Thus it is more necessary to resist [these criticisms]."[12]

Despite these comments, the majority at the Central Research Institute supported democracy and Wang Shiwei. On April 3, after summarizing the problems and lessons previously revealed, the Propaganda Department issued the "April 3 Decision." Three days later, on April 6, at the leading study group of the Central Committee, Mao emphasized that: "There exist three problems in the mobilization of the Rectification Movement." The last two problems were that: "The youth are dissatisfied and have uneasy feelings. There is also a problem of policy in the literary and artistic circles." The last problem was directly related to Wang Shiwei. According to materials now public, it seems that Wang Shiwei's name was not mentioned. However, the fact that Wang "provoked" the young people to "make complaints," demanded that leaders "listen to the 'complaints' of the young people from lower levels," and called upon artists to "aim at ourselves and our own camp first of all" was known to everyone. None of the participants would misunderstand the underlying meaning of what Mao had said, which was that in order to achieve the political purpose initially planned [i.e., attacking Wang Ming and Zhang Wentian], the dear old man had to deal with the obstacles personally [i.e., the discontent among the young supposedly engendered by Wang Shiwei] that had abruptly appeared from nowhere. Of course, what Mao said at that time was not as straightforward and explicit as what he would later say at the Seventh Party Congress in 1945:

> The party can only proceed if there is one unanimous thought; otherwise, there will be diverse ideas. The party cannot proceed if Wang Shiwei keeps declaring himself as king and autocrat. Wang Shiwei was the one who started the whole thing of putting up wall newspapers that attracted so many people outside Yan'an's south gate in 1942. He was the "general commander" and defeated us. We admit that we were defeated. That's why we will carry out this Rectification Movement thoroughly right now.

On April 7, the "thorough rectification" started at the Central Research Institute. "At the call of the Propaganda Department, cadres and activists in the Institute had a meeting. Comrade Kai Feng restated the 'spirit of the April 3 Decision' and criticized harshly erroneous tendencies in rectification at the Institute. This way, everybody was awakened and the Rectification Movement at the Institute was gradually put back on the right track."[13]

Readers should notice that this was the start of solving academic and ideological problems by organizational means.* However, the "gradually awakening" cadres, activists, and research fellows did not immediately abandon Wang Shiwei. They were still hoping that Wang would accept the criticisms, change his views, and become somewhat smarter.

Fan Wenlan said at the meeting:

> Over the past two months or so the party committee has talked with him eight times. I myself have talked with him on two or three occasions. Each time Wang quibbled, showing no sign of admitting his faults. Yesterday morning he said to me: "I've read your article criticiz-

---

*That is, severe punishments, including purges, imprisonment, and sometimes, as in Wang Shiwei's case, execution.

ing me in the newspaper. I am still unaware of why I am wrong."

The Institute's party committee entrusted five comrades to talk with Wang to help him realize his faults but Wang cursed them throughout the meeting. There were also some comrades who volunteered to talk to Wang but none of them succeeded in waking him up.

Wang was invited to participate in each forum but over the course of several weeks he turned down the offer each time. The forum entrusted some representatives to have further talks with him, which lasted for two whole days, but Wang just kept quibbling.[14]

Wen Jize, who was appointed as propaganda member of the Institute's party committee, was the most patient. He always considered Wang Shiwei as a comrade who had momentarily failed to change his mind. He thus went to see Wang even after the launching of the most serious criticism. Contrary to Fan Wenlan's description, Wang Shiwei actually changed his attitude in response to Wen's tireless efforts. Wang could not understand why he was being criticized for making correct criticisms to help improve the party. He felt that he was being treated unjustly beyond any reasonable expectations. Wen tried to console him:

> You surely didn't come to Yan'an from afar for the sake of yourself. All you have to do is to pay attention to your standpoint and the method you used with both your words and actions. Just think, where can you find true equality today?

Wang Shiwei was willing to accept soft rather than harsh criticism. After hearing Wen's words, he held Wen's hands and started to cry, saying:

> I will admit my faults. But what I've done was for the good of the party.

Wen Jize went to Li Yan, the party secretary of the Institute, and said:

> As far as I'm concerned, Wang has come to see his incorrect views on his own. Now that he has admitted his faults, do we still have to consider this a political issue?

Li Yan neither answered yes or no and after quite a while responded slowly: "Tell Wang to be more serious. You are representing the party committee. Don't let him sense that anything here is personal."

Wen Jize quickly explained: "I don't represent the party committee. I only represent myself."

The next day, Li Yan, with a rather serious look on his face, said to Wen as if it was he who had been criticized:

> I reported what you told me to Comrade Kang Sheng. He said you are sympathizing with Wang. And there's something else that you cannot reveal to anyone. Wang Shiwei is a Trotskyite and has engaged in some organizational activities. He is also a spy for the [KMT] Blue Shirts. He is different from other people. His problem is not an ideological one. You are working at the party committee. You should pay attention to what you do.

No matter how sympathetic Wen Jize was, he dared not insist on his own views on the Wang case. Thus he no longer saw Wang.

The next thing that happened was the involvement of the Central Social Department [Kang Sheng's secret police] that sent people to the Institute and ordered Li Yan to compose notes about Wang including his words and deeds in daily life.

Next, Li Yan was told to go to the Central Organization Department to examine Wang Shiwei's dossier (*dang'an*).

Arrow and Target was removed from the south gate. Once its erroneous tendencies were corrected, only two more issues of the newspaper —numbers six and seven—were published. Luo Mai restated his views about the March 18 meeting. Contrary to the disputatious situation that had prevailed among participants at the last meeting, this time the entire audience held their breath, and were quiet and agreeable.

Yan'an's Forum on Literature and Art ended on May 25. Mao's [Yan'an] talks given on the last day of the forum ended up being taken as the "bible" by artistic circles till his death. (One view holds that it is still the "bible" today.) The speech cleared up many errors and arguments on artistic issues, and "solved long-standing controversial issues in the modern Chinese art movement by systematically employing Marxist-Leninist perspectives. It also produced important results in solving the major division in the Rectification Movement between proletarian and petty bourgeois ideologies."[15] Ai Siqi listened to the speech and reported back to the Central Research Institute, where everybody ultimately came to realize the truth. For reasons of "promoting the cooperation of comrades in artistic and military fronts," Mao invited Wang Zhen, who "had engaged in struggles on the military front for a long time and had established a glorious military record," to head the rectification study group among artists. (Wang Zhen was then commander of the Yan'an Garrison Headquarters leading his troops in plowing fields in Yan'an. Wang Zhen had also voiced the most "explicit resistance" to the wall newspaper *Arrow and Target*. Wang Zhen "repeatedly claimed" that he "couldn't undertake this task." But Mao was very determined: "It is you that are appointed to do this work. It is because of your lack of much formal education that you should be appointed to deal with the literate.")[16]

On May 27, the forum on "Democracy and Discipline in the Party" was held at the Central Research Institute.

Chapter Five

The forum began on May 27. The intent and ultimate outcome of this meeting cannot be explained in just a few lines, nor even in a long article. It will require a thorough historical analysis by scholars at CASS who are studying the development and evolution of Chinese society and the revolution.*

The first five days involved discussions of party democracy and discipline, and rectification in general. The first people to speak made self-criticisms regarding their tendency towards extreme democracy revealed at the beginning of rectification. The extreme democracy tendency referred to the idea of "cutting off the big tails" (the leaders' tails) and negating the principle that all the leaders should be legitimate members of the rectification leadership. Some people, however, held a different view toward this idea.

Li Yuchao was the first to raise the issue of Wang Shiwei. Li stressed that "although there were quite a few people who exhibited erroneous tendencies, they differed fundamentally from Wang Shiwei." It can be imagined that Li's comments brought relief to quite a few people present at the forum. However, somebody spoke up and opposed Li's view, saying: "Li's style is nitpicking and has the remnants of subjectivism."

On the third and fourth days of the forum, there were no disagreements whatsoever. Luo Mai set the tone by saying: "Wang Shiwei's standpoint is contrary to the party's. Wang's mistake is not only an ideological one. It is a political one. His mistake cannot be viewed as the same erroneous tendency as some of our comrades."[17]

---

*Dai Qing is implying here that the internal dynamics of the meeting and the apparent willingness of intellectuals to launch assaults on their brethren reflected deeper psychological and cultural strains in Chinese society that require more thorough analysis by contemporary scholars.

Just like the dampness prior to a big rain, everybody sensed that a storm was brewing. Finally, the thunder came rolling in; it was one evening when: "Some comrades suggested to the chair of the forum committee that since the issue of democratic-centralism had been discussed extensively, the next session of the forum should focus on the nature of Wang Shiwei's ideology. The suggestion was adopted by the committee."[18]

The forum was then adjourned for the day. On the same day, Wang Shiwei's articles from the newspaper and wall newspaper were disseminated as study materials.

The main criticism session the next day attracted thousands of people. This was the so-called big forum held on the sports ground. The materials provided by Pan Fang and Liu Xuewei pushed the forum to its climax.

Liu Xuewei exposed Wang Shiwei's Trotskyite ideas—issues that had provoked frequent daily arguments between the two. Wang Shiwei attributed the failure of [China's 1927] Great Revolution to Stalin and Borodin, but not to Chen Duxiu. Wang thought that Chen Duxiu's ideas were not erroneous, but that he had failed in resisting the opposition's ideas. In literature, Wang asserted that he agreed with Trotsky's idea on the negation of proletarian literature mentioned in Trotsky's *Literature and Revolution.* In Wang's opinion, the bourgeois class, which had been in the dominant position for so long, could generate its own literature, while the proletarian class being subordinate to the bourgeois class, lacked its own culture and, after gaining power as society moved forward to communism, its class consciousness would quickly diminish. Thus, it would be impossible for a proletarian culture to appear.

Wang especially insisted on the theory of "human nature" (*renxing*). It was his belief that that "human nature played a major role in both politics in general and in the special circumstance of revolutionary politics." He also believed that "Marxists put too much emphasis on objects and that they focus too much on material things." He did not agree with the Marxist idea that once objective material conditions were changed human nature would then be altered. According to Wang Shiwei: "The work of altering human nature is independent and it is at least as important, if not more important, than the change in the social material environment."* He gave powerful evidence to prove his theory: After the [1927] revolution "the successful and newly powerful aristocrats of the new dynasty were uglier and more cruel in terms of human nature than that of the old Beiyang Warlords." Liu Xuewei commented: "That irritated Wang. Wang was more irritated by the fact that many of his 'old' friends had completely changed; as soon as the political atmosphere had changed they took their fathers as thieves and gained glory by selling out their friends. Wang also praised Trotsky's writing ability, by saying 'His skill can still be recognized even in [Chinese] translation.' "

Of course, Liu Xuewei objected to Wang's ideas and emphasized to him the danger of the "Trotsky-Chen [Duxiu] Liquidationist Faction." Xuewei also noted that art ought to serve class interests and reflect political views and pointed out that the key thing is to have the right standpoint; otherwise, the better the writing skill of an [incorrect] article, the more harmful it becomes. As usual, Wang Shiwei was not persuaded. Afterwards at the meeting:

> Comrades Xuewei and others stood up to present material proving that Wang Shiwei had been poisoned ideologically by his past associations with the Trotskyites. They reported that Wang had claimed that "Stalin's character is not praiseworthy," "[Karl] Radek is an admirable man,"† "the Comintern should be held responsible for the failure of the Great Chinese Revolution of 1927," "the charge of high treason against Zinoviev is dubious," "on certain issues Trotsky's theories are correct," and so forth.
>
> Wang's basic understanding of the Rectification Movement is fundamentally erroneous: He slandered the leading organ of the party by believing that some members were corrupt, he said that the Rectification Movement was "a unification under the leadership of Chairman Mao of upright people against immoral ones," and he said that Comrades Luo Mai and Fan Wenlan headed two factions on the question of democracy in our Institute. He also used the term *hard bones* to draw other comrades to his side and the abusive term *soft bones* to attack other comrades.

---

*This was another source of conflict with Chen Boda. See Chen's "Human nature, party nature, revolutionary nature," *Liberation Daily*, March 27, 1943, p. 4, cited in Stranahan, *Molding the Medium*, p. 69.

†Wang was obviously unaware of Radek's testimony against Bukharin in the Moscow trials. See Medvedev, *Nikolai Bukharin*, p. 133.

At the end of the meeting, Ai Siqi read aloud the article by Wang Shiwei in which he refuted the attacks against him by Qi Su in "Concerning 'Wild Lilies.' " In this article, [Ai continued] Wang not only slanders the party but promotes himself as a leader of youth. He claims to be the 'modern Lu Xun' and calls upon youth to shake his hand. Upon hearing these sickening phrases, the meeting roared with malicious laughter.[19]

At this point, it was too late for Xuewei to tell Wang Shiwei that he had unintentionally mentioned the discussions between the two of them to Xu Jiansheng. Xuewei had mentioned this to Xu because he considered the dispute between Wang and other people at the Institute to be serious and that Wang Shiwei had indeed held Trotskyite ideas. Xu passed what Xuewei had told him on to Li Yan who then reported it to Luo Mai. Luo then decided that Xuewei would expose Wang at the meeting.

Xuewei never expected that his speech would have such an impact. At a later discussion meeting he explained: "Wang had Trotskyite ideas, but it was not serious enough to be considered as an organizational issue." His attitude irritated Luo Mai.

Thirty-nine years later in 1981, Luo Mai entrusted Wen Jize and others to compile memoirs of people from the Yan'an Central Research Institute. As for those segments involving Wang Shiwei, Wen Jize asked: "No evidence was ever presented to prove he was a Trotskyite. Is it acceptable if we don't mention it anymore?" to which Luo Mai responded: "Let it remain as is. We really can't do anything about it now." Soon afterwards, Luo delivered a formal report to the Central Committee requesting a reevaluation of the Wang Shiwei issue.[20]

At the same time, Xuewei went to see Little Wen [a term of endearment for Wen Jize—Eds.] in the hospital and told him: "You must clear Wang's name. It was I who exposed him at that meeting. I never expected my actions would have such profound consequences. You must clear his name; otherwise, my heart won't be at ease even after I die."

But back in the 1940s, criticism and persecution was like a full-powered train—no one dared, nor was able to block it.

June 2 [1942]—

In the morning, Wang Shiwei presented his request to resign from the party to the Institute Party Committee. He explained that "the contradiction in interests between himself and the party had become virtually insoluble" and that he intended to "take the road he had chosen for himself."

After the meeting, everybody was still talking about Wang's resignation request. That night, several comrades sought out Wang and tried once again to save him.[21]

No one was sure who had talked with Wang. Anyway, Wang was obviously moved by it and thus participated in the June 4 meeting. According to Wen Jize's record:

> Today many people were present from the Central Political Research Office and the Literary Resistance Association (*wenkang*) as every window sill was filled. As soon as the bell rang starting the meeting, several hundred eyes turned toward Wang as he entered the auditorium from the door on the left. This was the first time Wang attended the forum.[22]

According to He Xilin's memoir: "Wang appeared at the meeting with that famous canvas reclining chair—he was probably already seriously ill [with tuberculosis]." Perhaps the young people in Yan'an in 1942 were different from the Red Guards in 1966. The former did not engage in physical torture "against the representative of the reactionary bourgeoisie within the party" (said by Ai Siqi). From this we can see that over the past thirty years the "revolution" has made progressive steps.

Also recorded by Wen Jize in his record of that day:

> After speeches by comrades Li Yuchao and Pan Fang, it was comrade Wang Shiwei's turn. He said in a low, deep voice: "I hereby withdraw solemnly and seriously my appeal to the party committee for resignation, made yesterday when I was in an abnormal state. . . . The 'love' of some friends whom I respect has moved me." One comrade interjected: "Is your political life determined by the 'love' of your friends?" Wang Shiwei replied: "I don't think that any 'love' or 'hatred' transcending classes exists. Just now Comrade Li Yuchao said that I am a Trotskyite, but I myself do not know. In the past I didn't have the slightest understanding of politics. . (?) . . If you've read my article on national forms of literature published in *Chinese Culture*, you would know that I have supported firmly the United Front . . . How can I have Trotskyite thought?"*
>
> A comrade stood up and interjected: "You should not tell lies! You

---

*Chinese Trotskyites, especially Chen Duxiu, strongly opposed the United Front with the KMT.

often spoke to me about the Trotskyite question and to this day you still believe that Trotskyites exist in the USSR and that they are not running dogs of the fascist bandit gang, that they are anti-fascist." Another comrade rose: "You told me the same thing." [Wang:] "I acknowledge everything I have said. Yes, I said that I hated the Trotskyites who organized against Stalin. But I am deeply moved by their alliance with the CPSU against fascism." Another intervention: "On what basis do you claim that Trotskyites still exist in the USSR? On what basis do you say Trotskyites oppose fascism?"

"Yes. You once said the same thing to me," another comrade replied.

In his subsequent comments Wang admitted that in 1929 he had contacts with Trotskyites for whom he had translated the *Lenin Last Testament*, (a testament revised by the Trotskyites). He also translated two chapters of Trotsky's autobiography [*My Life*], and published short stories in a Trotskyite magazine. Up until 1936, Wang continued to correspond with Trotskyites. He never forgot Trotskyite elements such as Chen Qingchen and Wang Wenyuan [Wang Fanxi]. "I think that the Trotskyite criticism of the Li Lisan line is correct." ("Sheer nonsense!" [the audience interjected]*) . . . "I've read the August 1 declaration [1935]. I believe that it more or less advocates the same idea as the Trotskyite call for a National Assembly." ("Sheer nonsense!") . . . "Only after I had read Lu Xun's letter to the Trotskyites, did I adopt a position in favor of the United Front."

Everyone was outraged by his unrepentant attitude and his blatant propagation of the theories of the Trotskyite bandits. The chair was asked to stop Wang Shiwei from straying from the subject and to reply to the questions clearly.

Another comrade stood up and asked: "Why did you say that during the purge of the party in the USSR people have ignored the crimes committed by Stalin? You made this statement." [Wang:] "I believe that during the purge of the CPSU, many enemies could have been turned into comrades. Stalin's character is too brutal." This slander of Stalin aroused righteous indignation. "Why on your arrival in Yan'an didn't you report honestly to the party about your association with the Trotskyites?" [Wang:] "When I first arrived in Yan'an I encountered discrimination everywhere . . . Right up to 1940 I criticized Chen Boda over the issue of national forms. During the polemic, he scolded me for being an opportunist of the Second International. If he wants to

*These interjections indicate clearly that during the purge of Wang Shiwei the CCP adopted the Stalinist style of show trials.

scold me as a member of the Fourth [Trotskyist] International what will that achieve? I reported to the party's Organization Department the links I had had with the Trotskyites." Beyond this, he grossly insulted Chen Boda: "He is a sectarian" (*zongpaizhuyi*); the chair silenced him.

Yet another comrade took the floor: "I ask that Wang Shiwei express his views on the following Trotskyite positions: (1) Trotsky's opinion on the question of the Soviet peasantry before the Twelfth Congress of the CPSU; (2) the question of the *Lenin Last Testament*; (3) the question of who, in the final analysis, should be responsible for the failure of the Great Chinese Revolution of 1925–27 . . . Wang Shiwei has debated these issues with me in the past. Wang Shiwei showed that he continued to preserve his 'original Trotskyite opinions.' " He [Wang] added: "If my opinion was incorrect, why didn't you educate me earlier?" [Another comrade:] "Did you ever discuss these matters with the party organization? Why didn't you ask the party to help correct your views? You prefer to spout off all around the place."

Wang Shiwei couldn't reply to these objections. When the meeting adjourned, I [Wen Jize] walked out of the meeting hall with Wang. He said to me: "Only I can rectify my errors. Others cannot shed light on them even if they are philosophers." I laughed coldly. He did not attend the meeting that afternoon.[23]

From then on, Wang never attended any other fora or conferences, including the "Meeting to Criticize Wang Shiwei" held on June 23.

During those nine days: "The movement shifted to the stage of examining and summarizing each individual's ideological background."[24] According to Ai Siqi: "Everybody analyzed the specific form of their own ideology and contradictions based on their social origin and historical development. Everybody also ruminated about the direction they would follow in the future. This historical (it can also be characterized as scientific though it was not scientific enough) examination made everybody clear about themselves. It also enabled everybody to figure out a more practical way of remolding oneself. Its role was far more significant than the half-baked self-examination and self-criticism on individual issues."[25]

Intellectual circles in Yan'an that two and one-half months earlier had been "chaotic and disputatious" now started to calm down. Wang Shiwei was dismissed from his membership in the Literary Resistance Association (the Yan'an branch of the All-China Literary Resistance Association) while "everybody else seriously analyzed themselves, and with great warmth helped each other. As a result, they got rid of their ideological burden happily and started to remold their view of the world conscientiously. Those comrades who had committed faults engaged in tearful self-criticisms." The contents of [their self-criticism] was very similar to that of the "anti-bourgeois liberalization" campaign forty-five years later [1987] in that: "Those who committed faults demanded democracy over party leadership; and freedom instead of party discipline."[26]

Ding Ling played an especially important role. Her comments at the meeting are still fresh in many people's minds: "I did not study well in the rectification of the three [evil work] styles movement. But now I've suddenly begun to be clear about quite a few of the issues that used to confuse me. I have the experience of 'turn around, and you will see the bank of the river.' Recalling my past frustrations, efforts, worries, and errors, I feel what Tang Sanzang [i.e., the Buddhist leader in the *Journey to the West*] felt when he was standing by the river on the border between heaven and earth—a feeling of suddenly realizing the whole truth.* I walk forward with steady and sure steps. There are still nine times nine equals eighty-one troubles waiting for me ahead."[27]

Author of "Miss Sophia's Diary" and "Thoughts on March 8," Ding Ling was later awarded the Stalin Prize for Literature for her book *Sun Shining on the Sanggan River* (Taiyang jiaozai Sangganhe shang). However, in her autobiography written in her later years, she only mentioned the work *Ghost World* (Guimei shijie) written in the 1930s and *Life Full of Wind and Snow* (Fengxue renjian) from the 1960s, while ignoring her great advancements after her great realization of the whole truth.

In contrast to this was another writer:

> In early June, Xiao Jun, along with comrades from the Literary Resistance Association, attended one of the big criticism meetings against Wang Shiwei. Xiao was upset about the chaotic conditions of the meeting and on the way home he voiced some complaints. His comments were overheard by a female comrade walking beside him who reported it to the Association's party organization. A few days later, the Institute

---

*Note the parallels to Bukharin's "conversion" as portrayed in Arthur Koestler's *Darkness at Noon*.

sent four representatives to Xiao Jun requesting that he admit his faults and apologize. But Xiao rebuffed them and then recorded what happened, collected materials, and delivered his opinions in a letter to Chairman Mao at the party center. Xiao styled that letter as a "memorandum" and read it aloud at the Association's rectification meeting. It prompted a big dispute between the five writers who were party members and who had participated in the meeting—Ding Ling, Zhou Yang, Ke Zhongping, Li Bozhao [Yang Shangkun's wife], and Liu Baiyu— and the two writers who were non-party members—Chen Xuezhao and Ai Qing. The meeting lasted from 8:00 P.M. to 2:00 A.M.—altogether six hours. There was dead silence in the audience. No one left the meeting early, for everyone was waiting to see the results. Xiao Jun was a "single tongue fighting a bunch of Confucians;" he thus became more and more excited. Wu Yuzhang, the chairman of the meeting, seeing that both sides were extremely resistant, stood up and said: "Comrade Xiao Jun is a good friend of our party. There must be something wrong in our work style that made Comrade Xiao lose his temper. We should focus on unity and criticize ourselves for what we did wrong!"

Old Wu's words calmed Xiao Jun down quite a bit.[28]

In fact, Xiao Jun had never met Wang Shiwei. However: "being sympathetic with Wang became a scar printed on Xiao's forehead forever. Thus, he lost the status of 'entering the circle' (joining the party)."*

This phase of ideological struggle ended with Zhou Yang's long article titled "Wang Shiwei's Views on Literature and Art and Ours" covering two full pages in the *Liberation Daily* [July 28 and 29, 1942] where Zhou argued that "Wang Shiwei is not worth mentioning anymore." However, he also pointed out that:

> The difference over literary matters between Wang Shiwei and us rests on only one issue—that is, whether or not art should serve the masses. That is the core of the issue. Neither the Trotskyites nor Wang Shiwei claim that art should serve the proletarian class and ordinary people. They all claim that art serves an abstract "mankind" and portrays an

---

*Xiao Jun had called for moderation on April 8 in his article "On 'love' and 'patience' among comrades" (Lun tongzhi 'ai' yu 'nai'), *Liberation Daily*, p. 4. Xiao's ideas were criticized by Mao in the May Yan'an "Talks," yet Xiao continued to publish independent, though restrained, articles between March and July 1942. Xiao Jun was famous for his hot temper. Perhaps his great fame in Manchuria inclined party authorities to avoid making a martyr out of Xiao—no need for bad press there.

abstract "human nature." In fact, they claim that art serves the exploiting class and the dark forces. They definitely don't believe that the masses are able to create culture and art. They take an aristocratic and condescending attitude toward the masses and separate art from politics. Above all, they separate art from the masses.

Forty-one years later [1983], when Zhou Yang finally realized that "the essence of human beings is the individual person," and when on the one hundredth anniversary of Marx's death he raised the issue of humanism and human nature, he was also criticized, though in a much lighter way—too light so it cannot be compared with the criticism of Wang Shiwei that involved coercion. This charge against Zhou Yang—if there was such a charge—could not have taken place in the 1950s, for many people cannot forget just how devoted Zhou Yang was to his work from 1953 to 1957. Thus, it is not hard to imagine how astonished Zhou was when Mao Zedong suddenly labeled the Central Propaganda Department as the "Palace of Hell" in March 1966. Such an intelligent man as Zhou should have carefully observed and drawn lessons from the situation in the fall of 1942 when on September 15 Mao addressed a letter to the head of the Central Propaganda Department, Kai Feng, that was not published until 1983. In that letter, Mao mentioned the "lack of articles in the *Liberation Daily* and also that the newspaper focused too much on art." Mao also drafted rules on "Methods of Soliciting Articles for the *Liberation Daily*" in which he requested that "the comrades listed below be responsible for soliciting articles in addition to those articles that have already been published in special editions of the newspaper or that were sent directly to the editor's office."[29]

More than ten people from artist and nonartist circles in Yan'an were listed in Mao's directive.* According to Shu Qun's memoir, Old Ke (poet Ke Zhongping) was one of the names mentioned under which Mao commented: "Focus on mass art and mass culture. Other topics

---

*Mao's September 15, 1942, Letter to Kai Feng and Mao's September 20, 1942, "Methods for Selecting Articles for Page Four of *Liberation Daily*" appear on pages 99–103 of *Selected Writings of Mao Zedong on Journalism* (Mao Zedong xinwen gongzuo wenxue) (Beijing: Xinhua chubanshe, 1983). The comrades Mao listed, in addition to Ke Zhongping, included Chen Huangmei, Jiang Feng, Fan Wenlan, Deng Fa, Peng Zhen, Feng Wenbin, Ai Siqi, Chen Boda, Zhou Yang, and a half dozen more. Page four was the miscellany page—including literature and art—of *Liberation Daily*, edited by Ai Siqi.

are minor. Twelve thousand characters per month." Although it's rare for a revolutionary leader to focus so much on culture and propaganda work during a hard-fought war, this struggle was a very intense ideological one that Mao felt compelled to enter. We Chinese of later generations may find it difficult to understand whether Zhou Yang realized that a great intellectual movement usually generates an unprecedented cultural flourishing. Perhaps he did not think much of it, or did not associate it with the revolution in China. Nevertheless, the criticism of "humanism and alienation" (*rendaozhuyi yu yihua*) was launched [in the early 1980s]. A year and a half later, Zhou Yang responded by suffering a severe stroke and being committed to the hospital. This year he is seventy-six.†

---

†Zhou Yang died in August 1989.

Chapter Six

What, then, was the relationship between Wang Shiwei and the Trotskyist organization?

After Wang's arrest on April 1, 1943, the Central Social Department could care less about accusations such as "Blue Shirt spy" and "anti-party gangster" that even Kang Sheng considered fishy and, since they were only used to scare people, could not endure. Instead, they focused on the contact between Wang Shiwei and the Trotskyists and brought Wang in for questioning on several occasions.

According to a memoir by Ling Yun, the first attempt was carried out soon after Wang's arrest at the detention office of the Central Social Department at Hou Gou, near Zao Yuan [Mao Zedong's residence in Yan'an]. Wang did not say a word to anyone upon entering the room, but proceeded directly to Lenin's portrait and bowed deeply. At that time, evidence was gathered by questioning the prisoner rather than sending people out to make investigations. The people at the Central Social Department were quite polite to Wang and did not use later [Cultural Revolution] methods such as "extorting a confession," "tricking one into a confession" or taking turns in interrogation. "The whole process often led to an opportunity for Wang Shiwei to give grand speeches" (said by Ling Yun).

Almost all of the questions were about two of Wang's former Beida classmates—Chen Qingchen of the Proletarian Society and Wang Fanxi of the October Society.

According to the memoir by Wang Fanxi:

> Wang Shiwei and I kept in touch for about one year in Shanghai—1930 to the spring of 1931. In fact, we did not meet frequently—in total we met about ten times—because he was busy translating books and I was organizing the Leftist opposition. Besides myself, as far as I

know, the only person Wang Shiwei contacted was Chen Qichang, whose real name was Chen Qingchen, who was frequently mentioned during rectification in Yan'an. (By the way, he was the Chen Zhong-shan who later wrote that letter to Lu Xun.) Chen Qichang was also dismissed from the party due to his tolerating the opposition. He belonged to the Chen Duxiu faction. Nevertheless, Wang Shiwei never joined the Trotskyites or the October Society that I joined or the Proletarian Society to which Chen Qichang belonged.

Politically, Wang generally agreed with the Trotskyite ideas, especially estimates at that time of the situation in China: Whether or not it favored direct revolution, or indicated that the revolution had failed. Wang agreed with the [latter] opposition's ideas. But he was also dubious about the possibility of establishing a revolutionary party led by Trotskyites. He wanted everyone to remain in the [existing] party and he never would have attempted to establish something new even if he had been dismissed from the CCP. I believe that it is due to this idea that Wang later managed to rejoin the party and went to Yan'an.

But these were not the topics of our occasional meetings. Instead, we discussed and argued over the issue of his "theory of human nature" that made him famous. . . .

At that time, I was involved in arranging a translation of the Trotsky autobiography [*My Life*] and asked Wang to help because of his excellent command of English. He agreed and translated two chapters—"New York" and "In a Concentration Camp." According to later Yan'an documents, Wang himself reported this fact to the party organization. The document also claimed that Wang translated the *Lenin Testament* for the Trotskyites, of which I know nothing. Perhaps it was arranged by Chen Qichang. The translation was published in a magazine edited by Wang Duqing.

If I remember correctly, those were the only contacts between Wang Shiwei and me, and between Wang Shiwei and the Trotskyites. In May of 1931 I was arrested by the Nationalists and never saw Wang Shiwei again.[30]

Wang Shiwei would never negate the "good human nature" he felt in his heart toward his "older brother" Chen Qingchen, even if he had confronted severe criticisms that would lead to personal disaster. This unnecessary stubbornness was the crucial evidence that proved Wang's "emotional contact binding him forever with the 'Trotskyite bandits' " [said by Kang Sheng in his accusation against Wang Shiwei]. Moreover, the examples Wang gave to prove Chen's good nature were trivial before the grand concepts of "standpoint," "consciousness," and "party principles."

In 1926, Chen's wife traveled from her hometown to visit him at Beida. Li Fen, Liu Ying, and some other female comrades went to see her after hearing that the "small-foot wife" of their "older brother," Chen Qingchen, had come for a visit. To their great surprise, Chen treated her extremely well. Later he explained to the female comrades: "She cried, thinking that I would abandon her to marry someone else. You think I would do that? I am determined to participate in the revolution. How can I bully a victim of the old system!"* Wang and his wife had the image of Qingchen as always coming in and out in a hurry carrying two pieces of corn bread. When Liu Ying had a miscarriage in 1930 and was penniless at home, Chen Qingchen out of the goodness of his heart gave the couple thirty kuai. Liu Ying still does not realize that the impoverished Chen raised the money by selling all of his belongings, while Wang Shiwei was never even informed of Chen's extraordinary charity.

As for the key issue of whether Wang Shiwei joined the Trotskyist organization, Wang Fanxi, who is still alive, provides testimony:

> As a witness with the status of an "accused," I'd like to propose the following statements to people who are possibly going to be responsible for reexamining the Wang Shiwei case. There is one sentence in my memoir. "Some Trotskyites (for instance, Wang Shiwei) who voluntarily went to work in areas controlled by the CCP were confronted with merciless struggle and were eventually killed."
>
> I should point out that this sentence is inaccurate. As recalled in the previous paragraph, although Wang kept in close touch with Chen Qichang and me for a long time, and although he was ideologically influenced by some of Trotsky's ideas (especially on literature), *he never joined any of the Trotskyite organizations in China* (original emphasis, Wang Fanxi).
>
> I can only say that Wang was once a sympathizer of the Trotskyist faction, but I can never say that he was a Trotskyist.
>
> My second statement is that Wang lost contact with the CCP from 1929 to 1934. He wandered between the "central faction" and the "Op-

---

*Chen's behavior toward his wife greatly contrasted with the cold, impersonal treatment by Mao and other top leaders of their traditional first wives.

position group" in order to rejoin the organization. He finally decided to join the former instead of the latter. It was his decision alone. As soon as he decided to rejoin the CCP, he broke off all contacts with his Trotskyist friends.

At this point there was absolutely no truth to the accusation that Wang had been "dispatched" to "penetrate" [the CCP for the Trotskyites].[31]

Liu Xuewei, however, insists that Wang Shiwei informed him of many issues engaging the Trotskyites as they competed for rank and involved themselves in splits, actions that Wang Shiwei found unattractive. For this reason, Xuewei suspected that Wang had, in fact, participated in Trotskyist activities.

Ling Yun, who was assigned to bring the prisoner before the court and to collect all the materials for the trial, remembers that Wang Shiwei himself had admitted that he joined the Trotskyite organization. The materials were destroyed at Wayaobao [a town near Yan'an] before the withdrawal from Yan'an in 1947. Ling Yun does not remember any other materials in which Wang Shiwei voluntarily confessed his deeds to the organization before 1940. That Wang Shiwei may have casually confessed due to his impatience with the trial should not be excluded. Ye Chengzhang who used to work in the Central Social Department and later was an ambassador to Malaysia, remembers words Wang Shiwei wrote on his cadre dossier. Wang admitted that he "once joined the Trotskyite organization." But Liu Xianglun (later a political affairs counselor to Belgium), who was also at the Central Social Department at the same time Ye Chengzhang was there and who escorted Wang to Xing County, Shanxi Province, remembers that Wang protested both during the trial and on the way to Xing County that he was not a Trotskyite.

Did Wang ever join the Trotsky organization?

History moves forward. All Trotskyite members of the "Leftist Opposition Faction" in the CCP who were arrested in 1952 were (if still alive) released in 1979. Zheng Chaolin, the leader at that time, is now a member of the Shanghai Political Consultative Congress and is still writing books. Even more noteworthy is that his release and new employment occurred even though he asserted that he would not alter his views or change his principles.

The accusation against Wang Shiwei as a Trotskyite has completed its historical fate and should also be ended.

Chapter Seven

In summer 1942, the scholar-officials (*caizimen*) in Yan'an were still depicting Wang's crime as being on the level of ideological criticism, though terms such as *antiparty thoughts* and *antiparty activities* were used.

The level of the crime was upgraded in the autumn on October 31. Five people were considered as enemies at the forum held by the Central Research Institute and the Political Research Office to condemn the Five Member Anti-Party Gang (*wuren fandang jituan*).

Yang Shangkun, the former party secretary of the Huabei Bureau of the Central Committee, had already been appointed to work at the Central Committee as the deputy director of the Central Study Committee (*zong-xuewei*). He had not previously participated in rectification work, nor in the criticism and determination of the [political] nature of Wang Shiwei carried out by the Central Research Institute and the Social Affairs Department. His speech [see Document 2.4] was obviously written following the dissemination of party regulations and guidelines. At the beginning he noted: "The forum held in the past ten days has exposed the antiparty activities of Wang Shiwei, Pan Fang, Zong Zheng, Cheng Quan, and Wang Li. Their Trotskyite thoughts, antiparty conspiracies, activities conducted in small groups, and methods used in their antiparty activities, and some other specific facts have also been exposed."

Among the hundreds of memoirs available today written by the "old people" from that unusual period in Yan'an, there are expressions of praises, feelings, and pity.* But none of them question why a month before the astounding "rescue movement" the issue of Wang

---

*Dai Qing is suggesting that these old cadres who "fondly" reminisce about Yan'an still neglect the fact that Wang was a setup for the notorious "rescue movement" orchestrated by Kang Sheng.

Shiwei was upgraded to such a high level. Perhaps in the political environment of that time, "ideological unity" had to be emphasized, for what Yang Shangkun was pointing toward in his speech was mainly the problem of "liberalism within the party":

> Why didn't we expose earlier the Five Member Anti-Party Gang? Why did they gain such success? Why did some comrades sympathize with them? Why were some comrades willingly used by them? . . . I think it's because of the serious weaknesses in their inner-party life, mainly the pervasive liberalism (*nonghoude ziyouzhuyi*) (a lack of political awareness, a political flu, a lack of a steadfast principled standpoint)![32]
> . . . In my opinion, inner-party life should be political and principled. It's erroneous to separate problems in inner-party life from considerations of politics and principle. Some party comrades enjoy making comments about others, tracking down other people's "secrets," and paying attention to other people's private affairs. Some of them even idle around after eating millet, act like "small megaphones" [i.e., rumor mongers] and "pay visits from door to door." They show no interest in and pay no attention to either politics or issues of principle. I do not consider those people to be qualified party members![33]

This total disregard for their qualifications as party members was most evident when [Yang Shangkun continues]: "They showed absolutely no aversion to hearing the antiparty speeches of the Five Members; on the contrary, they were quite pleased to hear them. They expressed no opposition to the antiparty articles by the Five Members; on the contrary, they praised them. They refused to report any of the antiparty activities by the Five Members; on the contrary, they tried to hide them from the party. . . . Is this the standpoint that a party member should take? It is instead sheer rotten liberalism!"[34]

[Dai Qing continues:] It seems apparent that "liberalism" was indeed the main enemy of the revolution, and was considered a much more serious problem than the feudal patriarchal system (*fengjian jiazhangzhi*),* arbitrary [decision making], the seeking of personal privileges through the abuse of power, corruption, and incompetence;

*Patriarchy (*jiazhang zhidu*) in Chinese politics and society, especially the family, had a been a major target of culturally iconoclastic criticism by Chinese intellectuals ever since the New Culture-May Fourth Movements (1915–21) and liberalism was considered most harmful to the revolution.*

Now that we know that the accusations against Wang Shiwei (spy, member of the antiparty gang, Trotskyite) were untrue, we can refer to this entire situation as a "frame-up" (luozhi). We should explore the question of just how Wang Shiwei was framed by these accusations. Of course, some will respond by saying: "You're being arbitrary by putting it that way! It may be that Wang was just hurt by mistake! Or, perhaps those involved in accusing Wang were too anxious and impatient. In actuality, the dire consequences resulted from a good heart! It is probably true that elevating the accusations against him into a political crime was incorrect. Perhaps its scope was slightly too large." Indeed, even today, He Xilin [a Yan'an era intellectual] still believes that the Wang Shiwei case was merely due to the party's inadequate experience in dealing with intellectuals [see Document 4.6]. The whole situation would have been different if Luo Fu had run the Rectification Movement.[35]

Now note what Kang Sheng said in his speech:

> At that time [1942], the policy of our leadership was to stress the democratic aspect of the April 3 [Central Committee] decision by calling on people to speak out boldly, advocating the publication of wall newspapers, and supporting criticism of leaders. We neither immediately counteracted nor suppressed some of the incorrect criticism. That brought about a fairly messy situation as party members with half a heart towards the party and counterrevolutionaries with two hearts [i.e., one pro-party, and one favoring counterrevolution] suddenly appeared . . . So you see, what level this phase of exposure had come to! [See Document 2.5 for the full text.]

Readers must feel that this strategy of "alluring the snake to come out of the cave"† used fourteen years later [during the 1957 Anti-Rightist Campaign] was nothing new.

But since the members of the "Five Member Anti-Party Gang" be-

---

even during the early period of the Chinese Communist Party under the leadership of Chen Duxiu.

*The reader should appreciate here, as in much of the book, that Dai Qing's sarcasm is stronger in the original Chinese.

†Yinshe chudong means to catch a snake (i.e., liberal intellectuals) by offering them something they like.

longed to three separate units, a problem arose as to how to launch criticisms against them as one group. Again let's read from Kang Sheng's account:

> The strategic aspect to this struggle was adopted from the Leninist strategy of winning over the majority and attacking the minority so as to destroy them one by one. Attacking them one by one was the heart of our strategy. . . . Instead of attacking Pan Fang, we promoted him. That way, the rest would think that since Pan Fang, despite having committed some errors, was promoted, they could also avoid punishment. At that point, we also thought about attacking Cheng Quan and Wang Li. But then because the masses at the Political Research Office did not support such a move, we figured that it would be difficult. We dared not hold branch party committee meetings because once any movement was started, it would be very difficult to put an end to it.

Lest we think that Kang Sheng was bogged down by such a small difficulty, he acted quickly by taking a person named Yu Bingran* as a test case.

[Kang Sheng continues:]

> Yu Bingran was at Zao Yuan. We were sure about the masses at Zao Yuan [i.e., that they would be motivated to criticize Yu]. Attack Yu Bingran first; later Cheng Quan and Wang Li, then Yu again. It was a detour [i.e., a roundabout way of getting at Wang Shiwei].

At the beginning, however, the masses were muddled. And the whole issue failed to be associated with the Wang Shiwei issue.

[Kang Sheng continues:]

> How could we spark a struggle at the Political Research Office when the masses lacked political consciousness? Our solution was to let the masses examine their leaders. Chen Boda as a leader probably had some problems. Examination after examination would cause the masses to become aroused. So we persuaded Chen to go to Zao Yuan to take a vacation. No matter how hard the masses scolded him, he was ordered

---

*In July 1942, Yu Bingran had challenged Chen Boda's assault on "petty bourgeois intellectuals" by arguing for evaluating individuals on merit, not class background, and opposing their need for ideological remolding. Stranahan, *Molding the Medium*, p. 67.

not to return to the [Central party] department until he received our letter. During the five days of the meeting, the problem of Cheng [Quan] and Wang [Li] was not even mentioned. The focus was solely on Chen Boda who was scolded in a bloody way. . . . On the fifth day, the couple [Cheng Quan and Wang Li] scolded Chen Boda from morning till the afternoon. What were they scolding him about? It was the human nature issue. At this point, the masses started to question the couple: "How come in the process of scolding [Chen Boda] you two have expressed the same thoughts as Wang Shiwei on the issue of human nature?" . . . At this point, the ideological struggle shifted from the Political Research Office to the Central Research Institute. Another detour. In this way both Pan Fang and Zong Zheng had exposed their Trotskyite thoughts. . . . After quite a few go-arounds, we shifted the focus to political struggle. That struggle was very circuitous and meticulous.

This was Kang Sheng's speech given at a training class in August 1943. Training! When we consider the nearly endless similar phenomena all over China in the past thirty-five years, it's not hard to think about the saying: "Excellent disciples are trained by excellent masters."

Not until 1982 was the incorrect accusation laid on the Anti-Party Gang cleared up one by one. Or perhaps I'm being inaccurate here for nothing has been done to clear Wang Shiwei's name yet, except for the footnote on the last page of the *Mao Zedong Reader* (Volume 2) where it is noted: "The accusation that Wang Shiwei was a hidden KMT spy was untrue."*

The real relationship between the two married couples [i.e., Cheng Quan and Wang Li, and Pan Fang and Zong Zheng] and Wang Shiwei was very shallow. At the end of 1928 when Wang Shiwei was teaching in Shandong, Wang Li, at the recommendation of her aunt who characterized Wang as "somebody with progressive thoughts," visited him twice. Wang Li and Pan Fang's wife—Zong Zheng—had been former schoolmates at Fudan University in Shanghai and later both went to Yan'an. There, Wang Li and Cheng Quan went to see Pan Fang and Zong Zheng and also paid a visit to Wang Shiwei who lived next door. Wang Li liked Wang Shiwei's ideas for "Wild Lilies" and told him: "Go ahead and write it. I'll supply the seeds!" That was the most

---

*See afterword for the recent decision by the Public Security Department in China clearing Wang's name.

serious sentence uttered in the twenty to thirty hours of contact involving the five people.

Among the group, Pan Fang, who was most willing to admit his mistakes, was the first to be released in November, 1943. Rather than going through the trouble of being transferred back to work at the Central Research Institute, he remained at the Central Social Department—directly transformed from a prisoner into an employee. Today, Pan Fang is a highly qualified consultant to the Ministry of State Security (anquan bu).* In his own words: "I was captured to work here forty-three years ago."

Zong Zheng was not as pliant as her husband. She firmly refused to discuss the issue of her readmission into the party with the party branch, and passed away five years ago still seething with anger. The tough Cheng Quan committed suicide during the Cultural Revolution despite the fact that Mao once commented on their case with poetic words: "It was a bayonet fight in the night that mistakenly injured our comrades." Wang Li, now in her eighties, is lying in bed, sick.

---

*This highly secret organization deals with high-level political crimes in the PRC and counterespionage.

Chapter Eight

On March 19, 1947, Hu Zongnan attacked the capital of the Shaan-Gan-Ning Revolutionary Base. The ensuing defense of Yan'an was one of the most mysterious dramas in Chinese military history.

Two days before the attack, on March 17, the Central Social Department sent Wang Shiwei, who had been imprisoned at the Security Department in Yan'an, to the rear areas—the Jin-Sui revolutionary base, which was east of the Yellow River and under the protection of General He Long. At that time, He Long was a member of the Seventh Central Committee and commander of the unified troops of the five provinces (Shaanxi, Gansu, Ningxia, Shanxi, and Suiyuan). He was also party secretary of the Jin-Sui regional bureau of the CCP and commander of the Jin-Sui military region.

From the time of their arrest on April 1, 1943, Wang Shiwei and the other prisoners had been imprisoned for four years. During this period they had raised pigs, grown vegetables, and woven thread. They were released one by one and all assumed new jobs. Their life of incarceration had not really been any harder than if they had lived outside the prison. Since he was one of the "big intellectuals," Wang Shiwei didn't engage in much manual labor in prison. It's apparent that at that time these prominent intellectuals were treated differently from what would have happened to them in 1967. Wang was imprisoned without ever having been brought before a court. By spring 1947, he was the only prisoner left at the Central Social Department.

Over those four years, Wang participated on several occasions in "foreign affairs activities": At the end of the summer in 1943, a group of Chinese and foreign journalists, including [Joshua] Epstein, were invited by Mao Zedong to visit Yan'an where they requested a meeting with "that writer." Wang Zhen, who received the guests, agreed immediately and a few weeks later, Wang Shiwei met with the journalists. According to a memoir by Wei Jingmeng, then a journalist for the [KMT] Central News Agency and now a "national policy consultant" on Taiwan:

> When Wang Shiwei met us, he immediately confessed: "I'm a Trotskyite." The only expression I saw on his expressionless face was fear.
> He said over and over again: "I'm a Trotskyite. I attacked Mao. So I deserve to be executed. I should have been executed a thousand times. But Mao is so magnanimous. He doesn't want me to die. He allows me to work. I am working diligently and have realized the great principle that labor is holy. I am extremely grateful for his mercy."

In spring 1944, another press delegation visited Yan'an. The delegation included Yang Xikun, then a member of the KMT Propaganda Department who in the 1930s had been a student [with Wang] at Beida. This was obviously a great chance for promoting United Front work. There was a rushed meeting of the "Beida Alumni Association" headed by Fan Wenlan and attended by Yang Xikun.

Wang Shiwei appeared again. The journalist Zhao Chaogou of the *New People's News* (Xinmin wenxue) wrote the following for his story "A Month in Yan'an": "A young man with a grey deadly look on his face was brought in by Ding Ling and he started to blame himself as if he was reciting from a textbook." But what we are discussing here in this book is obviously not that United Front conference that was attended by twenty-eight people. Yang Xikun was greatly surprised when Wang Shiwei was introduced. Wang gave an impromptu speech in which he said something like: "I made some mistakes in Yan'an but I am leading a good life. Xi'an [the KMT government] claims that I have been persecuted to death. (This referred to the comic play titled 'Funeral for the Living,' which had been performed in Xi'an a few years ago, that mourned for Wang Shiwei and others who were supposedly persecuted to death by the CCP.) Everyone has a family! If my family members heard of this, imagine their anxiety. Due to your [KMT] blockade, I cannot make contact with my family. Thus, I would be very grateful if my schoolmate Yang upon his return would inform my family of the truth. I shall be very grateful."

Unfortunately, "schoolmate Yang" did not take the task entrusted by the prisoner seriously. Maybe because there were no feelings between officials on the battle field at that time, or perhaps Yang took it merely as "superficial propaganda." In the end, neither "parents nor wife" were informed of anything about Wang Shiwei's fate.

On the night of March 17, 1947, a few young guards from the Social Department led the prisoner on the start of their journey. It took them more than a week—climbing mountains and crossing ditches carrying their own luggage. Forging the Yellow River, they used a makeshift wooden boat with a square bow that could have easily turned over. Wang Shiwei did not carry his own luggage, but on several occasions he lost his temper saying that he was "not a Trotskyite criminal, not a spy." The guards ordered him "not to make absurd arguments." Sometimes Wang couldn't walk and asked the young men to carry him on a stretcher.

Ling Yun ran into Wang while he was traveling between Lin and Xing counties. Wang, the former special research fellow, was wearing a grey cotton coat and pants, holding a stick, walking slowly by himself. No guards could be seen around him. As soon as Wang spotted this old acquaintance whom he had come to know three years earlier during his interrogation by the Social Department, Wang's spirits soared. Walking towards Ling and grabbing both of his hands, Wang told Ling that he had "withdrawn from Yan'an with the Social Department," and that he was "lagging behind because he was unable to walk any faster." Wang also complained that the young guards did not take good care of him. At that time, Ling Yun was working with the Land Reform Working group and offered Wang a bit of advice. Ling never expected that this would be the last time he would see Wang inasmuch as there was no fighting in Jin-Sui, and since Mao had issued explicit instructions: "Neither release nor execute Wang Shiwei."

Nevertheless, Wang was still executed by a prison guard from the Detention Section of the General Bureau for Preliminary Trial Procedure of the Jin-Sui Public Security Bureau.* The order could not have been given directly by the section chief, nor by the bureau director. It happened one day in late spring, 1947 . . .

Mao heard of the execution soon afterwards and became greatly agitated. He demanded that Li Kenong make amends by providing him with another Wang Shiwei. Li Kenong did not provide any explana-

---

*According to Dai Qing, Wang's executioner is still alive, committed to a mental institution.

tion, but only apologized again and again, asking in both oral and written form for punishment by the party. . . . Mao obviously found it difficult to calm down. The old man (*laoren*) had originally instructed that: "Since Wang has apologized, his case can be brought to a close." But now the Wang case was mentioned over and over again at meetings. The distraught Li Kenong passed away from a sudden cerebral hemorrhage in the late 1950s.

Was it Li Kenong who actually decided to have Wang Shiwei executed? It was indeed Li who took the prisoner transferred into his custody and incarcerated him in the security bureau at Zhou Xing near Yan'an. (Since all the other prisoners held by the Intelligence Department had already been released, the detention house was dismantled). After that, it was also Li who, despite the obvious difficulties, ordered the guards to evacuate Wang from Yan'an. Could it really be that Li actually searched for a different place in another province to kill Wang? It should also be noted that when Pan Fang ran into Li Kenong in Lin County and the two talked about Wang Shiwei, Li warned Pan in a joking way: "Be careful. He might curse you!"

According to the organizational system of authority at that time, departments under the Central Committee did not have the authority to issue direct orders to local security bureaus, nor could they pass on decisions for an execution to subordinate bureaus of the Central Committee. Furthermore, Li Kenong did not have the authority to make such a decision on his own. The decision on how to handle the Wang case should have been made collectively by a committee composed of several members . . .

The order could only have come from He Long. According to the memoir of a person who wishes to remain anonymous, following several self-criticisms by Li Kenong, He Long admitted: "It was I who approved the order." After hearing this Mao never said another word on the matter.

But why would He Long execute a prisoner incarcerated in his area by the Central Social Department?

At that time, many battles had broken out—the Shangdang and Handan battles, the Central China invasion and break-out, the Suzhong and Dingtao battles. The CCP and the KMT were involved in a life or death struggle. Someone has recalled that around this time there was a document or some kind of "spirit" (*jingshen*) originating in the Central Committee that granted local leaders the authority to execute prisoners during a wartime situation whenever it was inconvenient to bring them along with the troops.

But at that time there was no fighting in Jin-Sui. Moreover, Wang Shiwei was not the only prisoner in the Detention Section of the General Bureau for Preliminary Trial Procedure. So why was he singled out for execution?

Some people speculate that even after he was transferred to Jin-Sui, Wang Shiwei probably maintained his attitude of "going to his grave without admitting his faults." It is also possible that he did not maintain this attitude, but that's hard to say. Considering his reputation as "the famous person in Yan'an," would whoever had Wang killed not have been psychologically enthralled by the thought of "killing him merely for the satisfaction?" Isn't the "lurid seduction" of committing heinous acts something that has occurred throughout Chinese history? If we think of He Long's later confession of guilt and his harsh attitude in Yan'an back in 1943, it's apparent He Long deeply resented Wang Shiwei and his ilk. He once publicly cursed Ding Ling as a "stinking bitch." So how could He Long in the midst of all-out war have possibly sympathized with "a Trotskyite, KMT spy, and antiparty member"? Also, at that time He Long probably didn't know that executions needed to be cleared through a series of legal procedures.

No one is sure if He Long informed Li Kenong of his actions. Even if he did, it's unclear whether He Long let Li know before or after the execution. Li kept his mouth shut on this.

Years later in March, 1967, He Long was hidden by Zhou Enlai in a remote house in a suburb of Beijing to protect him from being seized and criticized by the "little fighters" [i.e., Red Guards]. There, he "completed his report 'On the problem regarding the execution of counterrevolutionaries in the Honghu Region [in Hubei]' " and asked Zhou Enlai to deliver it to Mao.* At the time of the party's victory in 1949, He Long, despite his many outstanding achievements as a soldier, had been assigned to the lowly position of national sports director. Just think of how many past events were roaring in the heart of this general who lacked a formal education and now [1967] could no longer harbor his guilty feelings, though he obviously did not think

---

*He Long, together with his elder sister, had directed much of this terror campaign that was subsequently glorified in the film *The Honghu Red Guards* (Honghu chiweidui).

about Wang Shiwei. Two years later [1969], he died from an "incorrect medical treatment" while still in hiding. Some believe he really died from "being purposely refused medical treatment."* As in the case of Wang Shiwei, He Long passed away without the company of his wife and children and still facing trumped-up charges.

---

*During the 1960s and 1970s, the People's Liberation Army Hospital No. 301 in Beijing was notorious for incarcerating political enemies of the Maoist leadership and then denying them medical cure, or even silently killing healthy "patients" with injections, such as may have occurred with Chen Yi on direct orders of Lin Biao. Immediately after the June 4, 1989, crackdown, however, the same hospital apparently refused to accept wounded soldiers and thus has been distrusted by the top leadership ever since.

Chapter Nine

Two and one-half years later, in August 1949, Liu Ying, accompanied by her two grown children—daughter Wang Jinfeng, now eighteen years old, and son Wang Xufeng, now thirteen years old, returned from Xiangxi to Changsha where they joined the crowd welcoming PLA soldiers. Both children had been named by their father who had a romantic feeling for the color red.* Jinfeng had only a slight memory of her father, while Xufeng had an even more vague notion formed only by his mother's secret words: "Your father has followed the brave soldiers and gone to fight against the Japanese." The family dared not expect to spot their father, whom they had not seen in eleven years, in the parade. Still they could not hold back their tears: "Our troops have returned! See how strong are the troops of our communist party!"

They waited to hear from their father—one month, two months, three months—without a response. Liu Ying sent a letter directly to the Central Organization Department. The return letter read: "When the enemy attacked Yan'an, the request of Wang Shiwei to volunteer for work at the front was approved. There has been no word from him since."

Liu Ying believed that Wang must have died in the enemy-occupied area. All she could do in the future was to continue with her husband's revolutionary work and concentrate on raising their children. She asked for work from the Twelfth [PLA] Division at Changsha and ended up being transferred to the remote north, in Jilin Province.

But her husband's death had still not yet been confirmed. Liu Ying inquired once more through her school organization where she was

---

*This refers to the Chinese character *feng* (red maple leaf) that appears in the names of Wang's two children.

working during the 1953 ideological movement [the Three Antis and Five Antis] about Wang's whereabouts. Without so much as uttering a word, the school leader gave her a pamphlet titled *Ideological Instructions* that contained an article by Chen Boda criticizing "Wild Lilies." Until then, Liu Ying did not know that her husband had committed errors in Yan'an.

What had happened to Wang Shiwei after committing these mistakes? In 1956, Liu Ying's daughter wrote directly to Lu Dingyi [then Propaganda Chief]. Again, the return letter was from the Central Organizational Department, but this time with different words: "Wang Shiwei went to Taiwan."

Liu Ying thought Wang must have been engaged in some kind of underground work in Taiwan—the most dangerous place—in order to make amends for his previous mistakes. This showed that he was still trusted by the organization. In 1978, Liu Ying, who had been sent to work in Jiaohe County, Jilin Province, heard Mao's words over the radio (which were quoted at the beginning of this book): "Wang Shiwei . . . the hidden spy . . . was arrested . . . executed."

Stunned, Liu Ying's hands and feet turned icy cold and her whole body trembled. Her son and daughter propped her up quickly and the whole family started to cry. The fact is that her children had known the truth for several years, but thinking that all was lost they had kept it from their aging mother. Their only wish was that she could live out her life in peace.

But for Liu Ying, who had demonstrated her commitment by joining the party in 1926, different thoughts occurred. She knew all too well her husband's penchant for directness. Wang Shiwei could lose his temper, blurt out dirty words, say things he shouldn't have said, but he would never be a spy or a Trotskyite, or do anything against the party. Never! Thus, in 1979, this seventy-three year old teacher, who had been selected as a model teacher in almost every year of her career, traveled south for the first time in over thirty years. But she was not going to her hometown: "Green mountains covered with trees in the distance, and green water without cold smoke." She was, instead, going to Beijing to make a personal appeal to the party.

Still another seven years passed by. The situation was one of "coming over like a fierce tiger, going away like a thin thread" [i.e., great hopes gave way to pessimism]. The family had grown, as Wang Shiwei now had a daughter-in-law, a son-in-law, a granddaughter and a grandson. They still waited, waiting like they had been for fifty years. Many of the family's relatives and friends had gone abroad and sent them money and gifts with warm affection after China had opened up to the outside world [after 1972]. But Liu Ying turned down all such gifts. Even though these friends and relatives claimed that all of it was money and things they had borrowed from Wang Shiwei in the 1930s, Liu Ying refused to deal with them.

A childhood friend of Wang Shiwei who is now a journalist in Hong Kong kept pestering Liu Ying for "brother [Shi]wei's photos, materials, and Liu Ying's appeal [to the party]" that he wanted to publish in Hong Kong. Liu Ying turned him down, saying: "This is an inner-party affair. It was the party that persecuted him. The problem is surely going to be resolved."

Liu Ying has only one small photo of Wang Shiwei in her possession. During the chaotic years of the Cultural Revolution, she burned everything except that last photo. Unwilling to part with it, she cut it into a smaller and smaller piece, and hid it behind a picture of her baby daughter.

Liu Ying is eighty years old this year [1989], and lives with her son in the famous city [Shiyan] in Hubei. She believes that she has said all that should be said. Now all she does is wait for the day when the case will be resolved. On that day, she will dedicate a glass of wine to her husband whose name will be cleared through the efforts of that pair of hands of hers that once kept secrets, spread pamphlets for the party, wrote the appeal for her husband, and held Li Fen's hands.

Notes to the Text

1. Zhang Ruxin, formerly a secretary to Mao Zedong, was heavily involved in the Rectification Movement. The author Shen Yi, in her "Remembering Comrade Zhang Ruxin" (Huinian Zhang Ruxin tongzhi) (included in *Memoir of the Central Research Institute in Yan'an* [Yan'an zhongyang yanjiuyuan huiyilu]) (Changsha: Hunan renmin chubanshe, 1984), [ed. Wen Jize, Li Yan, Jin Ziguang, and Qiu Dingyi (Beijing, 1984)], presented the following description that can help us understand Zhang Ruxin's personality:

"Comrade Jin Shizu, who used to work in the Political Research Office of the Central Research Institute, described the early stages of rectification in the following manner: "At that time everyone in our department viewed the Wang Shiwei case in their own way. In terms of the criticism of Wang Shiwei by Comrade Zhang Ruxin, some favored it and some opposed it. One day after dinner, a few of us were taking a stroll beside the Yan river toward Yangjialing where we spotted Chairman Mao hoeing his tomato garden. Seeing us, Mao stopped his work and engaged us in a discussion regarding the reaction in the Institute to the publication of 'Wild Lilies.' We informed him of the divided reaction. One of our group indicated that since it is a democratic discussion and everyone is allowed to express different attitudes and opinions, Wang Shiwei has a right to express his own views as do those who oppose Wang. Mao listened to our argument without comment, but as we departed he said that there's a lot to 'Wild Lilies.' Afterward we heard that later that night Mao demonstrated his great concern with ideological trends in the Institute reading by lamplight the article in *Arrow and Target*. Considering Mao's concern in light of the harsh criticism of Wang Shiwei by Zhang Ruxin, we can tell just how sharp were Zhang's thoughts and how hardline was his standpoint.

"Zhang Ruxin joined the revolution in 1925, took part in the Long March, and graduated from Sun Yat-sen University in Moscow. Following 1949, he was only appointed to two positions, president of Northeast Normal University and Director of the party History Department at the Central Party School. During the Cultural Revolution, he was cruelly accused of crimes concocted by Kang Sheng et al., and was imprisoned for four years, which had a profound effect on him for years to come. In 1976, after suffering a severe heart attack, he was denied the necessary medication. Premier Zhou's death accelerated his emotional and physical illnesses, and he passed away a short time later. Zhang kept mentioning the beloved Premier Zhou's name before his death because he had said many times before that Comrade Zhou Enlai took intellectuals seriously—comments by the author [Shen Yi]."

2. Li Yan, "Some Views Regarding the Rectification Movement at the Central Research Institute" (Dui zhongyang yanjiuyuan zhengfeng yundong de fandian tihui), in *Memoir of the Central Research Institute in Yan'an*, pp. 103–10.

3. Wang Fanxi, "Wang Shiwei and the 'Wang Shiwei Problem' " (Wang Shiwei yu "Wang Shiwei wenti"), *The Nineties* (Jiushiniandai), Hong Kong, May 1985, pp. 80–81.

4. Ibid.

5. Ibid., pp. 81–82.

6. The Youth League for the Three People's Principles (Sanqing) was not established until March 29, 1938, and thus Wang Shiwei could not possibly have made this statement in Changsha in 1936. Perhaps it was mentioned by Wang in one of his later letters addressed to his family and incorrectly recalled by Liu Ying—comments by the author [Dai Qing].

7. Wang Xuewen, *My Reminiscences* (Wode huiyi).

8. Rong Mengyuan, "Comrade Fan Wenlan in Yan'an" (Fan Wenlan tongzhi zai Yan'an), in *Memoir of the Central Research Institute in Yan'an*, pp. 180–87.

9. Li Yan, "Some Views."

10. See, "Comrade Mao Zedong advocates using newspapers to rectify the Three Work Styles," (Mao Zedong tongzhi haozhao zhengtun sanfeng yao liyung baozhi), *Liberation Daily*, Yan'an, February 1, 1942.

11. According to Ding Ling's memoir, criticisms of "Thoughts on March 8" and "Wild Lilies" were first raised at the senior cadres study meeting in Yan'an:

> Mao Zedong, Zhu De, Bo Gu [Qin Bangxian], and He Long were present at the meeting. Zhou Yang and I were the only two comrades from the literature and arts field. What left a deep impression and made me feel uneasy was the fact that Cao Yiou [Kang Sheng's wife] was the first one to criticize "Thoughts on March 8." I thought to myself at that time, Cao Yiou was not involved in literature and arts so why is it that she has become so concerned with these issues? Following Cao, many other comrades made speeches. He Long also criticized me, saying: "We are fighting battles at the front while you people are condemning our party from the rear!" (The interviewer inquired: "Somebody said that sentence had been uttered by Wang Zhen.") It was He Long who criticized me at the meeting. Comrade Wang Zhen later told me that he himself had said the same thing. (It seems that at that time Yan'an was not only short of physical materials, but also of words. Or perhaps that sentence was so fantastic that everybody competed in using it—comment by the author [Dai Qing]). I feel that many of the criticisms were very harsh. Many of the comrades were staring at me as if fearing that I could not stand it. Comrade Bo Gu came over and sat right next to me, and asked me quietly: "How are you?" I said, "I'm all right." I was fully at ease. The next day I went to visit Comrade He Long, a fellow provincial. I knew that he was a straightforward person and would not hide anything. I said to him that a good acquaintance was formed by fights and asked if he had any other criticisms. He laughed heartily, and did not mention any more. A few days later, Comrade He Long came to the Litera-

ture Resistance Association especially to see me. Mao Zedong made a summary speech at the senior cadres study meeting. In Mao's speech, he separated me from Wang Shiwei: "Comrade Ding Ling is not the same as Wang Shiwei. There were suggestions in her article as well as criticisms, while Wang Shiwei is a Trotskyite." In fact, I can say that it was Comrade Mao Zedong who protected me back then.

That "distinction" personally established by Mao was valid for several decades. In 1978 when Liu Ying traveled to Beijing to appeal for a reversal of verdicts, she did not have any personal connections (*guanxi*) in the capital. Finally, Liu Ying thought about Ding Ling who had been "involved in the same case" and whose students' homework Wang Shiwei had once corrected in the 1930s when he was desperately trying to make some money. Liu Ying figured that Ding Ling might tell the true story about the Wang Shiwei case. She got her telephone number from the Writers' Association and rang her up. The person answering the phone, after being informed of the whole thing, paused for quite a while, and then said: "Comrade Ding Ling is not at home." Although Liu Ying knew nothing about what had happened in 1942, including the "distinction" established by Mao at the senior cadres study meeting, Liu Ying finally experienced the pall cast over her husband. Liu never again tried to call that writer who had been tortured a great deal, though Liu knew that she would not be "not at home" forever.

12. Li Yan, "Some Views."

13. Ibid.

14. Wen Jize, "Diary of a Struggle" (Douzheng riji) in *Liberation Daily*, Yan'an, June 28 and 29, 1942. [See Document II:1 for full text.] The text of this quotation differs somewhat from the original appended version.

15. *Records of the Rectification Movement in Yan'an* (Yan'an zhengfeng yundong jishi).

16. In other words, Mao considered Wang Zhen's near illiteracy to be an important factor in making this appointment, something probably very galling to well-educated intellectuals in Yan'an such as Wang Shiwei. This added insult to the injury created by the appointment of Chen Boda to head the Translation Department despite his not knowing a foreign language.

Wang Zhen, "Hold a warm and wholehearted attitude toward the people's cause" (Manqiang reqing de duidai renmin shiye) *People's Daily* May 3, 1987. From then on Wang Zhen enjoyed the reputation of being the "sincere friend" (*zhi you*) of Chinese intellectuals. Even at the [recent] National People's Congress at which Wang Zhen was elected state vice president, journalists constantly mentioned Wang Zhen's reputation. Some take him as "China's General Patton." Whoever said such a thing knows nothing about military history, for the only similarity between the two is that both General Patton and Wang Zhen like to curse in public. Wang Zhen's unbridled curses, especially about students from Beida and People's University since 1976, are indeed unforgettable.

17. Wang Defen, "Xiao Jun in Yan'an" (Xiao Jun zai Yan'an), in *Historical Materials on the New Literature* (Xin wenxue shiliao), no. 4, 1987.

18. Wen Jize, "Diary of a Struggle."

19. Ibid.

20. Li Weihan [Luo Mai] passed away a year later. Six years after his death, Wen Jize, following Li Weihan's will, finished compiling the biographies of the martyrs who had died in the long revolutionary struggle of the CCP. He also kept appealing, delivering reports, and making numerous requests to get a reevaluation of the Wang Shiwei issue. . . . This process provided so much information that someone in the future could write a sequel to this present book [and, probably, assisted in Wang Shiwei's belated public rehabilitation in 1991, see afterword—Eds.]—comments by the author [Dai Qing].

21. Wen Jize, "Diary of a Struggle."

22. Ibid.

23. Ibid.

24. Ibid.

25. Tong Dong, "Extensive memoir of the Rectification Movement at the Central Research Institute" (Manyi zhongyang yanjiuyuan de zhengfeng yundong), in *Memoir of the Central Research Institute in Yan'an*, pp. 136–44.

26. Ibid.

27. Ibid.

28. Wang Defen, "Xiao Jun in Yan'an."

29. Others do not agree with the idea of this author [Dai Qing]. Comrade Wen Jize thinks that the reason why the Literature and Art Column in *Liberation Daily* was abolished was to make room for a comprehensive edition that was more rich and vivid than the literature and art section. He also thinks that after Mao's Yan'an Talks, the literary and art field prospered with many good works, such as "The Brother and Sister Plow the Barren Field" (Xiongmei kai huang) and the "White Haired Girl" (Baimao nü), and so forth. He also remembers a news report indicating that the reason for the uprising on the Yangtze River Ship in Nanjing was not due to any central document. Rather it was because those brave people were moved to begin their uprising by a broadcast of "The Story of Li Youcai" (Li Youcai banhua).

30. Wang Fanxi, "Wang Shiwei and 'the Wang Shiwei Problem,' " p. 82.

31. Ibid, pp. 87–8.

32. Yang Shangkun, "Activities of the Trotskyite Wang Shiwei and Liberalism in the Party," (Tuopai Wang Shiwei de huodong yu dangnei ziyouzhuyi) [see Document 2.4].

33. Ibid.

34. Ibid.

35. Zhang Wentian (Luo Fu), who after the Zunyi Conference was appointed general secretary of the party and concurrently director of the Propaganda Department, fully acknowledged the advanced and revolutionary character of petty bourgeois intellectuals in the democratic cultural movement. As early as the end of 1940, Zhang considered intellectuals a decisive power in a new cultural movement led by the working class. This estimation and prediction was considered to be backward in 1942. In 1943, the article "On the decision implementing the party's artistic and literary policy" (Guanyu zhixing dang de wenyi zhengce de jueding), written by the Propaganda Department of which Kai Feng was director, indirectly labeled Luo Fu's idea as "the liberal tendency of quite a few of our comrades"—comments by the author [Dai Qing].

Text Bibliography

"Comrade Mao Zedong advocates using newspapers to rectify the three work styles," *Liberation Daily*, February 1, 1942.

Gao Ao and Yan Jiaqi, *Ten-year History of the "Cultural Revolution"* (Wenhua "dageming" shinian shi).

Guo Jing and Nie Ye, "Two years at the International Relations Research Department" (Zai guoji wenti yanjiushi de liangnian), in *Memoir of the Central Research Institute in Yan'an*.

Li Yan, "Some views regarding the Rectification Movement at the Central Research Institute," in ibid.

"Records of the Rectification Movement in Yan'an."

Rong Mengyuan, "Comrade Fan Wenlan in Yan'an," in *Memoir of the Central Research Institute in Yan'an*.

Shu Qun, *Stories of Mao Zedong* (Mao Zedong gushi).

Tong Dong, "Extensive Memoir of the Rectification Movement at the Central Research Institute," in *Memoir of the Central Research Institute in Yan'an*.

Wang Defen, "Xiao Jun in Yan'an," in *Historical Materials on the New Literature*, April 1987.

Wang Fanxi, "Wang Shiwei and the 'Wang Shiwei Problem,' " in *The Nineties* (Jiushiniandai), May 1985.

Wang Xuewen, *My Reminiscences*.

Wang Zhen, "Hold a warm and wholehearted attitude toward the people's cause," *People's Daily*, May 3, 1987.

Wen Jize, "Diary of a Struggle," *Liberation Daily*, June, 28, 1942 [Document 2.1].

Yang Shangkun, "Activities of the Trotskyite Wang Shiwei and Liberalism in the Party" [Document 2.4].

Supplement to "Wang Shiwei and 'Wild Lilies' ": Notes on Liu Xuewei's Talk

TANG TIANRAN

The publication of Comrade Dai Qing's *Wang Shiwei and "Wild Lilies"* brought considerable public attention to the long-pending case of Wang Shiwei. The book has had a fairly extensive influence. Comrade Liu Xuewei was interviewed by the author. Not long ago, I visited the respected Xuewei who mentioned the book to me during our talk and who felt that the general character of the Wang Shiwei case was just as Dai Qing has described it. But a few points need to be supplemented and corrected.

According to Dai Qing's account, Wang Shiwei disseminated Trotskyite ideas during his argument with Liu Xuewei. Later on, Liu "unintentionally mentioned the discussions between the two of them to Xu Jiansheng." Comrade Xuewei said that, in actuality, he had made a formal report of his argument with Wang Shiwei to Xu Jiansheng, head secretary (*mishuzhang*) of the Central Research Institute, and to Li Yan, the party secretary. It was not "unintentionally mentioned." He also said that at that time it was not unusual for this kind of thing to occur. One can easily understand it if one is familiar with the movement to "Be Loyal and Aboveboard" (*zhongcheng tanbai*), and with the general political atmosphere in Yan'an that emerged following the return to China of Wang Ming and Kang Sheng from the Soviet Union, all of which were the prelude to the rectification in the party. Comrade Xuewei somberly said: "I should take responsibility for this case irrespective of the circumstances," words that made me appreciate the open-mindedness of an old comrade. In discussing what had actually happened without covering anything up, Liu's courage and spirit deserve respect.

Comrade Xuewei also said that, following the party's order, he subsequently gave a speech at a meeting of the entire Central Research Institute where the Trotskyite ideas disseminated by Wang Shiwei were exposed. He said that he should also take responsibility for that since it was his exposure that made the entire case more serious. But what happened to Wang Shiwei later on was beyond his expectation. He also said that at the beginning, he did not take Wang's words very seriously, thinking that it was merely a matter of ideological misunderstanding. He protested the fact that Institute leaders escalated the case without the slightest evidence by making Wang into an enemy—a Trotskyite spy. Liu reiterated his strong belief, at a departmental level party branch meeting (in the Institute), that escalating the case to a matter of political organization was totally without foundation. After that, Liu either refused to attend or was generally absent from the meetings held outside the Institute to criticize Wang Shiwei, though he avoided arguing publicly with Comrade Luo Mai while presiding over those meetings.

Comrade Xuewei also said that one part of Dai's description of the argument between he and Wang Shiwei over Trotsky's *Literature and Revolution* (involving the issue of proletarian class literature) must be corrected. Wang Shiwei agreed with Trotsky's views that it's impossible for "proletarian literature" to emerge and exist, while the only thing possible is for there to be a "classless literature" yet without a "proletarian literature" coming into being. Xuewei opposed such a view. But Xuewei never "emphasized that art serves the political view of classes." Xuewei said that he wrote articles criticizing Trotsky's *Literature and Revolution* (published in *Contemporary Monthly* (Xianshi yuekan). His argument with Wang Shiwei reflected his disagreement with Wang over Trotsky's idea in *Literature and Revolution*, [as Xuewei believed] that it in fact it is possible for proletarian literature to emerge and that indeed it had already emerged (such as in [Maxim] Gorky's works). Their argument never touched upon issues regarding the relationship between art and politics. Moreover, since the topic of "art serves politics" was at that time just being introduced into Yan'an, there were no such words as "[art] serves politics" in common use.

Ms. Dai also mentions in her book that Comrade Luo Fu [Zhang Wentian] had asked Liu Xuewei to "contact" Wang Shiwei so that Liu could "listen to Wang's many views and receive his help." As Comrade Xuewei had just begun work at the Central Research Institute, he was staying at the Literary Resistance Association. Luo Fu advised: "Since you have written on the history of contemporary Chinese literature, there's one person with whom you must exchange views." That person was Wang Shiwei. According to Xuewei, Ms. Dai's emphasis on Luo Fu's recommendation is a bit exaggerated.

Comrade Xuewei also said that the entire campaign to criticize Wang Shiwei—from the first criticism of Wang Shiwei at the Central Research Institute to Wang's eventual arrest by the Central Social Department—was led by Comrade Luo Mai. At that time, Luo Mai headed the Central Propaganda Department, and was concurrently head of the Department of Education. Since he was appointed by Comrade Mao Zedong to run the party organization at the Central Research Institute, he should bear responsibility for the disastrous consequences of the Wang Shiwei case. Having said this, it is important to note that following the [December 1978] Third Party Plenum of the Eleventh Central Committee [which under Hu Yaobang's leadership led to the rehabilitation of old political criminals in China, Eds.] Comrade Luo Mai was very active in clearing Wang Shiwei's name. This was also mentioned in Dai's book. According to Liu Xuewei, Comrade Luo Mai engaged in voluntary self-criticism, in which he assumed responsibility for concocting the case against Wang Shiwei. Time and again before he passed away, Luo Mai proposed to clear Wang's name. His attitude was serious and courageous.

Dai also recounts in Chapter Seven of the book that Comrade Mao Zedong himself in mentioning the so-called "Five Member Anti-Party Gang" commented on the Cheng Quan, Wang Li case. [Quoting Mao]: "It was a bayonet fight in the night that mistakenly injured our comrades." Liu Xuewei added that there was actually more to this story as Mao, probably in early 1945 during the "termination phase" of the Rectification Movement, had invited Cheng Quan and Wang Li over to his cave for a visit where he admitted to them that the whole case had been handled wrongly and then apologized. At that time, this news profoundly affected all of Yan'an. Wang Li is the niece of Wang Kunlun,* and Mao's apology was certainly helpful to the United Front. The Pan Fang couple were also released and began work at the Cen-

---

*Wang Kunlun (1902–1955) was a high-ranking official in the KMT who secretly entered the CCP in 1933 and later became vice-mayor of Beijing. He was later a victim of Kang Sheng's security apparatus.

tral Social Department. At that time, everyone expected that Wang Shiwei would be released soon, free of all the charges. But the outcome was totally different as Wang wasn't released and continued to be imprisoned at the Central Social Department, and was later executed.

Comrade Xuewei said that as a final gesture the most important thing to do now is to clear publicly the name of Wang Shiwei.

PART II
SELECTED DOCUMENTS

Compiled and with

Introductions by

Song Jinshou

Section One: Introduction

This section contains all the available works written by Wang Shiwei during the Yan'an era. The major articles are those that created the "Wang Shiwei problem": "Wild Lilies," "Politicians, Artists," and the political essays published in the wall newspaper *Arrow and Target*. The reason those essays were preserved was because they were criticized. They later appeared in the appendix to a book by Fan Wenlan titled *On Comrade Wang Shiwei's Ideological Consciousness*. It is impossible, however, to determine whether the omissions in the reprints were Fan's responsibility. (Though from the context of his entire work this does not appear to be the case. For instance, the second point in the section subtitled "A Few Explanatory Notes" was replaced entirely by an ellipsis. If that was Fan's original intention, why did he bother to list the succeeding point as "number two"?)*

As a writer (this is a controversial point. Some consider Wang Shiwei was a writer, others think not. Let's just use the term *writer* here), Wang Shiwei did not produce many works. Prior to going to Yan'an, he wrote some articles. During the criticism of Wang in the rectification, his short story, published in the magazine *Development* (Zhankai)—Wang Duqing was editor in chief—was mentioned. Some older comrades said that Wang Shiwei had an article in the magazine *New China* (Xin Zhonghua) (published in Shanghai in the 1930s). Up to now, we have not found those publications; therefore, we are not exactly sure of Wang Shiwei's total publications. However, we did find the novel by Wang Shiwei titled *Rest* (Xiuxi) in the Beijing Library (it totals about forty thousand words). It was published in 1930 as part of the New Art

---

*Song is suggesting here that the deletions were done by people other than Fan for political purposes. Fan's book, *Lun Wang Shiwei sixiang yishi*, is a collection of critical articles culled from *Liberation Daily*. Published by the Qi-Li-Yu Bookstore in 1944, it is currently available on reel three of the Yushode Bookstore Microfilm *Youguan Zhongguo Gongchandang cailiao* (Tokyo, 1970).

Book Series by the China Book Bureau, with Xu Zhimo as editor in chief. The novel, which recounts the suffering of a young student forced to become a post office worker, exposed thoroughly the darkness of the old society. At that time, it was considered a good novel from a political and artistic point of view. But due to its length, we did not include it here.

Perhaps more important were Wang Shiwei's translations. Starting in 1929, Wang was involved in producing translations for the *Complete Works of World Literature* (a series with Xu Zhimo as the editor in chief) for the China Book Bureau.* According to an article by Wang Fanxi published in the Hong Kong magazine *The Nineties*, Wang Shiwei also translated *The Return of the Native* (by Thomas Hardy), *Salambo* (by Flaubert of France), and two chapters from Trotsky's autobiography [*My Life*], an act that later constituted one of Wang's crimes. In all, Wang Shiwei translated many works.

After going to Yan'an, Wang Shiwei did not resume translations until the establishment of the Academy for Marxist-Leninist Studies in May 1938. A Translation Department specializing in translating Marx and Lenin's works was set up composed of Wang Shiwei, He Xilin, and Ke Bainian with Wang doing most of the work. Wang thus became famous in publishing circles. Works by Marx and Lenin translated during the resistance war era that can still be found in the Central Marx-Engels-Lenin-Stalin Compilation and Translation Bureau, the Central Party School, China People's University, etc., show that Wang Shiwei did the following translations: Two separate compilations in the Marx-Engels Series (altogether composed of twelve volumes of which we found ten); the first is the Series on Political Economy (Zhengzhi jingjixue congshu) (volume 6 of the Marx-Engels Series published in March 1939 by Liberation Publishing House), translated by Wang Xuewen, He Xilin, and Wang Shiwei. It includes two of Marx's works: *Employment, Labor, and Capital* and *Value, Price, and Profit*. The former was translated by He Xilin and the latter by Wang Shiwei. Wang Xuewen was the copy editor of the two books. The second is *Revolution and Counterrevolution in Germany* (volume 8 of the Marx-Engels Series, published in April 1939 by Liberation Publishing House). It was translated by Wang Shiwei and Ke Bainian, though, in fact, Ke only translated an article "Central Committee Letter to the Communist Alliance"

---

*See chapter three, p. 27 for a more extensive list of Wang Shiwei's translations.

located in the book's appendix. The main works in *Revolution and Counterrevolution in Germany* were all translated by Wang Shiwei.

From the *Selected Works of Lenin* (Liening xuanji) (originally twenty volumes of which eighteen are extant in the world) nine were made available in China as reprints of a Chinese language version published in Moscow, while nine others were translated and compiled by the Translation Department of which Wang Shiwei translated two and one-half volumes: The second volume (published in May 1940 by Liberation Publishing House), the fourth, and the first part of volume eleven (this volume was divided into two parts due to the length of the articles. The first part was jointly translated by Wu Liping and Wang Shiwei. Wang himself translated 180 pages—approximately eleven thousand words).

In addition, Wang Shiwei single-handedly or together with Wu Liping (Wu Liangping) also translated some short articles by Marx and Lenin. These were also published in *Liberation* (Jiefang) magazine and some were included in the book *Marx, Engels, and Marxism* (Ma, En, yu Makesizhuyi) (published in 1939 by Liberation Publishing House) and in *On Marx-Engels-Lenin-Stalin* (Lun Ma-En-Lie-Si) (also published by Liberation Publishing House). Some were also published individually. The article "Preface to 'Education and Cultivation of Youth' " included in this volume [Document 1.1] was written by Wang Shiwei for his translations of the Marx-Lenin works published by Seagull Publishing House. We reviewed all of Wang Shiwei's published translations of Marx and Lenin. Generally, there is an introduction by the proofreader or a preface that merely describes technical issues on either the translation or the publication. None covers the content of the work except the "Preface to 'Education and Cultivation of Youth' " where the translator expressed his basic attitude toward the works of Marx and Lenin. That is why we included it in this book.

The reason we have published the article "The Old Errors and New Erroneous Tendencies on the Issue of the National Form of Art" [not translated—Eds.] is that it alludes to Wang Shiwei's relationship with the Trotskyites as presented to the CCP Organization Department. But this is not the same article as "A Short Commentary on the National Art Form" also written by Wang Shiwei and singled out by Chen Boda when he accused Wang of being part of the Second Communist International. The former piece was a combination of two of Wang Shiwei's articles compiled by Wang himself. According to Chen Boda: "Most of the offensive content in that article was later omitted by Wang Shiwei when he had it republished in *Chinese Culture*."

Finally, according to our investigation and survey of materials, Wang Shiwei used the following pen names in his various essays, books, and translations: Shiwei (詩薇), Shiwei (實味), Shiwei (實薇), Wang Shiwei (王石巍), Shiwei (石巍), and Shiwei (石味).

Document 1.1

Preface to "Education and Cultivation of Youth," September 20, 1938*

WANG SHIWEI

Today's youth in China are starving and thirsty people searching for spiritual food. Having failed, however, to discover anything new in life from their families, from school, and after traveling to remote parts of the country [i.e., Yan'an], they have become depressed and frustrated. Innumerable young people have lost themselves in the middle of nowhere.

They eagerly long for spiritual food to fulfill their goal of enhancing their personal capabilities and self-cultivation and improving their ability to understand the world. In other words, they need to learn!

By all rights everyone needs to learn. Yet, this kind of learning, it should be emphasized, does not only refer to book learning, but also includes learning from the experience of life and from work. In this book, Lenin outlines a flexible learning method and specific skills for self-cultivation. I seriously recommend this book to young people and hope that you will benefit from it.

---

*This is the preface by Shiwei (a pen name used by Wang Shiwei [see above]) for Lenin's work entitled [in Chinese] *Qingnian de xuexi yu xiuyang*, published by the Seagull Publishing House in 1938 (and now entitled *Gongqingtuan de renwu*)—comment by Dai Qing.

Document 1.2

Politicians, Artists*

WANG SHIWEI

Our revolutionary work has two aspects: to reform society and to reform people—people's souls. The politician is the strategist and tactician of the revolution. He is the unifier, organizer, promoter, and leader of the revolutionary force; his duty is primarily to reform the social system. The artist is the "engineer of the soul" (*linghun de gongchengshi*) whose duty is primarily to reform people's souls (mind, spirit, thought, consciousness—here all one thing).

The darkness and filth in people's souls is the product of the inequity (*bu heli*) of the social system; before the social system has been fundamentally changed, a fundamental change in the human soul is impossible. The process of reforming the social system is also the process of reforming the human soul. The former expands the sphere of the latter, the latter speeds the completion of the former. The work of the politician and the work of the artist are mutually supplementary and interdependent.

---

*This document was translated by Timothy Cheek, who notes: We know from the May 26, 1942, denunciation of "Politicians, Artists" that this essay was written in the journal of Yan'an's Literary Resistance Association, *Spring Rain* (Gu Yu), Vol. 1:4. Until recently, the full text has not been available. It was reprinted in a set of documents on Chinese literary debates, *History of Thought Struggles in Contemporary Chinese Literature* (Zhongguo xiandai wenyi sixiang douzheng shi) (Sichuan, n.p., 1976), pp. 467–71, which dated Wang's article to February 17, 1942, and in Li Zhengjie et al., *Historical Materials on the Literary Movement During the Anti-Japanese War in Yan'an and Various Other Democratic Base Areas* (Kangri zhanzheng shiqi Yan'an jige Kangri minzhu genzhudi wenxue yundong ziliao), Vol. 1 (Taiyuan: Shanxi renmin chubanshe, 1983), pp. 348–57. All of the documents composed by Wang Shiwei and included in Dai Qing's text (except Document 1.1, the Lenin Preface) come from Li Zhengjie's collection, pp. 348–55. In the absence of the original publication the absolute authenticity of these reprints (which are identical) cannot be determined, but half of the present text already existed in the lengthy selections reprinted in the textual analyses attacking it on May 26 and June 16 in the *Liberation Daily*. There are no discrepancies between the overlapping sections, save a few typographical errors. Thus we assume the text is authentic.

The politician is primarily the commander of the material force of the revolution; the artist is primarily the instigator of its spiritual force. The former often is a sober and cool-headed person good at carrying out the actual struggle to eliminate filth and darkness and to realize purity and brightness; the latter, however, is often more passionate and sensitive, good at exposing filth and darkness and indicating purity and brightness and so, from a spiritual level, replenishing the revolution's fighting power.

The politician understands that in the revolutionary process the people of his camp are not faultless and that affairs can hardly be 100 percent perfect. Looking in terms of the big picture, he wants to assure that as the wheels of history progress light will prevail. The artist from a greater passion and sensitivity inevitably longs for people to become more loveable and for affairs to become more pleasant. Working from concrete details, the artist tries as much as possible to eliminate darkness and thus to make the wheels of history move forward with the greatest possible speed.

As the actual reformer of the social system, the politician emphasizes affairs; as the engineer of the soul, the artist demands perfection of the individual.

On how to unite, organize, and lead the revolutionary force and on how to carry out the actual struggle—the politician is superior to the artist. But the artist, too, has a superiority and that is by entering the innermost soul of humanity freely he reforms it—reforms himself in order to strengthen himself, reforms the enemy in order to disintegrate the enemy.

The politician and the artist each have defects. For the sake of successfully attacking the enemy, uniting with friendly armies and strengthening himself, the politician must be worldly wise, have an excellent command of cunning methods and be good at dealing with both enemies and friends. His defects come from just these merits. When these skills are used in revolutionary tasks, they become the most beautiful and glorious "arts of revolution." But apart from the truly great politician, none can avoid some desire to use these skills for their own reputation, position, and profit and thus to harm the revolution. Here we demand that the sharp claws of the cat will only be used to catch the rat and not to grab the chickens. Here is drawn the dividing line between the good politician and the self-seeking one. We must especially guard against the cat that cannot catch rats, but is expert at snatching chickens.

As for the defects of artists in general, the most important are arrogance, partiality (*pianxia*), unsociability, and eccentricity; they are poor at uniting with their own ranks to the point of mutual disdain and infighting. Here we demand that the engineers of the soul first reform their own souls to become pure and bright. To purge one's soul of the filth and darkness within is a difficult and bitter process, but it takes us along a great road that must be traveled.

The Chinese revolution is especially hard. On the one hand, everyone understands the difficulty of reforming social systems, but on the other not many understand the reason why it is so hard to reform people's souls. "The further one goes east, the darker society becomes." Old China is a pus-covered bloody society full of filth and darkness. Those Chinese who have long lived in that society have naturally become corrupted in it. Even ourselves—the revolutionary warriors creating a new China—cannot be an exception. This is a cruel fact. Only if we bravely face up to it will we be able to understand that in the process of reforming the social system we must at the same time seriously and deeply reform our souls in order to speed up the accomplishment of the first [task] and to guarantee its success.

Lu Xun fought all his life. But even those who have the slightest insight into him certainly can comprehend that in the midst of his fighting he was very lonely. He fought because he recognized the laws of social development and he believed the future would certainly be brighter than the present. He felt alone because he could see that the souls of his battle companions contained much filth and darkness. He could not help but understand this truth: the task of reforming old China will be only carried out by old China's children—who carry filth and darkness. But that great heart of his could not help but have some loneliness, because he so longed to see his battle companions be a bit more loveable, a *bit* more loveable!

The revolutionary camp exists in old China, and the revolutionary warriors are born out of old China; thus our souls cannot but carry filth and darkness. The nature of the current revolution also determines that aside from allying with the peasants and urban petty-bourgeois classes we must further carry other even more backward class strata (*jieji jieceng*) along the same road. Moreover since we must make a certain amount of compromise for them we must necessarily be contaminated by even more filth and darkness. Thus, the artist's work of reforming the soul is even more important, more difficult, more urgent. Bravely but appropriately we should expose all filth and darkness; wash them out. This is just as important as praising brightness: even more important. The work of exposure and cleansing is not just negative work, because as darkness decreases light will naturally increase. Some people think revolutionary artists should "close ranks," that if we expose our own defects this will provide the enemy with an opening for attack. This is a short-sighted view; our camp today has already grown so strong that it is not afraid to expose its own defects, though it still has not strengthened itself enough. Correct use of self and mutual criticism is the necessary method for consolidating its strength. As for those national pests in the anticommunist secret service, even if we really had no defects whatsoever they would still be able to start rumors to slander us. Actually, they hope we will conceal our faults for fear of criticism and so cause darkness to expand.

There are a few politicians who are arrogant; when they talk about artists their mouths float up in sarcastic smiles. There are as well a few artists who are conceited; when they mention politicians they, too, shrug their shoulders. In fact, objectively they both have some truth. It would be best if each took the other as a mirror in which to inspect themselves. Don't forget: we all are old China's children carrying filth and darkness.

The truly great politician certainly has a truly great soul sufficient to remold and cleanse by personal example (*ganhua*) the darkness and filth in the soul of others; here the great politician is also the great artist. The artist who truly has a great soul is also certainly able to unite, organize, mobilize, and lead the revolutionary forces; here the great artist is also the great politician.

Finally, with cordial sincerity and ardent hope, I respectfully call out in a thin voice to my comrade artists: Assume more fully the great mission of transforming the soul and first focus on doing work among ourselves and our own camp. Especially in China, reform the social system; it not only determines the speed at which the revolution will be completed but also will influence the success or failure of revolutionary work.

Document 1.3

My Criticisms of Comrade Luo Mai's Speech at the Mobilization Meeting for Rectification and Examination of Work

WANG SHIWEI

1. Short introductory explanation: Although I voiced my criticism of Luo Mai's speech at our institute, my criticism at the meeting was not fully explained and thus I would like to outline it here in written form; I am looking forward to a reaction from Comrade Luo Mai.

2. I'll state my conclusion at the beginning: I think that both the content of Comrade Luo Mai's speech and his attitude when presenting it contain remnants of the patriarchal style in the party that suppresses the masses' enthusiasm and incentive to struggle against the three evil work styles in the party.

3. A statement on evidence: The leadership principle before embarking on all struggles should be to try their best to generate enthusiasm among the masses and create an incentive for struggle. Combatting leftist tendencies should also be emphasized throughout the struggle. Comrade Luo Mai ignored this completely in that he suppressed the masses' high enthusiasm just when it had peaked with demands freely to elect members of the Examination Committees for the Rectification Movement. He acted like a vicious and tough parent, insisting that directors of the departments become automatic members of the committees and be responsible for leadership. This objectively demonstrates that he distrusts the masses, fears the masses, and severely suppresses the masses. He fails to understand that all the research fellows from the departments are knowledgeable in both education and politics. Some might be even more capable than some of the department directors.

It would be more beneficial to the investigation work by the committees if more democracy were permitted. Luo, however, stressed that "the directors are appointed by the Central Committee." "Those people have no choice but to come here to be directors;" "Not only have they come, but they will also be leaders." He never took into consideration how to get the work done well. His only concern is "leaders." He associated the issue of allowing articles to be published anonymously in wall newspapers with such scary words as anarchy. Is it true that the research fellows in this Institute are näive and innocent children who need to be succored by their parents?

My conclusion about Comrade Luo Mai's speech and his style of presentation is based on these views. As for whether it is correct, everyone should feel free to put forward criticisms. I also hope that Comrade Luo Mai himself will comment on this.

—Originally published in the first issue of *Arrow and Target* of the Central Research Institute in 1942

Document 1.4

Two Random Thoughts

WANG SHIWEI

1. Discriminate between good and evil.

The first task in the present rectification and examination of work is to discriminate between good and evil. The right spirit in the party must be elicited and the evil one eliminated; otherwise, there is the inevitable threat of ruining the country, the party, and ourselves. We should not focus solely on our own Institute, but also pay attention to Yan'an as a whole and the entire party, for there are people with the evil spirit everywhere, who hold up the banner of opposing the evil spirit to attack and scandalize people with the right spirit. Of course, it does not mean that people with the right spirit are completely without evil. Here we'll just follow the saying that goes: "When confronting two vicious things, choose the less vicious one." We shall definitely not let those with a more evil spirit be in a favorable situation. Comrades, be more alert. Open your eyes and discriminate between good and evil. Support a righteous spirit and attack the evil spirit.

2. Hard bones [strong-willed] and the soft bones [weak-willed] disease.

We need first of all to examine our own bones in this struggle. Ask ourselves a question: Comrade, is there anything wrong with your bones? Is it true that you dare not speak up to the VIPs (especially your boss) and would rather find fault with the small potatoes? Understand that the soft bones disease (*ruangu bing*) is a kind of evil spirit; thus, we must have real hard bones (*yinggutou*) in order to deal with it.

—Originally published in the first issue of
Arrow and Target in 1942

Document 1.5

Response to Comrades Li Yuchao and Mei Luo

WANG SHIWEI

1. How should a Marxist view things?

The major point of criticism Comrades Yuchao and Mei Luo have directed at me is this: Comrade Luo Mai's point is correct. It is I [Wang] who "twisted" his [Luo's] meaning—"said something out of excitement with my eyes closed." Here I will only respond with the hard facts—your so-called right point has been vetoed by a vote of 84 to 28 at the meeting.

A Marxist must examine the essence of an object by sweeping away all superficial phenomena. It should have been asked: What is the function of the basic spirit of the comrade's speech on rectification and examination of work? What kind of work style does it represent? Only by paying attention to this essential point will the argument be affirmed. Comrade Yuchao claimed that I "twisted" Comrade Luo Mai's meaning. I also feel that you two [Li Yuchao and Mei Luo] have "twisted" my meaning as well. The problem will never be solved if everyone plays on the choice and form of words.

2. A few explanations.

a. I do not deny the cynical, excessive nature of my speech on that day [Document 1.3]. Comrade Luo Mai's arbitrary and patriarchal style agitated me a great deal and also reminded me of the leader "more stupid than a pig" who caused the death of many comrades. I cursed Comrade Luo Mai. For this, I am willing to accept all kinds of criticisms.

b. . . . [in original—Eds.]

c. I neither suffered from serious "mistreatment" in the party in the past nor "mistreatment" by Comrade Luo Mai. The hypothesis formulated by Comrade Mei Luo is wrong.

d. I still respect you two regardless of the fact that we hold different views. I especially respect the fact that Comrade Mei Luo, a nonparty Bolshevik, expressed his criticism using his real name.

3. By the way, I'd like to discuss my own bones.

The bones that make a person into a real human being should be judged by those who understand him and the broad masses who have daily contact with him. The political bones of a party member should be judged by the Central Organization Department. No matter whether it's done from a kindhearted or vicious point of view, you should investigate thoroughly and speak up by standing at the forefront.

Attacking a person with rumors is the meanest, dirtiest act. Wang Shiwei is full of confidence. "His bones have never been soft and are not softer than others."

—Originally published in the third issue of the wall newspaper
Arrow and Target of the Central Research Institute

Section Two: Introduction

In this part, we have gathered together articles from publications in Yan'an criticizing Wang Shiwei. Two articles by Mao Zedong are very important and easily available: "Speech Given at the Conference on Reorganizing the *Liberation Daily*" and "Talks at the Yan'an Forum on Literature and Art." To save space only the titles of these articles are published here.

There were generally three phases in the criticism campaign directed at Wang Shiwei. The first started with the statement: "Some people do not speak from the correct standpoint." This is from a speech by Mao at a conference on reorganizing *Liberation Daily*. The criticism of Wang started gradually from then onward. Wang Shiwei was, for the first time, criticized publicly in the article entitled "Some Feelings after Reading 'Wild Lilies' " by Qi Su published in *Liberation Daily*, April 7, 1942. An article written by Fan Wenlan (on June 2) titled "On Comrade Wang Shiwei's Ideological Consciousness" was published in *Liberation Daily* on June 9. Articles criticizing Wang Shiwei from April 7 to June 9 in *Liberation Daily* can be characterized as criticisms among comrades. Most articles explained the reasons for Wang's deviation. We consider that criticism as ideological criticism.

The second phase of criticism involved political struggle. In fact, two meetings were held: One was the forum at the Central Research Institute, the other was the Seventy-two-day Meeting. The forum on "Democracy and Discipline in the Party" was held at the Central Research Institute beginning on May 27, 1942. In reality, it was an anti-Wang Shiwei struggle meeting. Prior to June 1, the main task was to involve the masses in the criticism of Wang Shiwei through discussions on democracy and party discipline. But after June 1, the forum was turned into an anti-Wang Shiwei struggle meeting [See Document 2.1, "Diary of a Struggle," by Wen Jize].

On the morning of June 4, Wang Shiwei participated in the forum for his one and only time. The reason why they demanded that Wang attend was to serve the purpose of "verification of evidence." On the same day, the historical relationship between Wang Shiwei and the Trotskyites was publicized by order of Kang Sheng. Actually, Wang Shiwei had voluntarily revealed his relationship with the Trotskyites to the Central Oganization Department in 1941. No one was aware of this, not even the leaders of the Central Research Institute. Publications on the relationship between Wang Shiwei and the Trotskyites quickly altered the views of the masses on Wang Shiwei. The forum was soon turned into a struggle meeting.

The scope of the forum was enlarged from June 8 onward. More than one thousand people from more than seventy units in Yan'an participated. During the last two days of the forum (June 10 and 11), the Institute leaders, including Luo Mai and Fan Wenlan, pronounced Wang Shiwei a "Trotskyite."

After the struggle meeting, the Seventy-two-day Meeting began on July 9 at both the Central Research Institute and the Political Research Office. Comrades Pan Fang, Zong Zheng, Cheng Quan, and Wang Li were criticized and labeled, together with Wang Shiwei, as the "Five Member Anti-Party Gang" (*wuren fandang jituan*).

The major speeches given at the Institute forum are included in this part of the book [none have been translated, but their main points are summarized in Wen Jize's "Diary of a Struggle," Document 2.1—Eds.]. The speech titled "Thoroughly Smash Wang Shiwei's Trotskyite theories and his antiparty activities" by Zhang Ruxin, summarizing Wang Shiwei's Trotskyite ideas and activities both past and present, was at that time considered as the most systematic criticism. That speech provides a typical example of how Wang Shiwei was labeled as a Trotskyite.

Kang Sheng played a decisive role in both the struggle against Wang Shiwei and the criticism of Pan Fang, Zong Zheng, Cheng Quan, and Wang Li. We could not, however, find Kang Sheng's articles and speeches from that period. But Kang's speech to a Cadre Training Class in August 1943 [Document 2.5] filled the gap. Kang himself said that "a strategic Marxist policy was adopted" in the criticism toward Wang Shiwei and the "Five Member Anti-Party Gang." This strategy of criticism was very skillful. In fact, this is the "live" stuff of Kang Sheng's "strategy for torturing people."

The third phase was the organizational conclusion in which Wang

Shiwei was deprived of his party membership in October 1942. It is said that Kai Feng drafted the decision approved by Mao Zedong.

In order to illustrate the argument between Wang Shiwei and Chen Boda over the issue of national form, we included Chen Boda's article titled "After Reading Comrade Shiwei's 'A Short Commentary on the National Form in Literature and Art' " [not translated—Eds.] to make it easy for comrades to examine the argument. Lastly, we also include Zhang Ruxin's "General Summary of Ideological Remolding in the Central Research Institute Since the Start of Rectification" [Document 2.3] and Ai Siqi's "How Our Learning Was Reformed" [not translated—Eds.]. Although these two articles did not criticize Wang Shiwei directly, they are linked to the Wang Shiwei issue and also help to enhance our understanding of the Yan'an rectification.

Document 2.1

Diary of a Struggle*

WEN JIZE

Wednesday, May 27

The forum of the entire Institute on "Democracy and Discipline in the Party" began at 9:30 A.M.

Today eleven comrades spoke. Everyone realized that at the beginning of rectification we manifested an extreme democratic tendency. Several comrades said that at the mobilization meeting we vetoed the original decision to have every director of the research departments automatically appointed to the examination committee. We thought that rectification was only a case of "cutting off the big tails" of the leaders, a tendency that was a manifestation of extreme democracy. A few comrades said that members of the investigation commttee should go through a process of election. This is something that vice-director Fan (Wenlan) agreed with in the earlier mobilization meeting. Therefore, it was believed that vetoing the idea that leaders immediately become heads of the investigation committees is not necessarily absolute egalitarianism. [Wen Jize:] This is a struggle question.

Comrade Fan Wenlan made a speech in which he made a deep and sincere self-criticism of his overly lenient attitude. This spirit of self-criticism deeply impressed everyone. Comrade Li Yuchao raised the question of Wang Shiwei. He declared: "There are many deviationists among us but the case of Comrade Wang Shiwei is fundamentally different. From his articles and his comments at the mobilization meeting and his subsequent individual activities one can see that his mistakes are consistent, severe, and not accidental." Another comrade said:

---

*Editors' Note: Douzheng riji appeared in Liberation Daily on June 28 and 29, 1942. This translation is taken from Anthony Saich, The Rise to Power of the Chinese Communist Party: Documents and Analysis (Armonk, N.Y.: M. E. Sharpe, forthcoming). Used with permission with minor alterations. Since the "Diary" covers the Central Research Institute forum from May 27 to June 11 we have placed it at the beginning of part 2 of the Documents section as a sort of summary.

"We should deeply and sincerely undergo self-examination. Our petty bourgeois consciousness is too deep. On this point, we can say that there is only a quantitative difference with Wang's mistakes. There is no qualitative difference." This is another point of discussion.

Thursday, May 28

Today the discussion lasted all morning. The majority of the speeches discussed the principle of democratic-centralism, for example the difference between democracy inside and outside the party.

A small number of speeches relaunched the discussion of the problem raised yesterday by Comrade Li Yuchao: Some comrades opposed his assessment of Wang Shiwei's mistakes and believed that his speech "made groundless accusations and manifested vestiges of subjectivism." Other comrades agreed with his assessment: "From the organizational point of view, Wang Shiwei is still our comrade. But from an ideological point of view, he has become our enemy." The debate over these two opinions has not yet been resolved.

In the morning, Comrade Ai Siqi made a report on Comrade Mao Zedong's conclusions at the forum on literature and art. The meeting reconvened in the afternoon. Three comrades spoke: "From the comments by Wang Shiwei at the mobilization meeting, from 'Wild Lilies' and 'Politicians, Artists' and from his other articles, one can see that he has abandoned the party's standpoint, has sown discord among lower and higher ranks and between politicians and artists, etc., and has opposed the party and its standpoint. The nature of our deviation is completely different."

Comrade Luo Mai intervened last and he systematically replied to the questions raised by the comrades on demcratic-centralism and party discipline. He expressed his opinion on the eradication of previous deviations and the question of Wang Shiwei. He also spoke on the question of deviations in the mobilization meeting. As for Wang Shiwei, he agreed with the ideas of Li Yuchao and the others. He analyzed "Wild Lilies" and pointed out that Wang opposed the party with an oppositional viewpoint. This was not only an ideological error but also a serious political error that was in no way similar to our deviation. Our deviations were accidental and derived from our näiveté.

In the evening, some comrades suggested to the chair of the forum committee that since the issue of democratic-centralism had been discussed extensively, the next session of the forum should focus on the nature of Wang Shiwei's ideology. The suggestion was adopted by the committee.

Sunday, May 31

The presidium edited and distributed Wang Shiwei's wall newspaper articles to all participants, to be used as reference material for the study of his thought.

Monday, June 1

Today, the central theme of the meeting progressed from eradicating extreme democratic tendencies to a discussion of Wang Shiwei's thought. The majority of the fifteen speeches in the day concentrated on this issue. The third speech was given by Li Yan. First, he gave some statistics: Many of our Institute's researchers more or less sympathized with Wang Shiwei when they first read "Wild Lilies." Even those who disliked this essay did not realize the fundamental mistake of the author's position. But over two months of studying rectification documents, and attending the meetings convened by the Central Committee Propaganda Department, studying [Mao Zedong's] "Combat Liberalism" and "On Egalitarianism," [Liu Shaoqi's] "How to Be a Good Communist Party Member" and other documents and the debates on "Wild Lilies" and "Politicians, Artists" have clearly enabled everybody to know the seriousness of the errors in thought and method contained in "Wild Lilies." (How necessary is thought reform! How important were the rectification documents!) Li Yan went on to report on the process of the six talks held between Wang and the party committee. Wang did not admit his mistakes until now. In order to "cure the illness to save the patient," we must completely expose Wang's mistakes and carry out a serious ideological struggle against him.

Afterward, Xuewei and other comrades stood up to present material proving that Wang Shiwei had been poisoned ideologically by his past associations with the Trotskyites. They reported that Wang had claimed that "Stalin's character is not praiseworthy," "[Karl] Radek is an admirable man," "the Comintern should be held responsible for the failure of the Great Chinese Revolution of 1927," "the charge of high treason against Zinoviev is dubious," "on certain issues Trotsky's theories are correct," and so forth.

Wang's basic understanding of the Rectification Movement is fundamentally erroneous: He slandered the leading organ of the party by believing that some members were corrupt; he said that the Rectification Movement was "a unification under the leadership of Chairman Mao of upright people against immoral ones"; and he said that Comrades Luo Mai and Fan Wenlan headed two factions on the question of democracy in our Institute. He also used the term "hard bones" to draw other comrades to his side and the abusive term "soft bones" to attack other comrades.

At the end of the meeting, Ai Siqi read aloud the article by Wang Shiwei in which he refuted the attacks against him by Qi Su in "Concerning Wild Lilies." In this article, [Ai continued] Wang not only slanders the party but promotes himself as a leader of youth. He claims to be the "modern Lu Xun" and calls upon youth to shake his hand. Upon hearing these sickening phrases, the meeting roared with malicious laughter.

At the beginning of discussions about "Wild Lilies" and "Politicians, Artists" some said that "Wang's position was incorrect but that his intentions were good." Others felt that his intentions were impure. Today the issue was resolved and no one stated that his intentions were pure. Today, the difference between Wang Shiwei's ideological errors and our deviations was clearly revealed. It was shown that all his words and provocative acts were the result of premeditated malevolence and that there was no question of regarding them in the same light as our spontaneous deviation.*

Tuesday, June 2

The chair decided to adjourn the meeting until the next day. Everyone was told to read Lenin's "Party Organization and Party Literature," Lu Xun's speech at the Founding Congress of the Left-Wing Writers Association, and the "Conclusions of the Yan'an Forum on Literature and Art" by Mao Zedong (notes), the first section of chapter ten of *History of the CPSU (Bolshevik), Short Course*, the *Selected Works of Stalin*, volume two, pp. 93–98 and 346–48. [All these passages are about experiences and lessons derived from crushing the oppositional conspiracies in the CPSU—Eds.]. These texts constituted an arsenal to fight against the Trotskyite thought of Wang Shiwei.

---

*This focus on the motives of individuals targeted for struggle was central to the CCP's evolving methods of thought reform.

In the morning, Wang Shiwei presented his request to resign from the party to the Institute Party Committee. He explained that "the contradiction in interests between himself and the party had become virtually insoluble" and that he intended to "take the road he had chosen for himself."

He is so stubborn he refused party education. What a dangerous and incurable road he is taking!

Wednesday, June 3

In the morning, members continued to read the documents. In the afternoon, the meeting continued.

One comrade spoke: "In the extremely difficult situation faced in the border regions involving political and economic affairs, Wang Shiwei has tried to undermine unity and propagate egalitarianism, etc. Under the slogan of opposing sectarianism, he has made provocations and under the slogan of opposing the black elements in the party and promoting democracy, he has opposed the leading organs. This is an exact copy of the old methods used by the Trotskyites in the Soviet Union. One can expect the worst if he does not correct his errors." Another comrade described briefly Wang Shiwei's family situation. This showed that Wang's thought was petty bourgeois derived from a small ruined aristocrat. Comrade Ai Siqi spoke last: "Wang Shiwei's viewpoints place him in the camp of the ultrareactionary petty bourgeoisie; he is the spokesman for the reactionary bourgeoisie in the party. Like a smuggler, he spreads Trotskyite thought that contains the following major elements: A hypocritical revolutionary zeal that conceals a genuine tragic pessimism; rejection of the United Front; the concept of a classless 'human nature'; and a factional view of inner-party struggle. His methods are truly ingenious! He knows how to make beautiful disguises (for example his slogans 'oppose subjectivism and sectarianism,' 'oppose formalism' [i.e., literally, the eight-legged essay in the party], 'oppose half-baked Marxism,' and so on. He uses provocative language and expressions).* He

---

*A classic Catch–22 situation for Wang Shiwei as his invocation of conventional party principles and slogans from the Rectification Movement is now turned against him as "evidence" of his "ingenious" criminal nature. This strategy of persecution presaged the attacks on various political factions during the Cultural Revolution who once out of favor were scurrilously accused of "waving the Red Flag to oppose the Red Flag."

makes use of the reactions of youth to pit them against the old cadres, subordinates against superiors and artists against politicians, etc." Comrade Ai Siqi concluded: "The most important lesson that we have gained in actual ideological struggle is the necessity to study correctly the twenty-two [official rectification] documents, rectify our thought, strengthen our political consciousness and take up ideological weapons."

After the meeting, everybody was still talking about Wang's resignation request. That night, several comrades sought out Wang and tried once again to save him.

Thursday, June 4*

Today many people were present from the Central Political Research Office and the Literary Resistance Association as every window sill was filled. As soon as the bell rang starting the meeting, several hundred eyes turned toward Wang as he entered the auditorium from the door on the left. This was the first time Wang attended the forum.

After speeches by Comrades Li Yuchao and Pan Fang, it was Comrade Wang Shiwei's turn. He said in a low, deep voice: "I hereby withdraw solemnly and seriously my appeal to the party committee for resignation, made yesterday when I was in an abnormal state. . . . The 'love' of some friends whom I respect has moved me." One comrade interjected: "Is your political life determined by the 'love' of your friends?" Wang Shiwei replied: "I don't think that any 'love' or 'hatred' transcending classes exists." Just now Comrade Li Yuchao said I am a Trotskyite, but I myself do not know. In the past I didn't have the slightest understanding of politics. . . . If you've read my article on national forms of literature published in *Chinese Culture*† you would know that I have supported firmly the United Front. How can I have Trotskyite thought?"

A comrade stood up and interjected: "You should not tell lies! You often spoke to me about the Trotskyite question and to this day you still believe that Trotskyites exist in the USSR and that they are not running dogs of the fascist bandit gang, that they are antifascist." Another comrade rose: "You told me the same thing." [Wang:] "I acknowledge everything I have said. Yes, I said that I hated the Trotskyites

---

*This is the start of Part Two of the account contained in *Liberation Daily*, June 29, 1942.

†*Zhongguo wenhua* 2:6, pp. 32–38.

who organized against Stalin. But I am deeply moved by their alliance with the CPSU against fascism." Another intervention: "On what basis do you claim that Trotskyites still exist in the USSR? On what basis do you say Trotskyites oppose fascism?"

"Yes. You once said the same thing to me," another comrade replied.

In his subsequent comments Wang admitted that in 1929 he had contacts with Trotskyites for whom he had translated the *Lenin Last Testament*, (a testament revised by the Trotskyites). He also translated two chapters of Trotsky's autobiography [*My Life*], and published short stories in a Trotskyite magazine. Up until 1936, Wang continued to correspond with Trotskyites. He never forgot Trotskyite elements such as Chen Qingchen and Wang Wenyuan [Wang Fanxi]. "I think that the Trotskyite criticism of the Li Lisan line is correct." ("Sheer nonsense!") . . . "I've read the August 1 declaration [1935]. I believe that this more or less advocates the same idea as the Trotskyite call for a National Assembly. ("Sheer nonsense!") . . . Only after I had read Lu Xun's letter to the Trotskyites, did I adopt a position in favor of the United Front."

Everyone was outraged by his unrepentant attitude and his blatant propagation of the theories of the Trotskyite bandits. The chair was asked to stop Wang Shiwei from straying from the subject and to reply to the questions clearly.

Another comrade stood up and asked: "Why did you say that during the purge of the party in the USSR people have ignored the crimes committed by Stalin? You made this statement." [Wang:] "I believe that during the purges of the CPSU, many enemies could have been turned into comrades. Stalin's character is too brutal." This slander of Stalin aroused righteous indignation. "Why on your arrival in Yan'an didn't you report honestly to the party about your association with the Trotskyites?" [Wang:] "When I first arrived in Yan'an I encountered discrimination everywhere . . . Right up to 1940 I criticized Chen Boda over the issue of national forms. During the polemic, he scolded me for being an opportunist of the Second International. If he wants to scold me as a member of the Fourth [International] what will that achieve? I reported to the party's Organization Department the links I had had with the Trotskyites." Beyond this, he grossly insulted Chen Boda: "He is a sectarian"; the chair silenced him.

Yet another comrade took the floor: "I ask that Wang Shiwei express his opinion on the following Trotskyite positions: (1) Trotsky's opinion on the question of the Soviet peasantry before the Twelfth

Congress of the CPSU; (2) the question of the *Lenin Last Testa-*
ment; (3) the question of who, in the final analysis, should be responsible for the failure of the Great Chinese Revolution of 1925–27 . . .
Wang Shiwei has debated these issues with me in the past. Wang
Shiwei showed that he continued to preserve his "original Trotskyite
opinions." He [Wang] added: "If my opinion was incorrect, why didn't
you educate me earlier?" [Another comrade:] "Did you ever discuss these
matters with the party organization? Why didn't you ask the party to help
correct your views? You prefer to spout off all around the place."

Wang Shiwei couldn't reply to these objections. When the meeting
adjourned, I [Wen Jize] walked out of the meeting hall with Wang. He
said to me: "Only I can rectify my errors. Others cannot shed light on
them even if they are philosophers." I laughed coldly. He did not
attend the meeting that afternoon.

Fifteen comrades spoke during the meeting and criticized his Trotskyite viewpoint. Those who had not recognized the true face of Wang
Shiwei saw clearly today that he was a Trotskyite and that his errors were
particularly serious and dangerous. To help Wang Shiwei understand his
errors, the meeting designated three delegates to speak with him after the
meeting. At the end of the session, the chair adjourned the meeting for
two days to allow everyone to read the *Selected Works of Stalin*, volume
two, pp. 85–156 (againt the opposition) and volume three, pp. 101–106
(on the question of Lenin's testament); the August 7 Manifesto [1927]; and
the directives sent by the Comintern to the CCP during the great revolution. We need these weapons in order to smash the Trotskyite opinions
that Wang Shiwei has retained on a number of concrete problems.*

Monday, June 8

Beginning at 7 A.M.† some one thousand participants from more than
seventy organizations and schools came to listen. The public surrounded
the chair and spread out over the sports field (the provisional meeting
place). When the chair announced "the meeting will begin," the comrades could not stop from laughing. Never before had there been such
a gigantic meeting!

At first, the chair made a brief report about the meetings of the

---

*Other party members obviously agreed with Wang's views.
†The fact that Wen Jize notes that the meeting began at 7:00 A.M. instead of the
previous time of 9:30 A.M. suggests that the mobilization phase had clearly begun.

previous two weeks in order to let recent arrivals learn about the background. Comrades Li Yuchao and Liu Xuewei addressed relatively systematically Wang Shiwei's Trotskyite thought, his historical links with the Trotskyites, his incorrect ideas about the party, his complete misunderstanding of the Rectification Movement and his activities during the movement, etc.

During the lunch break, the chair decided to ask every organization and school to select representatives to attend the afternoon's meeting. (It was impossible to hold a forum of one thousand people.) The meeting continued in the afternoon, and the presidium declared that those invited would also have the right to speak. A few comrades presented new documents on Wang's personal life. These documents made it easier to evaluate how disgusting and filthy Wang Shiwei's soul really was.

Tuesday, June 9

Two magnificent speeches by Comrades Chen Boda and Ai Qing highlighted today's meeting.

Comrade Chen Boda began by criticizing the Trotskyite viewpoint in Wang Shiwei's manuscript on national forms. Then he described Wang Shiwei's egotistical behavior at the Translation Department of the Academy for Marxist-Leninist Studies and the Central Research Institute: "This kind of person has no 'spine' but is like a spineless leech! There is no 'greatness' about him, he is as minute as a mosquito; like the kind that sneak in silently to bite you."*

Comrade Ai Qing declared: "Wang Shiwei's articles are impregnated with a gloomy spirit. Reading them gives me the feeling of entering the temple of a spirit that protects the town. His style is mediocre . . . He depicts Yan'an as dark and sinister, he pits artists against politicians, old cadres against the young and stirs them up. His viewpoint is reactionary and his remedies are poisonous. This 'individual' does not deserve to be described as 'human' let alone as a 'comrade.' "

The speech of another comrade set off a violent debate. He declared that "it is undeniable that Wang Shiwei ideologically is a Trotskyite but we cannot prove that there is an organizational problem." This idea

---

*Such organic terminology comparing political dissidents to insects has been a staple of Chinese communist ideology up through the recent post-Tiananmen criticism of democracy movement activists.

was challenged by six or seven comrades who thought that Wang Shiwei's mistakes were not limited to ideology and politics but extended to organizational questions. Everybody clearly saw that the serious mistakes of Wang Shiwei had been proved.

Wednesday, June 10

In the morning, Zhang Ruxin made a systematic analysis and criticism of Wang's thought. First, he outlined the important points of Wang's thinking: The theory of human nature that forms the foundation of his philosophy of life; his theory of "degeneration," that is his ideological weapon to oppose the party; extreme democracy and absolute egalitarianism that are intimately linked to the previous two. Then, he analyzed Wang Shiwei's methods: Using a leftist guise Wang exploits the weaknesses of youth, he sows discord, he is two-faced. His history confirms the consistency of his thought and activity and shows that they are no accident. Then Zhang criticized Wang's Trotskyite thinking (notably on the question of the purge of the party in the Soviet Union, the *Lenin Last Testament*, the National Assembly, the Li Lisan line, the winning-over of the Trotskyites etc.) as well as his understanding of the party's problems (the difference between a proletarian party and a party of peasants and petty bourgeois elements under the leadership of the proletariat, utilitarianism, and the relationship between the party and its members). Finally, he appealed to us to strengthen our unity in order to smash Wang Shiwei's Trotskyite thought, his influence, and his politics.

The meeting continued in the afternoon. All branches of personnel and research departments at the Institute as well as the Political Research Office demanded unanimously that Wang Shiwei be expelled from the party. The chair decided that the party committee of the Institute should handle the affair. Twenty comrades spoke.

Thursday, June 11

The last day of the forum. The crowd was particularly large today. The grand hall thronged with people.

Comrade Ding Ling spoke first. She rejected the insults of the Trotskyite element, Wang Shiwei, about the cultural sphere in Yan'an. Then she made a self-criticism about her own essay "Thoughts on March 8." Comrade Luo Mai followed her and made five points:

1. He explained that the debates, over the past two weeks, had

eradicated past deviations and had thoroughly exposed Wang Shiwei's counterrevolutionary thought and his antiparty activities. Everyone had made progress in politics, in principle and methods of ideological struggle, and in form of thought. This is a great achievement of this meeting.

2. Wang Shiwei's thought is dominated by the Trotskyites, it is the ideology of the bourgeoisie. Those elements of petty bourgeois thinking that he possesses are merely those of the bankruptcy of the petty bourgeoisie and its systematic sabotage, its stupidity, and its psychological desperation that are characteristic of Trotskyite elements. His words and deeds not only have political goals but also organizational objectives. Responsible and ordinary members of the Institute have all tried to help him and we have adopted the method of curing the illness to save the patient. However, he has not accepted our help sincerely. At this point, Luo Mai declared: "I agree that the question of his party membership should be decided by the committee, but, at the same time, we should say: Wang Shiwei should have one last chance to pull himself out of his counterrevolutionary shit pit (*maokeng*)."*

3. This struggle and debate, Luo Mai explained, has great educational and serious political meaning. At this time of difficulty in the war of resistance, it is necessary to purge antiparty thought, antiparty activists, and the influence spread by Wang Shiwei.

4. He explained that the deviation by others and Wang Shiwei's thought had similarities but also were distinct. It is necessary to see the nature of this deviation clearly and compare it to the reality of Wang's thought in order to triumph over the deviation and to develop the struggle against Wang Shiwei. Over the past eighty days, everyone has gone through the process of studying the documents and continuous self-examination. This has been a great gain from this meeting. We know much more clearly the force of the party documents and the importance of the rectification documents.

5. Luo Mai expressed several hopes: He hoped that we would continue and extend the self and mutual criticism, study the documents more concretely and deeply, and examine our consciences. He wished sufficient courage to those lacking the courage to engage in self-criticism. Our slogan is not to let a single comrade retain or hide his or her faults. Finally, he hoped that comrades would take advantage of the

Maokeng—an earthy term for large and not very private latrines generally located in China's rural areas.

situation to criticize leading responsible comrades, especially with respect to remolding their ideology and work-styles.

Fan Wenlan made the final speech. He asked: "Who is Wang Shiwei? He is a Trotskyite." He divided his comments into two parts. First he explained that the party tried to save Wang Shiwei. The party committee already knew about Wang's counterrevolutionary thought and activities. We have continually shown generosity and we tried to cure the illness to save the patient. Comrade [Hu] Qiaomu criticized him face-to-face and by letter; the party committee spoke with him on two or three occasions and charged five people to help him; and other comrades criticized him on numerous occasions either verbally or in writing. However, he always refused a self-examination. We tried everything to pull him out of his shit pit but he wanted to drag us down with him. This is outrageous! Now, we should declare: Wang Shiwei has one last chance to climb out of his counterrevolutionary shit pit.

In the second part, he drew out the lessons of the struggle and indicated the points that were worthy of general attention: A resolute and total opposition to liberalism, strict adherence to discipline, a complete ban on rumor-mongering, heightening of our political vigilance, improving our study of the [rectification] documents, and increasing the seriousness of our self-examinations.

At the end of Fan Wenlan's speech, the entire hall applauded enthusiastically. Amidst this enthusiastic and victorious applause, the chair announced the conclusion of the meeting.

Document 2.2

Resolution of the Yan'an Literature and Art Circles Forum on the Trotskyite Wang Shiwei, June 18, 1942

1. We unanimously agree that Wang Shiwei's fundamental thought and activities are Trotskyite. It is antiproletarian and harmful to the communist party and the revolutionary cause. All revolutionaries and their sympathizers should firmly oppose it.

2. We unanimously* agree that Wang Shiwei's "Wild Lilies" and "Politicians, Artists" are propaganda reflecting his incorrect thought. It is inappropriate for the Literature and Art column of *Liberation Daily* and *Spring Rain* to print them instead of exposing and criticizing them.

3. We unanimously agree that the criticism of Wang Shiwei by the Central Research Institute and *Liberation Daily* is necessary and correct. It is of great educational significance to all literary circles and ourselves; therefore, we unanimously support this struggle.

—Originally published in *Liberation Daily*, June 20, 1942

---

*Note all this "unanimity" compared to the divisions generated by Wang's proposals for elections to rectification committees.

Document 2.3

General Summary of Ideological Remolding in the Central Research Institute since the Start of Rectification—Report on Party Rectification in the Central Research Institute, September 1942*

ZHANG RUXIN

Since rectification began this year on March 18 in this Institute, it has gone on for exactly half a year. In the initial stage, erroneous tendencies (*pianxiang*) appeared and we exposed Wang Shiwei's anti-party activities. Afterward, the erroneous tendencies were corrected. This period is merely six months time, but it is undoubtedly comparable to a few years in terms of its content and effect on our comrades. Everyone thinks this half year has provided us with much valuable experience and has taught us many lessons. These experiences and lessons need to be carefully summarized to guide our future practice.

Here I am only going to discuss several issues, experiences, and lessons regarding ideological reform in the Rectification Movement. This is the core of my summary that deserves careful attention and meticulous examination.

---

*This document, published in two parts on October 31 and November 1, 1942, is a classic statement of inner-party struggle methods developed during the Rectification Movement. The rectification study methods described here were expanded to the entire Communist party, and after 1949, throughout China's educational system. For a detailed history of rectification, see Frederick C. Teiwes, *Politics & Purges in China: Rectification and the Decline of Party Norms, 1950–1965* (Armonk, NY: M.E. Sharpe, 2nd edition, 1993).

A. General exposure and the origins of the erroneous tendencies at the beginning of rectification

As for the reasons for the appearance of erroneous tendencies, this must be discussed before we address the issue of the struggle over ideological remolding, a struggle that overcame the erroneous tendencies that had appeared at the beginning of rectification. The basic content of the ideological remolding in this Institute has been the appearance but also the correction of erroneous tendencies.

Now everyone admits that at the beginning of rectification there were erroneous tendencies and that they have undergone self-examination both in theory and in practice. However, we must be clear about the content and the genuine characteristics of erroneous tendencies.

We think that at that time the erroneous tendencies were mainly reflected in the following three respects:

1. They came from the incorrect understanding of the basic spirit of rectification. Now everyone knows that this rectification aims at remolding the ideology and work style of party cadres and members of the entire party. It is a very significant event that further Bolshevizes our party. It is the darkness before the dawn. It is also a general ideological mobilization of the entire party that strives for victory in the anti-Japanese struggle. But at that time, the majority of our comrades did not understand the significance of rectification, thinking that it was the same procedure as the previous examination of work involving mobilization, examination, and summarization with no special ideological or political significance. That is why many comrades, after listening to Mao's speech, still considered rectification as an "old cliché," needing no further attention or discussion.

Another even more significant way of thinking that at that time unduly influenced most of our comrades was that the only purpose of this rectification was to torment cadres—i.e., those so-called great masters. They either failed to realize or did not pay enough attention to the fact that rectification aimed at remolding their own ideological standpoint. That is why most comrades welcomed the editorial on "Dogma and pants" (Jiaotiao yu kuzi) in *Liberation Daily*, while they felt uneasy and disliked the editorial "How to begin self-criticism" [April 6, 1942]. This thought is the fundamental basis of their erroneous tendencies.

2. The above-mentioned thought caused the erroneous tendency to-

ward extreme democratization (*jiduan minzhuhua*). The change in attitude of people with the erroneous tendency toward cadres in the leading organs was due to the fact that they considered rectification to be a means of tormenting cadres and the "great masters." This erroneous tendency led them to ignore the importance of the leading organs and cadres. They opposed the idea that all departmental directors are guaranteed members of the rectification committee, thinking that ordinary comrades should hold the leading power and that the development of rectification would be hindered if [high-level] cadres reinforced their leadership. For this reason, cadres in that period were ruthlessly attacked in an unprincipled manner. The majority of comrades advocated the idea of "boldness first," thinking that it would be acceptable as long as they boldly criticized the cadres without considering organizational principles and the tone of the criticism.

During that period, even some of the departments of the Central Committee and some important cadres in Yan'an were criticized in wall newspapers. These phenomena obviously manifested the erroneous tendency of extreme democratization that idolized and took democracy to the extreme and separated it from centralism. Democracy was incorrectly developed, centralism was ignored, and principles were diminished. Of course, one thing needing elaboration is that it does not mean that the leading organs and the leading cadres cannot be criticized during rectification (it's the same in ordinary times); on the contrary, accurate and principled criticisms within the organization are necessary, beneficial, and are a must both in the past, present, and future. For instance, I myself have a lot of faults. Good criticisms from comrades can be very helpful to me. My point here is that at that time the attitude toward the leading organs and the majority of cadres violated the basic spirit of rectification in ideological and organizational terms. It also destroyed the party's organizational principles and weakened party discipline. Thus we consider it an erroneous tendency.

3. Some comrades more or less adopted the attitude of liberalism in dealing with Wang Shiwei's Trotskyite thoughts and his antiparty activities. From the very beginning of rectification, Wang Shiwei actively used any opportunity to spread his Trotskyite ideas and carry out his antiparty activities. His speech at the "March 18" mobilization meeting [Document 1.3] greatly strained comradely relations by scolding leading cadres. Afterward at the discussion in his department, he publicly exposed his ideas on "human nature" and his "theory of de-

generation" (*tuihua lun*). Next, he spread his "hard bones" theory and at that time published his articles "Politicians, Artists" and "Wild Lilies." None of these antiparty activities by Wang Shiwei were criticized and brought out by the majority of comrades; on the contrary, in certain respects it won their support. For instance, Wang Shiwei's speech at the Rectification Mobilization meeting and his "hard bones" theory contributed to our comrades' misunderstanding of the basic spirit of rectification and in the meantime reinforced the erroneous tendency toward extreme democratization. Also, "Wild Lilies" aroused sympathetic feelings for egalitarianism in the hearts of quite a few comrades. Our comrades have admitted to this unanimously.

Two factors contributed to Wang Shiwei's incorrect words and his antiparty activities having such an impact: One is that our comrades' ideologically erroneous tendency offered space for Wang's thoughts to penetrate. The second is that our comrades lacked political and ideological awareness. Besides, before and after the Rectification Movement, Wang Shiwei blatantly disseminated his Trotskyite theory (praising the Trotskyite faction and scolding Stalin and the CPSU). These comrades, with only a few exceptions, neither counteracted him, nor reported it to the party organization. This is even a more serious case of liberalism.

The above-mentioned three issues constituted the main content of the erroneous tendency at the beginning of rectification. These three are connected, and among the three the most prominent is the issue of extreme democratization. It was the most apparent and explicit example of the erroneous tendency.

Of course, besides the three problems, other incorrect ideas were exposed such as egalitarianism, and the self-protective attitude of the minority toward the erroneous tendency (mainly the erroneous tendency of extreme democratization). However, the above-mentioned three aspects represent the most important incorrect ideas.

What is the basic nature of erroneous tendencies? Now everyone admits that it is petty bourgeois. This is a correct estimate, for the attitude toward the basic spirit of rectification, toward the relationship between the individual and the party, the superior and the subordinate, and toward Wang Shiwei's thought and his activities, were indeed a petty bourgeois instead of a proletarian point of view. Moreover, these views and attitudes were given a proletarian form. That is to say, the majority of the comrades with the erroneous tendency considered their standpoint as the only accurate one. They also thought that only by following that method could the goal of rectification be reached. But in reality theirs was the erroneous tendencies of the petty bourgeoisie.

As for the reasons for the erroneous tendencies, I would indicate the following:

1. The most important reason is that most comrades are new and young party members with a petty bourgeois background (according to one estimate, 82 percent are intellectuals; as for the length of party membership: 74 percent joined the party after the outbreak of the anti-Japanese war; in terms of age: 79 percent are between twenty and thirty years old). These comrades, generally speaking, lack experience with struggle both in and outside the party; they also lack any cultivation of ideological consciousness, organization, or discipline (according to one estimate, 68 percent who came to Yan'an to study lacked work experience). Therefore, many people have only a few years' experience as party members, and suffer from petty bourgeois ideas such as individualism, individual prominence, considering oneself as always right, and arrogance, as well as subjectivity and one-sidedness in terms of ideological methodology. They can only observe and handle issues reflecting their own subjective wishes and their own trivial experiences.

In addition, those comrades were under the vicious influence of the past dogmatic educational policy in Yan'an's schools (according to one estimate, 84 percent were educated in Yan'an). As a result, their ideology and work style was seldom remolded; on the contrary, their learning was not applied in practice and theory was disconnected from practice. This contributed to a work style that does nothing but engage in boasting instead of being practical. Petty bourgeois individualism and dogmatism are the foundations of erroneous tendencies.

2. Furthermore, it cannot be denied that there are other factors behind erroneous tendencies. For instance, Wang Shiwei's antiparty propaganda, that aimed at alienating relations between comrades, to some extent promoted the development of erroneous tendencies. The publication *Light Calvary* with its vicious influence in Yan'an acted as a model to comrades. Also, although the leading organs of the Institute had a basically correct understanding of the Rectification Movement at its beginning and made several arrangements, they did not carefully investigate the internal thoughts of comrades regarding themselves. The lack of careful preparation and mature meditation beforehand con-

tributed to erroneous tendencies and thus the majority on the examination committee adopted a let-it-go attitude that is another reason why erroneous tendencies spread throughout the Institute.

There were also other influential factors such as the conflict between the domestic and overseas situations, the difficult economic conditions in the frontier regions, and the shortcomings of certain work in the leading organs. All these undoubtedly contributed to erroneous tendencies.

B. The policy and method used in correcting erroneous tendencies and the process of correcting them

As everyone knows, afterward the erroneous tendencies were corrected, and now not even one comrade supports them. How were erroneous tendencies corrected? What policy and methods were adopted? What was the process of correction? These issues are, from today's point of view, indeed interesting. To draw lessons from the past, these issues must be clarified.

First, the policy adopted at that time was nothing but the rectification policy stated by Chairman Mao in his rectification report. This policy was composed of eight great [Chinese] characters: "Learn from past mistakes to avoid future ones, and cure the illness to save the patient." What does it mean to "Learn from past mistakes to avoid future ones?" It means that all kinds of mistakes, no matter how old or new, partial or holistic, ought to be exposed during rectification without any irresponsibilities or compromises. Exposing mistakes does not simply mean roundly cursing others, but to analyze and criticize them scientifically so as to be clearly aware of the causes and to look for better means to correct them.

As for "cure the illness to save the patient," it indicates that our purpose in exposing those mistakes is to save the wrongdoers, not to "rectify them to death."* Thus, we welcome and help any comrades, high or low, who committed mistakes and are now willing to correct them. A more cautious attitude and method should be adopted in curing those who committed ideological and political errors. The leaders of the Central Research Institute adopted this policy in correcting the

---

*The tragedy—and another reason for Dai Qing's sarcasm—was that Wang Shiwei was "cured" (i.e., he ultimately confessed to political crimes), but was killed, not "saved."

erroneous tendencies. They also held the view that the nature of most comrades is good and that under the right leadership and through the comrades' individual determination and effort, the erroneous tendencies would definitely be corrected. This proved to be true.

Relying on this policy is not enough, however, for there must also be a whole set of concrete methods. These include the decision on discussing the rectification report made by the Propaganda Department on April 3. This decision was the concrete form of the Central Committee's policy of "learn from past mistakes to avoid future ones, and cure the illness to save the patient." This is the policy adopted by the leaders of the Institute during rectification. As for the specifics of the April 3 decision, I will only make the following points:

1. In order to intensify the study of central documents, the Institute's committee decided to extend the study period. They made the decision to study first the documents on party work style based on the family background of comrades, their political level, and the nature of their erroneous tendencies at the beginning of rectification. A senior study group was also established at the Institute in order to intensify the study of the documents. This group functioned as the ideological core for leading the study and later on they became standing members of the Examination Committee at the Institute.

2. The most important aspect to studying documents is to remold our attitude toward study and our learning methods. Here we refer to how to carry out the Propaganda Department's April 3 decision: "Read, make notes, and discuss each item or group of items intensively in small groups.* Everybody ought to think deeply and examine his work, ideology, and entire life." Ignorance of party documents and the past method of studying them dogmatically by separating theory from practice should be eliminated.

3. Intensify ideological leadership and connect the study of each document with the remolding of each person's ideological consciousness, especially the causes behind their erroneous tendencies. On the one hand, the tendency of studying documents alone without examining oneself should be overcome; on the other, the tendency of describing one's own history without studying the documents should also be overcome.

---

*It is in such small groups that the psychological pressure on wavering members could be maximized.

4. The use of research and persuasion gradually to increase and deepen our comrades' subjective consciousness (by way of studying the documents and conducting self-examination), especially the cautious and responsible attitude adopted in the struggle against Wang Shiwei, was adopted in criticizing and clearing accounts of erroneous tendencies; coercion should not be used nor advocated in either the various departments nor the entire Institute (under the condition that the majority of comrades have not yet prepared themselves ideologically). While studying the documents and engaging in self-criticism to correct erroneous tendencies, instead of embarking on an overall criticism and self-examination, we solved problems one by one. Also, in examining erroneous tendencies, we carried out the examination in accordance with the principle of seeking truth from facts (*shishi qiushi*) and in line with the essence of central documents; the emphasis on personal attack and condemnation should be avoided, that is, the focus is on substance not people.

Furthermore, the process of examining the various kinds of erroneous tendencies began with major cadres first, then involved ordinary comrades. During this time, cadres were urged to set examples in self-examination both in terms of written and oral presentations so as to promote the development of the movement in the entire Institute. In the process, the leading organs followed the direction of the ideological shift among comrades and their degree of development closely and provided specific instructions.

Though the above-mentioned methods were not implemented flawlessly, they were basically successful. Due to this policy and method, the erroneous tendencies that had appeared at the beginning of rectification were eventually corrected and Wang Shiwei's thoughts and activities were finally exposed and smashed.

What about the process of correcting erroneous tendencies? I'd like to discuss this question according to the following phases:

The first phase was the exposure phase at the Institute that began at the March 18 meeting and ended on April 7 at the forum held solely for the Institute by the Propaganda Department. The situation in this phase was analyzed above.

The second phase started at the meeting held by the Propaganda Department and ended right before the discussion of the central documents on party style (April 7 to early May). One thing that characterized this phase was the necessity of having a preliminary understanding of the aim of rectification and the shift from erroneous to correct tendencies. At the forum mentioned above, Comrade Kai Feng pointed out the aim of the movement and gave an initial criticism of the erroneous tendency advocating extreme democratization. This encouraged the minority of comrades with the correct standpoint to stand up and criticize the erroneous tendencies at the forum. The majority of the comrades who had committed some mistakes then started to question their previous standpoint. Some did a self-examination and admitted to an erroneous tendency. However, no one was courageous enough to stand up and expose other people's mistakes. Some comrades refused to admit to erroneous tendencies or took the erroneous tendencies as something that could not be predicted and that could only be corrected after they occurred. Some emphasized that during the process of correcting them it was useless to talk about erroneous tendencies.

The discussion held after the forum on the April 3 decision helped everyone in holding to the correct attitude toward rectification. It also touched on topics such as the relationship between leadership and democracy as well as the standpoint and method carried out in criticism and self-criticism. During that discussion, a few comrades still attempted to distort the meaning of the documents by singling out a few words to alter the entire meaning in order to defend erroneous tendencies. The self-examination of erroneous tendencies among a minority of comrades had begun, though the self-examination was far from deep and profound. In spite of the fact that the self-examination did not deeply expose erroneous tendencies in ideology, it developed in the right direction.

The third phase started with the discussion on the documents concerning democracy and discipline and ended with the forum criticizing Wang Shiwei (early May to mid-June). The characteristic of this phase is that through the study of documents the majority of comrades gradually mastered the ideological weapon, participated in the struggle to clear away the erroneous tendencies and participated in the struggle against Wang Shiwei. The study of documents on party style began with the essay on democracy and party discipline. This document helped everyone to understand the essence of the party's democratic-centralism and how to put democracy into practice. Some departments associated this discussion with the tendency of extreme democratization and did a self-examination. But other comrades attempted to disguise that tendency by adopting another one, such as attributing the ultimate responsibility to the leaders and emphasizing that the erroneous tendency was "legal" (that is, that the election of directors was actually approved by leaders at the mobilization meeting).

Next, the study of "Combat Liberalism" and "On Egalitarianism" was begun pushing the entire movement one step forward. The Institute's party branch printed materials for reference by comrades depicting the various kinds of liberal tendencies in the Institute. The majority of comrades to a certain extent did self-examinations. For instance, one comrade said during the discussion: "After reading the documents, I felt that each item in the document was pointing at my heart like a needle." But at that time, few people associated their self-examination with erroneous tendencies. The document "On Egalitarianism" made everybody aware of the fact that egalitarianism was an illusion of the petty bourgeois class. Comrades also criticized the egalitarian ideas that existed both in the Institute and in Yan'an. Quite a few departments started the criticism of Wang Shiwei's "Wild Lilies." The discussion of [Liu Shaoqi's] "How to Be a Good Communist" was the key for the ideological preparation of this phase. This document helped comrades realize the significance of ideological cultivation to party members, especially new members, and the harm of petty bourgeois liberalism to the party. It also helped comrades understand the party's methods and policies carried out in various struggles and the difference between methods and policies employed within the party and those employed outside. The self-examination of erroneous tendencies both in discussions and on wall newspapers increased. Quite a few comrades were able to carry out analysis and criticism from the perspective of considering the origin of the ideology of erroneous tendencies.

Dissatisfaction with and criticism of Wang Shiwei's ideas also proceeded one step forward as the Institute, following the demand of some comrades, held a conference in different departments on Wang Shiwei's "Politicians, Artists" and "Wild Lilies." The majority of comrades considered Wang Shiwei's ideas backward and petty bourgeois and his speeches to be detrimental to the party and the revolution. Those who in the past had committed the error of liberalism toward Wang's thoughts engaged in partial self-examination. However, a very few comrades still emphasized that Wang's subjective motivation was correct. Some comrades did not express any opinions. All in all, as a result of the study of the documents on party style that lasted for nearly a month, the majority of comrades were basically prepared in ideological terms for criticizing erroneous tendencies and Wang Shiwei's ideas.

Thus, the Institute decided to hold a forum for all its members to criticize erroneous tendencies and Wang's ideas. The issue of democratic-centralism was discussed in the first few days of the conference to resolve completely the past tendency toward extreme democratization. The majority of comrades made candid and honest self-criticisms, while in the last week of the forum Wang Shiwei's ideas were examined. Because prior to the forum all the comrades were ideologically well prepared, which helped reveal more of Wang Shiwei's materials and activities, all comrades concluded that Wang Shiwei's thoughts were not simply backward and petty bourgeois; rather, they were the rotten and reactionary thoughts of the dying class. Everybody agreed that adopting an attitude of liberalism toward such thoughts is absolutely impermissible.

The last phase extended from the anti-Wang meeting to the summation on party work style (mid-June till early September). The major task of this phase was to deepen the struggle against erroneous tendencies and bring about more concrete individual examinations as well as a general examination of everybody's personal history. After the anti-Wang meeting, discussions were held in each department for a week during which time the ideological behavior exhibited at the beginning of rectification by each person was examined, and everyone wrote a memoir of their initial impression of Wang Shiwei's "Politicians, Artists" and "Wild Lilies." During this examination, many comrades examined themselves honestly and candidly.

There was also mutual criticism among comrades (before this, self-criticism was done, but there was very little mutual criticism). Later, in the discussion of documents on opposing factionalism, many comrades revealed the factors that had caused them to demand independence from authority at the beginning of the movement. After completing the study of the rectification documents, every comrade wrote an ideological autobiography, which was then discussed in each department for about ten days. During that discussion, many comrades voluntarily exposed their erroneous thoughts and conducted a general examination of the ideological problems that had appeared at the beginning of the movement. Discussion of the ideological autobiographies was not flawless, for instance some comrades were insufficiently candid and honest, and some comrades' way of analyzing their own thoughts still needed improvement. However, there was a major shift in the standpoint of the majority of comrades toward the party. And they were determined to pay more attention to remolding their ideological consciousness and developing themselves in the right direction. That was the significant harvest from this discussion of autobiographies.

All in all, after their initial appearance it took about a half year to overcome erroneous tendencies, and to deepen the struggle. The process was a twisted one. At the beginning, the majority insisted on the correctness of their erroneous tendencies. Later on, they started to weaken. After going through several self-examinations, they finally overcame their misdirection. As for Wang Shiwei's ideas, some comrades were influenced by them at the beginning of the movement. Then they became dubious and shaky. After that, partial criticism of Wang's ideas was carried out. In the end, Wang's entire ideology was reversed. This twisted process is the general principle of ideological remolding, especially the remolding of young party members from an intellectual background. Since the appearance of erroneous tendencies was not incidental, it was by no means easy to overcome them. The lesson of this twisted process helped affirm our comrades' recognition and understanding of the profound truth. Thus, the twisted process was not detrimental; on the contrary, it was good for our comrades.

Our purpose in correcting erroneous tendencies was to "cure the illness to save the patient," not to "cure the illness so as to harm the patient." Hence, those comrades who in the past had committed mistakes by exhibiting erroneous tendencies were asked to examine themselves voluntarily and admit their mistakes to the party. This is the so-called: "Though the role of the leaders is important, he who tied up the bell should be the one to untie it!" (*jieling haixu jilingren*, i.e., "people who create a problem should solve it").

C. Some lessons from the summary of ideological remolding

There are, indeed, quite a few lessons that can be learned from the ideological remolding of the past six months. Because of the limits of my personal ability, I can only come up with several points for your reference and for discussion:

1. The experiences of the past half year have documented cogently that the Central Committee's policy of carrying out this rectification is absolutely necessary and correct. It has also demonstrated that this is

indeed a great remolding of all thoughts and work styles in the party. The participants in the movement have learned much. It is unanimously* acknowledged that if rectification had not been carried out the fruits of the ideological remolding would not have been so great. This is also a powerful reply to the very few comrades who ignored the rectification.†

In the meantime, these experiences tell us that rectification is a struggle between destroying the old and establishing the new. The remolding of each comrade's ideology and work style in this movement has included two aspects—destruction and construction. What we aimed at destroying was the various kinds of remnant non-proletarian thought and work style (mainly from the petty bourgeoisie) and what we aimed at establishing was a more perfect and more thorough ideology and work style of the proletariat. New members constitute 90 percent of the party's membership and most are from petty bourgeois backgrounds (farmers and intellectuals). With their brief membership in the party, they lack the party's education and practical work experiences in political struggle. Besides, they have brought with them considerable petty bourgeois thoughts from the old society that, if not eliminated, will definitely become the scourge of the party and lead to more erroneous tendencies. This was demonstrated by our experiences at the beginning of rectification.

Our experiences have also demonstrated that petty bourgeois thought appears subjectively in a proletarian outlook and consistently opposes the correct three work styles of the party. Moreover, that thought is deep-rooted and by no means easy to correct. This means that our new party members must be more determined in destroying the remnants of their petty bourgeois thought. As for older party members, although they have endured the party's tests for a long time and have gained much in terms of ideological construction, the influence of the old society has not been eliminated completely‡ and remnant erroneous tendencies in the party still more or less dominate their mind.

---

*Declarations of unanimity on rectification was crucial in creating an image that the dissent symbolized, but not restricted to, Wang Shiwei had been overpowered and crushed.

†Perhaps a reference to Xiao Jun, who remained adamantly opposed to the rectification.

‡Ironically, this was also a point raised by Wang Shiwei in "Inevitability," "The Sky Is Not Falling," and "Triviality."

Thus, older members still need to continue to destroy and construct. No matter how old or young, you must go through a series of struggles to destroy and construct. It is impossible to destroy thoroughly and construct perfectly without a struggle. The form of this rectification is peaceful and not bloody; however, its nature is a serious ideological revolution. It is a great debate between proletarian and petty bourgeois thought. It is also a massive battle to topple the ancient backwardness and to establish the new brightness!

The majority of the comrades at the Institute are new party members from petty bourgeois backgrounds and since rectification began they have undoubtedly learned much from the ideological remolding. Generally, we can say that most comrades have come to understand more about the relationship between individuals, and between the parts and the whole. They have also realized more clearly the fallacies and detriments of petty bourgeois thought. Therefore, they have made some progress in shifting from the petty bourgeois to the proletarian standpoint. This great achievement cannot be obliterated, for it is the result of our party's education. However, our comrades definitely cannot be satisfied with these achievements because what must be eliminated has not been eliminated completely and what must be established is far from being established fully. The ideological revolution is a long-term revolution. The remolding of party members cannot be achieved overnight. Our comrades still need to improve the relationship between individuals and the party, and to continue to improve in practical terms the relationship between the party and the masses.

Also, issues regarding ideological methods and work style have not yet been discussed earnestly, let alone mastered fully. All these skills must be acquired over the long term in future rectifications and work. Also, this Institute is the place where cadres specializing in theoretical work (*lilun gongzuo ganbu*) are cultivated. These comrades will eventually work hard on the theoretical front. To be a Bolshevik theory worker, one must not only master theory, but also possess a steadfast party spirit (*dang xing*) and a communist viewpoint. Without these basic factors, it will be impossible to become a fighting theorist able to master and protect the truth, and to fight against all kinds of erroneous thoughts. Also, the cultivation of party spirit cannot be realized simply by relying on personal and subjective desires; it must go through the process of long-term ideological remolding and practice!

2. The half year ideological remolding has also given us many valu-

able experiences in . . . the methods of leading ideological struggle. First, this experience has demonstrated that the method of "Learn from past mistakes to avoid future ones, and cure the illness to save the patient" is the only correct method for leading struggles within the party. Our party will surely become stronger and more consolidated if such a policy is adopted in resolving all struggles, including the present one, in the party. Older party members with relatively longer experience in the party are acutely aware that our party has had quite a few bad experiences in this regard. For instance, there once was a popular work style that can best be described in eight [Chinese] characters: "Those supporting me survive, those opposed to me perish" (*xunjizhe chang, nijizhe, wang*). Such was the leading line of the leaders at that time. It was the almighty "absolute truth." Those sharing the same views were considered "the loyal carriers of the international policy" and "good Bolshevik cadres" and were granted titles and positions. As for those with different views, they were scolded bitterly as "right opportunists," "surrendering to class enemies," and deserving to be "fought against ruthlessly" and "attacked unmercifully." The result of this struggle and attack was that people were either blacklisted or dismissed from their jobs and examined. This method was applied to those with different political and ideological views. This kind of struggle not only undermined the activism and initiative of all party members, it also destroyed the unity and fighting ability of the party.

Since the Zunyi Conference [1935], the policy of "Learn from past mistakes to avoid future ones, and cure the illness to save the patient" has been advocated by the Central Committee headed by Chairman Mao. It is the opposite of the above-mentioned approach in that it separates the method of dealing with class enemies from the method of handling inner-party struggles. It also combines an uncompromising attitude toward erroneous thoughts with the policy of curing the illness of comrades who have committed mistakes. The method of persuasion and education was adopted to deal with these comrades. Harsh punishment was applied solely to those hopeless "black sheep." This method was used with great success in the fight against Zhang Guotao. This Rectification Movement is, of course, not the same as the struggle against Zhang Guotao for it is an ideological revolution for the entire party. It is a great debate between proletarian thought and the petty bourgeoisie thought that makes it far more difficult and arduous when compared with the struggle against Zhang.* Thus, the policy of "Learn from past mistakes to avoid future ones, and cure the illness to save the patient" should be adhered to strictly. The rectification of erroneous tendencies in this Institute has followed the essence of this method in that no organizational enforcement was used during the movement. Instead, only the methods of persuasion and education have been adopted. Everyone has gone through a subjective and conscious process of realization. Erroneous tendencies have been corrected without anyone being hurt. Wang Shiwei's erroneous thought and antiparty activities have also been smashed. This valuable experience deserves to be studied and learned by everyone.

Apart from the above-mentioned policy, the experience of fighting over a half year also alerts us to the following points when leading ideological struggles:

a. The leadership of ideological struggle is a science, so it needs to be carried out technically.† The leading organs should not only possess a firm and correct policy, a serious and responsible attitude, as well as a whole set of flexible and appropriate methods; they should also carry out meticulous investigations both prior to and immediately after the struggle, understand the ambience, origin, nature, and degree of erroneous thoughts, and pay attention to the ideological dynamite and the movement of the pulse in each period so as to master the process of the entire ideological development and provide concrete instructions. Upon analyzing the situation, we should make sure to distinguish the advanced from the middle and backward people, the ideological position of the minority as opposed to that of the majority—the minority's understanding cannot represent the majority's and an individual's action cannot be taken as that of an entire sector or the whole party. Only through scientific investigation and research, as well as understanding the entire process of struggle, together with the adoption of the above-mentioned policy, can the aim of ideological struggle be achieved.

b. The creating of the ideological struggle cannot be successful without ideological preparation. As for the scale of preparation, it de-

---

*Considering the large military forces that Zhang Guotao once commanded, this statement indicates just how seriously Mao and the party leadership took Wang Shiwei's ideological and political challenge.

†The printed text, used by Dai Qing, gives *yishu* (art/artistically), which we take to be a misprint for *jishu* (technically).

pends on the nature of erroneous thoughts, their depth of influence as well as both their subjective and objective environment. Generally speaking, it takes time to prepare, for otherwise those who have behaved erroneously will not adopt the correct view, nor overcome the erroneous side. In fact, this kind of preparation cannot be done by holding one or two meetings. Generally, the greater the influence of erroneous thought and the deeper its origin, the more necessary it becomes to have good preparation work that usually takes quite a while.

Thus, the leading organs should select the opportunity to start a struggle on the basis of the level of consciousness for struggle among the masses. It is certainly detrimental to start a struggle too early. For instance, since the ideological preparation among our comrades was not yet ready, the anti-Wang Shiwei struggle would have been premature if it had started in the first half of May. It was right to begin it in the second half of May since by that time the ideological preparation was basically completed.

c. In ideological struggles, the task of the progressive people is, first, to stick to the correct standpoint and possess the steadfast, anti-trend spirit whenever needed (especially when the majority exhibit erroneous tendencies). However, they should also be adroit at attracting the majority of comrades to the right side. Ideological remolding cannot be forced upon or performed for individual comrades because each differs in terms of the level of their thought, personal experiences and views. Moreover, the aim of the ideological struggle is to remold everyone's ideology, not just that of a few individuals. Thus, when confronting the situation where most comrades cannot yet accept correct thought, the progressive people should, first, wait and should not assume that what they consider obsolete is also considered obsolete by the masses. Do not take careless actions.

Second, they should try their best to persuade people with erroneous tendencies by using the appropriate, step-by-step methods so as to raise their consciousness gradually. They should also unite and help the middle people, and encourage and push the passive ones (*xiaoji fenzi*). As for those with serious erroneous tendencies, criticize them, but, in the meantime, try to win them over. In this Institute's anti-Wang Shiwei struggle, some progressive people stood at the very beginning of the struggle on the correct side and were with the steadfast, antitrend spirit. That was good. However, they were not adept at uniting and winning over the majority. And they attempted to start the struggle before everybody was ready, taking what they considered obsolete to be considered obsolete by others. This resulted in conflict between them and other comrades for some time. And they were separated from the masses. This lesson should be noted.

d. Flexibility in the leadership style of ideological struggle should be combined with high principles. There must be a right principle in the leadership of ideological struggle. All disputes must be resolved in accordance with the party's principles and following the method of seeking truth from facts. Tendencies of attacking without principle, taking revenge, and engaging in sectarianism must be corrected in this struggle. The criticism of past mistakes should be aimed at the mistakes themselves instead of at people. Problems of responsibility can be pointed out whenever necessary. One thing must be emphasized, that is, mistakes belonging to different categories must be distinguished. Mistakes of different natures and degrees must not be confused. The leading organ of this Institute adopted the party's principles of clearing up its mistakes by taking on problems one by one. Also Wang Shiwei's erroneous thought at the very beginning was separated from those of the majority. This sort of highly principled leadership is absolutely necessary.

e. Lastly, in ideological struggle, first unite senior cadres and activists, raise their ideological consciousness, organize and use them to influence and push the development of self-criticism by the majority. This can be significant in overcoming erroneous thought as was demonstrated in the struggle in our Institute.

The above are a few experiences in the methods of ideological struggle. This struggle, for me as well as all comrades, was a good learning experience. Of course, we must anticipate the nature and characteristics (composition, location, and conditions) of this struggle. Do not mechanically use these methods in other situations. It is the spirit of the above-mentioned methods that is worthy of attention.

3. The half year experience has clearly demonstrated that in the process of ideological remolding Marxist theory has a great instructive function. In the past, everyone has either heard or read what Marx once said: "Once the ideology is controlled, the masses can turn it into a material power." Lenin also said: "Only a party that is armed with advanced revolutionary theory can carry out the role of the vanguard." However, our comprehension of these classic sayings was dogmatic

and abstract. Now that we have experienced this struggle, these lines become far more vivid and specific. Our ideological remolding this time was waged completely under the banner of Marxism. The twenty-two [rectification] documents are moving and concrete examples of Marxist theories. Our comrades corrected their own erroneous tendencies and eliminated Wang Shiwei's influence by relying on these theoretical weapons. Let's recall: Why could our comrades not eliminate those petty bourgeois thoughts before they studied the party's documents on our work styles? What contributed to the enormous change after study? The reason is nothing other than that our comrades mastered the theoretical weapon of Marxism. This mastery turned the documents into a material force. Relying on this force, we cleared the erroneous tendencies and criticized Wang Shiwei's erroneous thought. This shows that the twenty-two documents have a great instructive function and the rectification movement is powerful. The remolding of the party's ideology and work style will, if all comrades master these weapons well, surely make a great step forward. This is also a profound lesson to those who have ignored the documents, theoretical study, and rectification.

This experience also tells us how to study and master Marxist theory —that is, to master the spirit and core of the theory and remold our own thought and to solve present problems in accordance with it instead of reciting its quotations and conclusions. Our ideological remolding this time used such a method. The half-year experience splendidly confirms the truth of the new study method and clearly proclaims the bankruptcy of the dogmatic method adopted in the past.

A summary of study methods and other experiences has already been made. Here I am not going to repeat it. What I will do is to review the Rectification Movement over the past half year as a new method. I think the following points are key features of the movement: (a) Rectification itself carried out the spirit of shooting the arrow at the objective and seeking truth from facts. The documents and the entire arrangement aimed at the concrete situation and the needs of cadres and party members. There was a clear aim in terms of educating cadres and party members. Also, there was preparation prior to the movement. (b) The content of education was based mainly on documents containing Sinified Marxism and on basic international experiences (for instance, the conclusion of the [Stalinist] party history of the CPSU, and the twelve points of Bolshevism). This marks the difference between the content of education in the past when the original works of Marx, Engels, Lenin, and Stalin were the main content.* (c) Rectification study indeed served as a conscious process of realization and enlightenment (*qimeng*) that developed the remolding of our ideology and work style. (d) The weapon of Bolshevik self-criticism was adopted on a large-scale in this study and thus created and developed methods and experiences of self-realization (*fan xing*). . . . (e) Engendering the function of the leading organizations was coordinated with individual and collective study methods (casual discussions, fora, discussions, wall newspapers, visits, and exchange of notes).

We can say that rectification itself is an experiment in practicing these new teaching and learning methods on a large scale. These initial experiences are worth further study and development.

---

*Original works by Marx, Engels, and Lenin were now expunged from the curriculum in favor of writings solely by Mao and Stalin. As translator of the former writings, Wang Shiwei was in a position to challenge any ideological "heresy" of the Maoist leadership.

Document 2.4

Activities of the Trotskyite Wang Shiwei and Liberalism in the Party, October 31, 1942

YANG SHANGKUN*

This is a speech by Comrade Yang Shangkun at the forum on the "Five Member Anti-Party Gang" held by the Political Research Office of the Central Research Institute. It is reprinted here so comrades will understand the truth about Wang Shiwei's Trotskyite activities and so everyone will be aware of the importance of enhancing the political consciousness of our party members and their ability to discriminate between correct and erroneous thought as advocated by Comrade Mao Zedong in his report on the rectification of the three kinds of work styles.

—Editor, *Party Life*

Comrades:

The forum held in the past ten days has exposed the antiparty activities of Wang Shiwei, Pan Fang, Zong Zheng, Cheng Quan, and Wang Li. Their Trotskyite thoughts, antiparty conspiracies, activities conducted in small groups, and methods used in their antiparty activities, and some other specific facts have also been exposed. Thanks to the exposure of the Five Member Anti-Party Gang, we are provided with a living antiparty example. It also enables us specifically to investigate the conspiracies and the methods used in antiparty activities conducted by antiparty members and to realize fully the harm they have brought to the party. I believe that this forum will surely improve our political

---

*Although Yang Shangkun was a relatively minor player in the Rectification Movement, Dai Qing has stated that she included this speech in the collection because Yang is still a major political figure in China and should "look into the mirror." Unpublished comments, presented to the colloquium "On Revolutionary Intellectuals: The Case of Wang Shiwei," Yale University, November 13, 1992.

consciousness and awareness so that those with a liberal attitude toward inner-party life will be greatly shocked and the principles that a party member should possess will be reinforced. Some comrades did not have a chance due to time limitations to study this issue at the forum. It is my hope that in the future they will continue with their study and self-analysis of their learning style (at the Central Research Institute) and of the party's work style (at the Political Research Office).

Regarding inner-party life, Comrades Fan Wenlan and Chen Boda have made many good points. I agree with both of them. Here I only want to make a few points to be taken as reference for our comrades in their continued studies.

1. The Five Member Anti-Party Gang is a small organization that is antiparty and destructive to the party. Wang Shiwei, the Trotskyite, participated in it and led it. The combination of those five people was not merely based on a "relationship among friends." It was a political combination.

According to available documents, we can see that the five have much in common ideologically. The nature of their ideology is Trotskyite (such as the theory of human nature, and the theory of degeneration). The five played the same role in terms of political behavior. That is why they all engaged in concocting rumors, casting aspersions, and instigating splits to destroy the party.

The antiparty activities of these five people were organized activities. Both the goals and the methods of their activities were based on mutual consultation and discussion. Wang Shiwei exchanged ideas with the other four regarding his antiparty articles ("Wild Lilies" and "Politicians, Artists"). During rectification, Wang Shiwei consulted Pan Fang and Zong Zheng over articles opposing the leaders and party efforts to oppose erroneous tendencies by publishing the wall newspaper at the Central Research Institute. In fact, some of those articles were written by the five together but published in the name of one person.

They consciously adopted a two-faced means to coax the party in a well-planned way. In terms of dealing with our comrades, they purposely attempted to maintain a close relationship to those with an unsteady standpoint who were dissatisfied, plus those who were emotionally distressed due to certain illnesses. The five adopted the means of adulation and collusion. To further expand their influence and conduct their antiparty activities, they also tried to align themselves with those who lagged behind politically, who enjoyed boasting and being small megaphones (*xiao guangbo*) [i.e., rumor mongers].

Therefore, this Five Member Anti-Party Gang possessed Trotskyite thought in terms of ideology (the word ideology should be put in quotes here), conducted Trotskyite-type activities to destroy the party, and used the Trotskyite way of destroying the party in all their actions. The five have a lot in common in these basic aspects. This small antiparty organization was formed and organized voluntarily on the basis of their common thought, common political activities, and common means of carrying out their activities.

Of course, apart from their common points, we can also see that there are some differences between Pan Fang, Zong Zheng, Cheng Quan, and Wang Li in that Cheng and Wang voluntarily exposed their faults to the committee and the branch committee while Pan Fang and Zong Zheng were forced to admit their faults after the true facts were publicized.

However, those differences can neither be used as an excuse to reduce Cheng and Wang's antiparty faults, nor be used as their "bunker" for self-protection. Cheng and Wang should clearly be aware of the seriousness of their antiparty faults and that they cannot separate themselves from Wang Shiwei, Pan Fang, and Zong Zheng. They should also be aware of the fact that they cannot attribute their own faults to other comrades. They should try to find the causes of their faults in their own ideological consciousness.

As for what Pan Fang, Zong Zheng, Cheng Quan, and Wang Li did in the past and their activities before coming to Yan'an (Pan Fang and Zong Zheng were in Shanghai, Cheng Quan and Wang Li were in Shandong), as well as whether or not they joined the Trotskyite organization, it is my hope that the branch party committee of the Central Research Institute and the branch party committee of the Political Research Office will continue to collect and exchange materials.

2. This forum exposed the activities of this small-scale organized, Trotskyite, antiparty gang. It is also the continuation of the previous anti-Wang Shiwei meeting held at the Central Research Institute. This meeting mainly exposed their Trotskyite thought while the present forum aims at exposing their activities. In terms of basic nature, this forum somewhat surpasses the scope of inner-party struggle; in fact, it is in the nature of a struggle outside the party [i.e., 'enemy' vs. 'people' in Chinese communist terminology].

From this we can see that the Rectification Movement contains two kinds of struggles. One is the inner-party struggle, the struggle of proletarian ideology versus petty bourgeois ideology. Its purpose is to remold the ideological methods of both cadres and party members, improve their work style and party spirit, and consolidate unity so as to further Bolshevize the party.

The other struggle is the one that exposes and opposes those Trotskyites and dissidents who snuck into our party to destroy and undermine it. They took advantage of some of the weak points in our inner-party life (such as a pervasive liberalism *nonghoude ziyouzhuyi*) and seized the opportunity (the Rectification Movement) to carry out their activities, attempting to achieve their purpose by using this movement to destroy the party. Confronting such a situation, every party member ought to stand up and expose their conspiracy and smash their attempt at alienating party members from the organization. We shall never allow them to insult our party, our leaders, nor any of our comrades. For me, this forum fits the latter kind of struggle. Chairman Mao admonished us a long time ago that rectification contains these two kinds of struggles. Our own participation in this forum proves once again the accuracy of Mao's instruction.

Although the nature of this struggle belongs to the second type, we adopted a serious but comradely attitude toward Pan Fang, Zong Zheng, Cheng Quan, and Wang Li, patiently listening to their reports and speeches without being in the least antagonistic. Why? It's because the party wishes them to realize their mistakes and confess the activities of their Five Member Antiparty Gang and expose the evil people in the party. It is actually a test to determine whether they still wish to be party members and be loyal to the party. It provides them a chance to turn over a new leaf.

In my opinion, our comrades grasped such a spirit with a good sense of propriety in this forum, though there were some inappropriate points (such as some comrades' speeches). A few comrades made rather caustic remarks in their speeches and even proposed to make an organizational conclusion (*zuzhi jielun*) right at the forum. I do not consider that as too drastic. Their assailing standpoint toward the five was absolutely correct despite the fact that the content of their speeches may not have been appropriate.

Comrades! A party member should consider the party's interests above everything else. He should consider the party's interest as more important than his own life! Can we be considered party members if we do not stand up to speak for the party when it is endangered and adopt an absolutist attitude toward those attempting to undermine the party? This forum is a test of all the comrades present.

The article on inner-party struggle by Comrade Liu Shaoqi summarizes our party's experiences of inner-party struggle in the past in both theoretical and practical terms. It is a very good article that warrants study by our comrades. It is said that some comrades, after having read that article, think that the tone of the forum has gone too far, that it is not "benevolent" enough. I do not think this is right, for Comrade Liu Shaoqi's article refers to inner-party struggles, while this struggle is a struggle outside the party. This problem can be resolved after comprehending this principle.*

3. Why didn't we expose earlier the Five Member Anti-Party Gang? Why did they gain such success? Why did some comrades sympathize with them? Why were some comrades willingly used by them? . . . I think it's because of the serious weaknesses in their inner-party life, mainly the pervasive liberalism (a lack of political awareness, a political flu, a lack of a steadfast principled standpoint)!

Our comrades should deeply understand that to undermine our party ideologically is certainly the most vicious counterrevolutionary ploy. This is actually spreading ideological poison (what Wang Shiwei labels as "sowing flower seeds")! To deal with such poison, we need to have the most acute political sense. Only with that can we discover and expose this conspiracy in time. Those suffering from the political flu and whose political sense is not acute are likely to be poisoned. The reaction of the majority of comrades at the Institute toward "Wild Lilies" before it was exposed proves that the above-mentioned principle is correct. It also fits Comrade Mao Zedong's admonition at the beginning of the movement to improve political awareness.

Comrades! Chairman Mao warned us a long time ago that there

---

*Yang is admitting here that party members who read Liu's article and perhaps even Liu himself supported less forceful means in dealing with Wang Shiwei's purported deviation. In 1937, Liu Shaoqi had, in fact, complained that line struggle in the party, which he traced to the meetings in 1927 purging Chen Duxiu, prevented rational discussion and deliberation in party councils as every disagreement was met with highly politicized charges. See Liu Shaoqi, "Letter to the party center concerning past work in the White areas," March 4, 1937, in Saich, *The Rise to Power of the Chinese Communist Party.*

existed a pervasive liberalism in our party. That is why he once wrote
that article opposing liberalism. After the beginning of the anti-Japanese war, our party expanded on a large scale. More than 80 percent of
party members are new. Old party members count for only a small
percentage. Moreover, the majority of new members come from
farmer and petty bourgeois backgrounds. With such backgrounds, they
have no source of ideological consciousness. Their training in inner-party
life is insufficient and they lack experience in political struggle . . . ,
they lack a steadfast standpoint and are likely to commit the mistake of
liberalism. Especially those from a petty bourgeois background are
soft-hearted and pay too much attention to friendship . . . That is
exactly what nurtures liberalism.*

The disease of liberalism has also increased among some older cadres due to their lack of correct understanding concerning inner-party
struggle (Comrade Shaoqi's article solved this issue) and the effect of
the ambience of the United Front after the start of the anti-Japanese
war. Thus, at present, we need to strengthen inner-party life, consolidate the principled standpoint, intensify party spirit, and firmly oppose
liberalism. In places such as the Central Research Institute and the
Political Research Office where intellectuals with petty bourgeois
backgrounds dominate, there are serious problems in inner-party life
stemming from the basic nature of liberalism.

In my opinion, inner-party life should be political and principled.
It's erroneous to separate problems in inner-party life from considera-
tions of politics and principle. Some party comrades enjoy making
comments about others, tracking down other people's "secrets," and
paying attention to other people's private affairs. Some of them even
idle around after eating millet, act like "small megaphones," and "pay
visits from door to door." They show no interest in and pay no attention to either politics or issues of principle. I do not consider those
people to be qualified party members!

Comrades! This forum has exposed many of the rumors that, concocted by the Five Member Anti-Party Gang, scolded our party and its
leaders. This is a vivid demonstration of their extreme aversion toward
the party and their efforts to destroy the party. Some of the rumors,
however, were spread by the "small megaphones." See how harmful

*Yang is virtually admitting here that Chinese society breeds liberalism and
that only the Communist party can combat it.

the "small megaphone" is to the party! The "information" from the "small megaphones" was welcomed by the Five Member Gang and other anticommunist die-hards. Everyone has heard that their information was reprinted in the magazines *True Words* (Liangxin hua) and *Central Weekly* (Zhongyang zhoukan) [a KMT publication—Eds.] and was disseminated as materials to oppose our party. We should condemn these "small megaphones" and admonish them to stop offering voluntary help to the Trotskyites and anticommunist spies. Always remember that you are a party member and a revolutionary soldier!

Of course, we should not view all "small megaphones" in the same vein as the Five Member Gang. We should know that the reason why some of the "small megaphones" engaged in their activity is because of their lack of political principles and party standpoint, their näiveté, and ignorance . . . Of course they are incorrect and should be educated. They can be forgiven if they correct their mistakes!

No one can deny that our party has shortcomings or even faults in various kinds of work. We should engage in criticism in order to make the party correct them. Didn't Chairman Mao propose correcting subjectivism (*zhuguanzhuyi*), sectarianism (*zongpaizhuyi*), and party formalism (*dang bagu*) that in the past existed in our party by advocating rectification of the three work styles? However, comrades, hasn't Chairman Mao also admonished us that the purpose of rectification is to intensify unity instead of weakening unity, to create the situation of "having the same morality and heart" instead of "deviating from the same morality and heart"? In a word, the purpose of criticizing the criticisms voiced by the Five Member Gang (Wang Shiwei's "Wild Lilies," Cheng Quan's letter to Chairman Mao, the criticisms proposed by Pan Fang, et al. toward the leaders at the beginning of the movement) has been to protect the party (not to undermine it), and to intensify the party's power (not to weaken it). Their criticisms are not consistent with either the spirit or the principle of our criticisms. They aimed at ruining the relationship between our comrades, at creating factions, opposing the leadership, and undermining and destroying the party.

Their antiparty activities were not conducted in one day. Some of the comrades present have heard their speeches and watched their actions, have even been taken as objects to be converted, and have done some work for them. How come those comrades were so blind and servile and were taken advantage of? I think it's due to the effects of liberalism.

[This disregard for their qualifications as party members was most evident when] they showed no aversion to hearing the antiparty speeches of the Five Members. On the contrary, they were pleased to hear them. They expressed no opposition to the antiparty articles by the Five Members; on the contrary, they praised them. They refused to report any of the antiparty activities by the Five Members; on the contrary, they tried to hide them from the party . . . Is this the standpoint a party member should take? It is instead sheer rotten liberalism!

Does it mean that liberalism is the cause for all these faults? No. I only refer to some of the comrades. For other comrades, it is not only an issue of liberalism; rather, it is because they have something in common with the Five Members. For instance, some comrades tried to amend some of the antiparty articles instead of counteracting them. Can we say that this is merely liberalism? Another example: Some comrades participated in, advocated, and propagated some of the antiparty activities instead of reporting them to the party. Is this merely liberalism? Obviously, those who have committed such mistakes cannot be disguised and defended with the label of liberalism. It is my hope that these comrades undergo a thorough self-examination.

There are also some other comrades who, though they did not follow the Gang by participating in antiparty activities, have shown something in common with them in terms of discussing some of the issues regarding inner-party life. I also hope that they will undergo a close self-examination.

Comrades! The Central Committee has advocated that we engage in self-examination to expose faults in our own ideology. Take off the pants to cut off the tail.* I hope that these comrades will strictly examine themselves. Don't try to hide or shy away.

Honestly take off your pants! Cut off the tail if you have one! If you have a tail, the onlookers can see clearly. It is impossible to hide, for the fact that the tail is attached to your body is an "objective fact!"

Hence, every one of us should use the lesson of this forum to examine ourselves, to check if we possess a firm political standpoint and explicit principles, whether we have committed some liberal mistakes, what problems we have and what caused our liberalism, etc.

*An earthy phrase, *tuo kuzi ge weiba* means to expose and criticize people's faults in public.

Only by this kind of profound self-examination can we consolidate the achievement of this forum.

We should remember Chairman Mao's words: "As a party member, you should be upright, honest, loyal, and highly motivated. Put the interests of the revolution before your personal interests and be willing to sacrifice your personal interests. No matter when and where, always stick to the correct principles, and fight against all kinds of erroneous thoughts and conduct yourself tirelessly in order to consolidate the party's collective life and the relationship between the party and the masses, care more about the party and the masses than yourself, and care more about other people than yourself. Only by doing this can one be considered as a 'qualified party member.' "

Comrades! some of our comrades take good care of themselves, pay more attention to their own lives, status, gains, and losses—everything regarding themselves. They ignore important issues regarding conduct against the party and people opposed to the party. To them, there are only personal affairs and personal complaints, no public affairs or public anger. They only care about protecting their pots and jars. Whether the party's interests have been destroyed or antiparty articles have been disseminated all over the place, is of little concern to them. This is the worst kind of liberalism!

Those five always claimed so-called friendship. Pan Fang claimed Wang Shiwei as his "sincere friend" and that their "friendship" was a true friendship. They even claimed that "there's no friendship in the party." Is it right? Some comrades have been trapped and taken advantage of by such "friendship." Thus it is imperative that I mention it here. I feel that the relationship between we party members is the noblest and purest friendship. It is built on a common view of the world and on certain political principles. It is a kind of class love, comradely love, and the great love of collectivism. It cannot be compared with vulgar "friendship." Our friendship is constructed on the basis of the party's principles without which such friendship cannot exist. The "friendship" advocated by the Five Member Gang is actually a signboard that helps cover their small-scale, organized antiparty activities. They attempted to use the unprincipled soft-heartedness of the petty bourgeoisie in order to attract those people to their side. Don't the activities of Wang Shiwei and Pan Fang, and their lot indicate what kind of "friendship" they had?

4. Chairman Mao once admonished us that ideological struggle is

extremely subtle work and thus cannot be addressed with a rough attitude. Comrade Liu Shaoqi also admonished us that ideological struggle is the most serious obligation. It must be dealt with seriously and responsibly and not carelessly. This forum and the recent struggle have demonstrated the accuracy of such instructions.

This struggle began by summarizing the learning style of people in the Political Research Office and by partially examining the leaders of the [Central Research] Institute. During the process of examining the leaders, some of the comrades' speeches had serious erroneous tendencies in that they attacked the leaders personally, even though the leaders of the Office and of the Study Committee, and the chairman of the meeting at that time, suppressed no one. The leaders aimed at listening to all kinds of criticisms from comrades (both correct and erroneous) in order to promote their own self-examination and improve future work.

After Cheng Quan reported his own antiparty activities to the entire party, the leaders of the Office, of the Study Committee, and of the branch party committee all adopted an extremely serious attitude in collecting objectively and meticulously materials for research. The dialogue between the branch party committee and Wang and Cheng lasted for half a month.

As for Pan and Zong, the leaders of the Institute and its party committee also spent considerable time examining them. After Cheng and Wang had exposed Pan and Zong, to test Pan and Zong, the Office and the Institute branch party committees had two dialogues with them (September 16 and September 12 [as written]) during which none of them expressed loyalty to the party; instead, they continued to hide everything, and even attempted to hide things for Cheng and Wang. Prior to that, the Institute party committee had a few more dialogues with them. Comrade Kai Feng also talked with them. However, they still did not confess.

Comrades, we spent quite a long time in dealing with the Five Member Gang. This forum alone lasted for two weeks. From the very beginning to the present, it has been seventy-two days! Though it took a long time, the lessons we have drawn from it are significant. It is my hope that we can understand and absorb the spirit of the struggle. The same attitude should be adopted in the continuation of this issue.

This experience in struggle has informed us that ideological struggles must have preparation, organization, and leadership. It cannot be done in an uncontrolled manner, for in all kinds of struggle (including ideological struggle), there are bound to appear active members (with a more acute sense and awareness of the nature of the issue and the correct line), less progressive members in the middle, and addle-headed backward members. The responsibility of the leaders is to unite the activities around the party and organize them on the basis of principles and the correct standpoint, and to use this force to improve the understanding of the members in the middle, and to win over the backward ones. Thus it is essential to discover and organize the active members in the struggle. It is impossible to win a victory and to generate new struggle without having active members.

As for the responsibility of active members, on the one hand it is to stick to the party's principles and fight firmly against all antiparty thoughts and people; on the other, it is to use the party's principles and standpoint to improve the middle people and win over the backward. They must be with the masses. Never separate from the masses, for once separated from the masses, the active members become useless.

Comrades! These are the few points that I have made. It is my hope that you give some thought to them.

Document 2.5

Abstract of Kang Sheng's Report to a Training Class, August 1943*

The first phase [of the rectification in 1942] was from the time Mao gave his speech in March to the anti-Wang Shiwei meeting held on June 23. At that time, the policy of our leadership was to stress the democratic aspect of the April 3 [Central Committee] decision by calling on people to speak out boldly, by advocating the publication of wall newspapers, and by supporting criticism of leaders. We neither immediately counteracted nor suppressed some of the incorrect criticism. That brought about a fairly messy situation as party members with half a heart toward the party and counterrevolutionaries with two hearts [i.e., one pro-party, and one favoring counterrevolution—Eds.] suddenly appeared . . . So you see, what level this phase of exposure had come to! Here I will not reveal more about specific cases. I'll just take literature as an example. There were Wang Shiwei's "Wild Lilies" and his "Politicians, Artists," Cheng Quan's several letters to the chairman, Yu Bingran's letter to Ren Bishi, and the attacks on the party by the wall newspaper *Light Calvary*. The Central Research Institute's wall newspaper *Arrow and Target*, the Northwest Bureau's *Northwest Wind*, the *Liberation Daily's* wall newspaper (the title of which I cannot remember clearly), the Three Frontier's *Camel Bell*, *Suide's* XX, and Guanzhong's *New Malan*, plus Ding Ling's "Thoughts on March 8." All of them are counterrevolutionary ideological poison.

At that time, the incorrect thoughts of many party members were revealed. Comrades on the front line would be frightened to death once they discovered how those counterrevolutionaries acted, how much hatred they had for the revolution, and how they expressed their ideas in literature. I'm not sure if comrades from the front lines have read "Wild Lilies" and "Politicians, Artists." These things must be read in order to carry out rectification. You people can read page 4 of *Liberation Daily*.

One thing you don't know about is the letter Cheng Quan wrote to

___

*This is the original transcript of Kang Sheng's speech as made at the time; it has not been revised.—Dai Qing.

Chairman Mao. This letter was written to Mao three days after the chairman gave his speech on the problem of stereotyped writing [the eight-legged essay] in the party [February 8, 1942]. Cheng Quan also followed the stereotyped tendency. That bastard's [literally, "bastard turtle's spawn"] hatred toward the party was beyond our expectations. It seems that all the legs in his eight-legged letter were connected like the chapters of a novel. That is what counterrevolutionaries call X. The first line goes something like: "Sound, color, dogs, and horses." Sound refers to a gramophone, color refers to beauty, dogs refers to raising dogs, and horses refers to riding horses [i.e., leisure activities]. "Great cadres walk by ostentatiously." The rule is eight characters in one line. The next line is "People with coats and hats" that judges people according to the clothes and hats they wear. "Low ranking party members, janitors and doormen" (*chuanda limen*). This is the first leg of his letter.

Let's look again at what Cheng Quan said: Great cadres and low-ranking cadres are mutually antagonistic. What is the second leg? It goes: "There is a distinctive gap between the bigwigs and the humble" and: "He who works with his hands is only worth half a *kuai*." Labor is only worth half a *kuai*! The next line runs: "No equality between the rich and the poor" that puts mental laborers at the top. In this way, physical laborers and mental laborers are separated into the rich bigwigs and the poor and the humble. The two groups are set against one another. What about the third leg? It reads: "The healthy are being taken care of." The healthy ones seek free health care everywhere: Iron walking-stick Li is injected with glucose, healthy people get sick* . . . eat fine rice. See how much hatred he has. The fourth leg describes: "Three classes of foods": big, medium-sized, and small pots, and "Three categories of clothes": grey, black, and blue of which some are bright and others dark. There is something else described as: "The rich are peculiarly rich. . . cadres discard their former wives and chase new wives, old women." This sets women cadres against the rest. Next he accused the frontier districts of "Arrogance toward authority, and cheating of subordinates." As a result, the leaders of those self-reliant frontier districts left their positions and returned home. Giving up rank and returning home, the local emperors self-destructed. The seventh

---

*Kang Sheng is accusing Cheng Quan of castigating high-level cadres for abusing the rudimentary health care system. For further details on Cheng's letter to Mao, see Document 4.3, Dai Qing's Interview with Wang Ruqi.

leg announces: "Scratching for oil and absorbing water, try every means to gain benefit." The eighth leg goes: "Eating meat and drinking milk." Thus everyone, including the children of the cadres that were involved in the above, were classified into different classes and set against one another. These are the eight legs. . . . That's why I am informing you people now.*

Consider this exposure phase. To what extent have problems been exposed! There are many other such things. For instance, the Northwest Bureau's *Northwest Wind* scolded Comrade Gao Gang as a poisonous snake and a fierce beast. The scolding was made by cadres from the Cadre Bureau of the Organization Department. See how counterrevolutionary they are. The "soft bones and hard bones" mentioned by Wang Shiwei in the wall newspaper are extremely vicious. In a word, Wang's whole idea is his "theory of human nature" and "theory of degeneration." There is also the erroneous tendency among party members favoring extreme democracy and egalitarianism and Ding Ling's "Thoughts on March 8." At the March 8 public meeting [commemorating international women's day] she strongly scolded and cried out in her heart. There were even some people who after the April 3 decision still opposed exposure. People at the Academy for Marxist-Leninist Studies described the April 3 decision as "the incantation of the golden hoop" (*jinggu zhou*)† that no party member can escape. It's a pity that this hoop is not really made of gold! Instead, it's made of iron. No matter who you are, you must abide by this iron principle. Even Central Committee members must follow it. If you don't rely on it, you must favor the "Realm of Freedom," "Fruit Mountain," or "Water Fall Cave" [i.e., places occupied by ghosts and supernatural creatures described in the classical Chinese novel *Journey to the West*—Eds.]. And you then become the "wisest man in heaven." Where would the position of the party be!‡ There are still these kind of people even after the April 3 decision. Their thought still needs more exposure. That is why we label this phase as the exposure phase.

---

*At this point in the text the date "February 10" appears. Since Kang's speech is dated "August 1943," this interpolation (or remainder of an excised portion?) remains obscure.

†A powerful spiritual force originating in Buddhism.

‡That is, people cannot become powerful spiritual beings but must, instead, rely on the party. Kang Sheng is accusing them of putting themselves above the party.

What is the advantage of this exposure? This is a deliberate exposure that has three advantages: First, conditions among subordinates involving bureaucratic behavior that are not easily made known can now be revealed to those in authority; second, wrong ideas and thoughts among party members can be exposed; and, third, the deeper those counterrevolutionary ideas are exposed, the more effectively rectification will be carried out. One thing we don't fear is exposure. Before, we scolded Chen Boda from head to toe. Cheng Quan asserted that he would add another vicious style to the three vicious styles pointed out by Chairman Mao in his speech. Cheng claimed that in Yan'an, the treatment of human beings is not upright. At New Year's, he sent Chen Boda an eight-legged essay on the subject of party style, claiming that a human being should be treated as a human being and should not be forced to eat his own words. That's what he did. In a word, the Political Research Office was all messed up by the Central Research Institute's wall newspaper that was attached to a big piece of cloth and hung outside the south gate of Yan'an where everybody went over to read it just like they were attending a fair. This exposure phase is beneficial to us and also to the future goal of examining and investigating cadres.

The second phase began with the successful anti-Wang Shiwei meeting on June 23. To when? To November, the end of the Seventy-two-day Meeting, the conclusion of the party school's criticism of Li Guohua and Wu Xiru. At that time, it was characterized by ideological counteraction on one side, and deeper ideological struggle on the other. This is exactly what is mentioned in the April 3 decision! There was an anti-Wang Shiwei meeting at the Central Research Institute. There was also an anti-Yu Bingran meeting in August at Zao Yuan. In September, there was an anti-Li Guohua–Wu Xiru meeting at the party school. This meeting lasted for about a month! The Five Member Anti-Party Gang meeting was held at the Political Research Office, which was the Seventy-two-day Meeting. In October, the Eighty-three Senior Cadres meeting was held in a frontier district.

During this phase of ideological struggle meetings were long-lasting. What is the advantage of holding such meetings? On the one hand, they can readjust ideologically erroneous tendencies among party members; on the other, they can isolate counterrevolutionary thoughts. Thus, stressing the April 3 decision meant stressing the issue of leadership, not democracy. This ideological struggle should have been carried out to the fullest extent possible and by October it had almost been completed. Since during this time everyone studied the correct party style, some cadres were involved in it from general study to self-examination and personal practice, and from general examination to self-confession. Thus, it was ideological autobiography and historical autobiography. The issue of antiliberalism was proposed in the leading organs. In the meantime, the struggle against Wu Xiru started. The process went from examining his ideological problems and his political problems to the problem of his engaging in spying. It was probably October 7. Wu withdrew from the party in October when his role as a spy was proved. So, the ideological struggle was shifted to a anti-counterrevolutionary struggle.

Besides Wu, there were eleven people at the party school who were exposed as spies. At that time at Zao Yuan there was the struggle against the political problems of the spy Yu Bingran. In early November, Yu's wife confessed that she was a spy under Dai Li [head of the KMT's secret police—Eds.]. In the meantime, the case of Luo Jiming was addressed at the Military Committee auditorium. Luo Jiming was once on the political committee in the Instruction Group. He opposed the party committee and Chairman Mao. He scolded the party at the last party affairs meeting. Luo was arrested on November 30. See, at the party school there was the Wu Xiru problem, at Zao Yuan there was the problem of Yu Bingran's wife, and at the General Political Committee (*zongzheng*) there was the Luo Jiming problem. Ideological rectification was already associated with individual organs and individual persons, with examining cadres and ferreting out spies. Thus, the focus of the movement was shifted from study to examining cadres, from proletarian or non-proletarian issues to revolutionary or counter-revolutionary issues.

Let me discuss once again the issue of Wang Shiwei and the Five Member Anti-Party Gang. The strategic aspect to this struggle was adopted from the Leninist strategy of winning over the majority and attacking the minority so as to destroy them one by one. Attacking them one by one was the heart of our strategy. During the anti-Wang Shiwei struggle, after a few struggles, we ended up attacking four more people (Pan Fang, Zong Zheng, Cheng Quan, and Wang Li). We can see from the struggle that these four people were associated with Wang Shiwei. Wang Shiwei at that time, however, refused to admit his faults or confess to being a counterrevolutionary. On the contrary, he sometimes tried to draw some people over to his side. But materials regarding those people's relationship with Wang were not sufficiently concrete for us to attack them except that after the publication of Wang Shiwei's "Wild Lilies," 95 percent of the people at the Central Research Institute favored that article. They were sympathetic with Wang's counterrevolutionary thoughts. It was vicious. That is why after attacking Wang Shiwei, we continued to attack Pan Fang, Zong Zheng . . . one by one. That was the strategy.

Later, we made Pan Fang secretary of a study committee and director of an administrative office. Was it deliberate or accidental? (Zhang Zhongshi answers: It was deliberate.) Instead of attacking Pan Fang, we promoted him. That way, the rest would think that since Pan Fang, despite having committed some errors, was promoted, they could also avoid punishment. At that point, we also thought about attacking Cheng Quan and Wang Li. But then because the masses at the Political Research Office did not support such a move, we figured that it would be difficult. We dared not hold branch party committee meetings because once any movement was started, it would be very difficult to put an end to it. Cheng Quan scolded Chen Boda viciously. At the meetings, the branch party committee could do nothing but be the mediator that sometimes involved favoring one side and sometimes favoring the other. The masses were not conscious enough; therefore, the attack should not have been carried out. Even if the attack were carried out, we figured that it would not have been successful.

We did a further study on the case and figured out that the Five Member Anti-Party Gang was in reality composed of two groups. The Gang was actually composed of six members. Pan Fang and Zong Zheng belonged to the group at the Central Research Institute with Wang Shiwei as the superficial head. The real head was Pan Fang. Cheng Quan and Wang Li belonged to the group at the Political Research Office with Wang Li as the head. But in reality, the head was Yu Bingran. Yu was at Zao Yuan. We were sure about the masses at Zao Yuan. Attack Yu Bingran first; later Cheng Quan and Wang Li, then Yu again. It was a detour [i.e., a roundabout way of getting at Wang Shiwei]. The attack lasted for quite a few days. The wall newspaper at the Social Department [Kang's secret police center] made the attack comprehensible to the masses. Realizing how serious his faults were, the first time he was attacked Yu thus admitted to all of them. He said, I am a Chinese who has the style of a real man. A real man has the courage of admitting his faults. He labeled himself with an ideological hat only. He was fairly cunning. What he said made some of the new party members think that once he admitted his faults, he should be forgiven. But the old party members figured that Yu must have serious problems and that it was insufficient for him simply to admit his faults. They also thought that the struggle against Yu should be continued. An ideological hat was insufficient. He should be labeled with a political hat.

We gave an order that only ideological problems could be discussed and that neither historical nor political problems should be touched. What problem did Yu have? The old cadres understood it, but the masses were muddled. We let the masses alone to be muddle-headed. Once Yu started to confess, the Rectification Movement would go on smoothly. Yu, in order to protect himself, had to attack others, had to attack Cheng Quan and Wang Li. I said to him, now that you have confessed, how come Cheng Quan and Wang Li have not confessed? You should try to make them confess, too. Yu said: I know how to make them confess. Thus the delegation was organized at Zao Yuan with Yu as the head but in secret there was a more reliable comrade as the real head. The delegation went to the Political Research Office and started the struggle there. Later on, Yu, in order to show his sincerity, became very active in exposing the Trotskyite ideas of Cheng Quan and Wang Li. Why did he do that since neither Cheng or Wang were Trotskyites? He did it so as to disguise the fact that Yu, Cheng, and Wang were all members of the [KMT] Blue Shirts. To admit that they were Trotskyites would be beneficial both to Yu, and also to Cheng and Wang. In the beginning, Cheng and Wang refused to admit that. But later on, they finally did. We exposed that part. Yu also touched on that part. How could we spark a struggle at the Political Research Office when the masses lacked political consciousness? Our solution was to let the masses examine their leaders. Chen Boda as a leader probably had some problems. Examination after examination would cause the masses to become aroused. So we persuaded Chen to go to Zao Yuan on vacation. No matter how hard the masses scolded him, he was ordered not to return to the [Central Party] department until he received our letter. During the five days of the meeting, the problem of Cheng and Wang [Li] was not even mentioned. The focus was solely on Chen Boda who was scolded in a bloody way [literally, "to cover the head with dog's blood"] . . . On the fifth day, the couple [Cheng Quan and Wang Li] scolded Chen Boda from morning till the afternoon. What were they scolding him about? It was the human nature issue. At this point, the masses started to question the couple: "How come in the process of scolding [Chen Boda] you two have expressed the same thoughts as Wang Shiwei on the issue of human nature"? . . . At this point, the ideological struggle thus shifted from the Political Research Office to the Central Research Institute. Another detour. In this way both Pan Fang and Zong Zheng had exposed their Trotskyite thoughts . . . After quite a few go-arounds, we shifted the focus to political struggle. That struggle was very circuitous and meticulous.

The masses were now suspicious and claimed that the two had Trotskyite thoughts, which was inexcusable. So on the fifth day, the focus shifted from Chen Boda to Cheng and Wang. The delegation joined in. And Yu Bingran gave a speech in which he verified that Cheng and Wang held Trotskyite thoughts. That speech changed the entire situation of the meeting. Everybody started to attack Cheng and Wang. The attack eventually lasted for seventy-two days. We exploited the contradiction between Yu and Cheng and Wang. Of course, Yu also exploited the contradiction between Cheng and Wang and us. Both Pan Fang and Zong Zheng had exposed their Trotskyite thoughts and their antiparty activities. How did Yu know that? Once again for the purpose of attacking others to promote himself, Yu said that it was Pan and Zong who had given him the information. I said: As long as they do self-criticism, things will be all right. You should talk to Pan and Zong. Yu found Pan and Zong and scolded them harshly.

At that time, the ideological struggle had shifted from the Political Research Office to the Central Research Institute. Another detour. Then came the climax to the struggle against the Five Member Anti-Party Gang when both Pan and Zong were labeled as Trotskyites. See how we exploited contradictions: The contradictions between Yu and Cheng and Wang Li were now applied to Wang Shiwei. We successfully attacked Pan and Zong by exploiting the contradiction between them and Cheng and Wang Li. They all exposed themselves one by one. But until the Seventy-two-day Meeting Yu was not included among the Five because of one issue. The struggle against Yu at Zao Yuan was not that serious because at that time the focus of the struggle had already shifted to the Political Research Office. And when it came to attack Pan and Zong, Yu appeared to be more active. As a result, there was only the Five Member Anti-Party Gang. Yu Bingran returned to Zao Yuan. He used the strategy of attacking first to protect

himself by asking his wife to confess the first evening after he returned. He did this solely for the purpose of sacrificing another to
protect himself. He told his wife to confess on her own and not to tell
anybody that he knew all about that. His wife indeed came out to
confess. Yu made a good arrangement.

As soon as the Seventy-two-day Meeting was over, Yu wrote a
letter to me, similar to Wang Shiwei's, appealing to withdraw from the
party. Yu's case was different from that of Wu Xiru's. Wu claimed
that he had been wrongly accused, while Yu said: "The real reason
why I want to withdraw from the party is that I am not qualified to be a
party member in that my friends were Cheng Quan and Wang Li and
my wife was a spy. I don't consider myself as a true party member for
these reasons. I request that the party dismiss me and transfer me to the
front to be a soldier so that I can devote myself to the party." Yu
wanted to make us talk to him and thus to put us in a passive position. I
ignored him for two days after receiving his letter. He gradually realized that he was trapped and became very worried. He wrote another
letter, claiming that he made a mistake by asking to withdraw from the
party and that he wished his [original] letter would be returned as soon
as possible. Zao Yuan let him know that his letter had already been
submitted to the party committee and that he should be serious about
party membership: Either withdraw or don't withdraw. Yu then coun-
terattacked us by asking the meeting to discuss his letter and requesting
a divorce from his wife the spy and separation from her as soon as
possible.* Of course, Yu figured that we wouldn't do that, but to his
surprise, we accepted his request and warned him that once separated
from his wife, he could never see her again.

Here appeared another contradiction. Yu said to his wife: "Why do
you have to be the one to be sacrificed? Where on earth is there such a
wife like you?" He succeeded in persuading her to admit that it was Yu
who had asked her to confess. That is how we exploited the contradiction between Yu and his wife. Later on, we enlarged that contradiction.
That was how we struggled against Yu. Eventually we arrested Yu
who confessed to the whole process. Then we attacked Cheng and
Wang. That was the second round. After the Seventy-two-day Meeting, Cheng and Wang attacked us again. He [Cheng Quan] wrote a

*Such "political" separations and divorces would also occur during the Anti-
Rightist campaign and the Cultural Revolution.

letter in which he told the truth. He said: "I admitted that I was a Trotskyite at the meeting. In fact, I am not. If in the future this is found out, it should be cleared." He was telling the truth. We knew that he was a KMT member. But we merely labeled him as a counterrevolutionary and kept ignoring him until after Yu confessed everything. After that, we got some materials to work him over with again!

We arrested Pan and Zong on April 1 [1943]. That was another round of attack in the struggle. Another triangle. This struggle is fairly meticulous. Some comrades at the party school found out about Wu Xiru's problem first. That struggle was extremely circuitous. We began by attacking Li Guohua, not Wu. Later on, Li owned up. But this was only the ideological phase. After quite a few go-arounds, we shifted the focus to political struggle. That struggle was very circuitous and meticulous. Chairman Mao has said these four lines (1) cure the illness to save the patient; (2) when a melon is ripe, the stem will surely fall off, don't pick melons that are not yet ripe, when a melon is ripe, it will just drop off; in struggle it won't do to be rigid; (3) one's accomplishments are revealed in the details; (4) welcome progress. We appreciated Yu Bingran's progress. These four lines were actualized through the intense struggles in Yan'an though they seemed simple.

Section Four: Introduction*

This section includes the actual documents obtained from investigations and interviews. They were recorded by us and have been reviewed by the interviewees.

The recorded interviews completed before 1981 are rather vague because it was unclear whether the Wang Shiwei case would be considered as a historically unresolved case and whether Wang Shiwei's name would eventually be cleared. As a result, the interviewees' answers could possibly have been affected by these unresolved questions. However, information offered by those comrades is of great significance.

At that time, the main purpose for collecting information was to provide references for Comrade Li Weihan's [Luo Mai's] *Reminiscences*. Before Comrade Li passed away, he wrote the following paragraphs based on the information we had collected and his renewed attention to the Wang Shiwei case in the third section ("The Rectification Movement at the Central Research Institute") of the third draft of his *Research Work and the Rectification Movement at the Central Research Institute*:

"Part Six: Unsettled Case"†
by Li Weihan
(and other information on the handling of the Wang case
compiled by Dai Qing)

"The issues regarding Wang Shiwei as a Trotskyite and the Five Member Anti-Party Gang (Wang Shiwei, Cheng Quan, Wang Li, Pan Fang,

---

*Section Three of the documents collected by Dai Qing is not included in this translation; these documents include articles and reports on the Wang Shiwei case made in the KMT press in the 1940s. The gist of the KMT view of this case is available in Warren Kuo, *Analytical History of the Chinese Communist Party,* 4 vols. (Taipei, Taiwan, 1966–78).

†The published version (see citation below) was not "Part Six," but has a "Part Three" on "Criticism and Struggle of Wang Shiwei," pp. 491–94, which seems to be the highly revised version of this text.

and Zong Zheng) appeared after I finished my instructional work on the Rectification Movement at the Central Research Institute. Recently, I received a letter from Wang Shiwei's wife, Comrade Liu Ying, in which she requested a reevaluation of the Wang Shiwei case. It is said that Comrade Wang Li (Wang Ruqi) has also applied to the Central Party Discipline Inspection Commission [to reevaluate the Wang case]. The Central Investigation Bureau is also in the process of reevaluating the Pan Fang and Zong Zheng case.*

[Wang Shiwei] is an unresolved case. It is my hope that the Organization Department will eventually be allowed to come to an accurate conclusion. I was one of the people involved in that case. In order to be responsible to the party, I am obliged to give my personal opinion on this.

I have suggested to the Organization Department that it reinvestigate the Wang Shiwei case. As we look at it today, the following points are correct: First, the Wang Shiwei case was mainly an ideological issue, not an issue between enemy and people; second, the relationship between Wang and the Trotskyites was an historical issue, not a contemporary one; and, third, the Wang case was a personal problem. He was not involved in organizing a gang to carry out counterrevolutionary activities. Therefore, the so-called Five Member Anti-Party Gang was actually an incorrect accusation, and it should be cleared. Whether the accusation against Wang Shiwei as an individual is right or wrong can be concluded through reinvestigation. If it turns out to be an incorrect accusation, Wang Shiwei's name should be cleared even if he is already dead.''

[Dai Qing continues:] Of course, this case needs to be reinvestigated since it is an unresolved one. Later, some of the relevant [party] departments expressed that there were real difficulties in reexamining the Wang case and that it would be difficult to alter the conclusion. Due to this, Comrade Li Weihan had to change his view toward the Wang case and he crossed out the above section of his book. He also made some changes in his views in accordance with the abovementioned condition. Obviously, he avoided the word "Trotskyite." Instead, he merely asserted that Wang had "Trotskyite thoughts." See Li Weihan, *Reminiscences and Research* (Huiyi yu yanjiu) (Beijing: CCP Party History Documents Publishing House, 1986, pp. 491–94).

---

*The Central Discipline Inspection Commission and Central Investigation Bureau are involved in examining cases of purported political crimes in the CCP.

In February 1982, the CCP Organization Department formally cleared the name of the Five Member Anti-Party Gang (see the afterword in this book). But nothing was mentioned regarding Wang Shiwei as an individual.

On June 2, 1986, Comrade Hu Qili said at the forum with intellectuals in Shanghai, that Comrade Hu Yaobang had often told comrades at the Central Secretariat Department that many lessons could be drawn from party history. From the criticism of Wang Shiwei during the Yan'an era to the criticism of Hu Feng later on, to the criticism of the "Three Family Village" during the Cultural Revolution, all these experiences tell us that conclusions (of cases) made on the basis of carrying out movements (*yundong*), beating with sticks, turning ideological issues into political issues and then punishing by organizational means are of little staying power. No matter what, ideological issues cannot be solved by organizational means. Hu Yaobang's attitude toward the Wang Shiwei case as passed on by Comrade Hu Qili helped to resolve the Wang case smoothly. According to the interpretation in the *Mao Zedong Reader* published by the CCP Documents Compilation and Editing Committee in 1988, there was a reevaluation of Wang Shiwei. The label of "KMT special agent, spy" put on Wang was also removed. (See: *Mao Zedong Reader*, vol. 2, p. 890, n. 486.)

One thing that needs elaboration here is that during the criticism in Yan'an of Wang Shiwei, Wang was only accused of being "a Trotskyite." Wang was never labeled as a "KMT special agent, spy." According to internal documents, Kang Sheng was the only one who accused Wang Shiwei of being a spy and a member of the [KMT] Salvation Association. Thus, we are puzzled as to where Mao Zedong's version of "KMT special agent, spy" originated.

Recently, we did some additional investigation to determine the following: First, whether labeling Wang Shiwei as "a Trotskyite" was based on solid evidence; second, what did Wang Shiwei actually do during his life? And, how do we evaluate him? Some of the information gained from these investigations was recorded and has been reviewed by the interviewees. Some, however, was not recorded, but it is reflected in the introductory sections of this book.

Document 4.1

Conversation with Li Yan on the Question of Wang Shiwei as a Trotskyite, May 9, 1980

The Trotskyite faction existed during the anti-Japanese war era. At that time, the Trotskyite label referred to those anti-CCP and anti-revolutionary gangs who were extreme leftists, fabricated rumors, instigated conflicts between our comrades, and destroyed overall anti-Japanese unity. They were running dogs of Japanese imperialism. And most of them were traitors to our party such as Zhang Mutao in Shanxi and Ye Qing [Jen Cho-hsuan, an ex-CCP member and later member of the Left Kuomintang—Eds.] in Xi'an. These people were allowed to exist in KMT controlled regions. Ye Qing was made an official in Xi'an. Those people were absolutely not allowed in the anti-Japanese bases, especially in the Shaan-Gan-Ning Border Region.

How did Wang Shiwei come to be labeled a Trotskyite?

Wang Shiwei acted differently during the early period of rectification when, suffering from tuberculosis, he seldom appeared. But after rectification began, he became extremely active by publishing several articles in succession, such as "Wild Lilies," "Soft Bones and Hard Bones," etc. in both the *Liberation Daily* and the wall newspaper *Arrow and Target* of the Central Research Institute. He advocated focusing rectification on the leadership of the party.

Comrade Wang Zhen went to read *Arrow and Target* and bitterly cursed the authors of those articles. Wu Yue, who came from the [army's] 359th Division and was working at the Central Research Institute, also wrote some articles. Wang Zhen asserted on the spot that in the past Wu had been a traitor. At the end of March, Chairman Mao went to read the wall newspaper. Kang Sheng probably also went there.

In late April, Wang Jiaxiang [a Russian returned student], of the Central Social Department (Kang Sheng was the director of this office specially charged with struggles against enemies) sent somebody to the Central Research Institute and asked me to make a report about Wang Shiwei's behavior at the Institute, including his "Wild Lilies" and other articles he had published in *Arrow and Target*. I finished the report that noon without taking a lunch break. The person from the Central Social Department took the report back to Wang. A few days later, Wang came over and told me that the party leaders had read my report. Comrade Wang Jiaxiang commented that it was well done and was not in the style of the "eight-legged [stereotyped] essay." But Wang Jiaxiang also pointed out that there were defects in the report and that I should accept criticisms. In fact, he meant to tell me to prepare for criticisms. Next, he asked me to join the cadre meeting at the Social Department at which I was bitterly criticized by Kang Sheng for the section describing Wang Shiwei's behavior that had been hastily done. At the end of the report, I meant to write that the words uttered by Wang Shiwei were "naturally expressed" without any pressure from the outside. Instead, I wrote down "enthusiastically expressed." Kang Sheng inquired, what's this "enthusiasm?!" It is "counter-revolutionary enthusiasm!" Where is your proletarian standpoint?! Kang also said that Wang Shiwei's "Wild Lilies" was published in a Hong Kong newspaper in April. The Central Committee paid considerable attention to the fact that the article was published in Hong Kong. Kang actually considered the Wang case as a conflict between enemy and people. Only the issue involving the publication of Wang's article in Hong Kong was mentioned at that meeting; nothing else about Wang came up. After that meeting, I reviewed Wang's dossier at the Central Organization Department in order to learn more about his past. There I read Wang's own report to the Organization Department about his relationship with the Trotskyites.

The whole issue about exposing Wang's Trotskyite thoughts was reflected at the forum held by the Central Research Institute. That is all I know. As for whether there were additional materials, we did not know. The Central Social Department never informed us either.

The forum on Democracy and Discipline in the Party held at the Institute was actually a meeting to criticize Wang Shiwei. Fan Wenlan presided over the forum. Department directors such as Zhang Ruxin and we party committee members were also present. In reality, the forum was directly led by Kang Sheng and Yang Shangkun. Kang attended a few times. Comrade Yang Shangkun was present all the time. Both of them were leaders of the Study Committee that was responsible for guiding study in all organs affiliated with the Central Committee. A wrong tendency appeared at the beginning of the Rectification Movement at the Institute, especially with the Wang Shiwei case. Therefore, it was necessary to expose Wang Shiwei so as to educate everybody. Afterward, the forum was enlarged, as people from literary and art circles and the Central Political Research Office at Yangjialing [a site near Zao Yuan] were accepted. Speeches by Chen Boda and Ding Ling were probably arranged by Kang Sheng.

In winter 1942, Wang Shiwei was arrested by the Central Social Department as a Trotskyite and was imprisoned till 1947 when the Central Committee withdrew from Yan'an. I am not sure what happened to Wang after his arrest. Not until after 1961 did I hear that Wang had been persecuted and then killed during the Yan'an withdrawal.

There were two couples in Yan'an who, due to the fact that they were in daily contact with Wang, were included in the Five Member Anti-Party Gang. They were Pan Fang and Zong Zheng, Cheng Quan and Wang Li. They were criticized at the meeting jointly held by the Central Research Institute and the Political Research Office under the leadership of the Central General Study Committee of Units Directly Subordinate to the Central Committee at Yangjialing. They were also arrested in winter 1942. Now it is clear those four people were wrongly accused.

As for whether Wang Shiwei was really a Trotskyite, it should be investigated. It is said that Wang's daughter has sent a request to the Central Organization Department to reevaluate her father's case.

At that time, Trotskyites were considered to be like gangsters, extreme leftists, involved in activities that were anti-CCP, counterrevolutionary, and contrary to anti-Japanese unity, and in instigating conspiracies. Wang Shiwei was naturally considered a Trotskyite due to his behavior during the Rectification Movement, his past relationship with the Trotskyites, and the publication of "Wild Lilies" in a Hong Kong newspaper.

Note: Comrade Li Yan was secretary of the general branch party committee at the Central Research Institute in the 1940s. Sub-branches under the general branch committee also existed at the Institute.

Document 4.2

Wen Jize on a Few Limitations of the Wang Shiwei Case, June 9, 1980*

I would like to say a few words about the Wang Shiwei case:

1. When the criticism of Wang Shiwei first began, I considered his problem an ideological issue, not a political one. Nobody accused Ding Ling of being "antiparty" although she had written the article "Thoughts on March 8." At the Yan'an Forum on Literature and Art, Xiao Jun said in front of Chairman [Mao] and General Zhu De: "You say you will rectify. I don't believe you will be able to change anything!" Xiao was extremely tough and rude. We seriously criticized him, but again we did not accuse him of being antiparty.

2. Wang Shiwei had already on his own reported to the party his problem with the Trotskyites. He had already broken off his relationship with the Trotskyites. It was a historical question. As for whether it should have been considered as a contemporary issue, this needs to be studied. Kang Sheng accused Wang of being a member of the [KMT] Blue Shirts. What evidence did he base this on?

3. On the issue of whether the Wang Shiwei case is an individual problem or a problem involving a gang, I was dubious about the accuracy of labeling Wang Shiwei as a member of the Five Member Anti-Party Gang together with Pan Fang, Zong Zheng, Cheng Quan, and Wang Li.

---

*Comrade Wen Jize was in the Cultural and Ideological Research Office of the Central Research Institute in the 1940s. During rectification, he was transferred to work at the general branch party committee to help collect materials on Wang Shiwei.

Document 4.3

On the Circumstances of Yan'an's "Five Member Anti-Party Gang"

An Interview with Comrade Wang Ruqi
[Wang Li], January 7, 1981

The so-called Five Member Anti-Party Gang headed by Wang Shiwei was attacked during the movements for the rectification and examination of cadres from 1942 to 1945 in Yan'an. The following is what I remember from those events:

A. The origin of the "Five Member Anti-Party Gang" and information regarding the five members:

1. Members of the "Five Member Anti-Party Gang" and their relationships: The members were Wang Li, Cheng Quan, Zong Zheng, Pan Fang, and Wang Shiwei.

I was addressed in Yan'an as Wang Li (my original name is Wang Ruqi). I joined the CCP in 1938, and went to Yan'an in 1940 where I was involved in research on the women's movement. In winter 1941, due to my illness, I went to stay at the Central Political Research Office where my husband Cheng Quan was working.

Cheng Quan (original name Cheng Chuangang) had also joined the CCP in 1938, and went to Yan'an in 1940 where he was appointed provost of the Administration College. In 1941, he was sent to study at the Academy for Marxist-Leninist Studies. In the winter 1941, he was shifted to the Central Political Research Office to do research on economic issues.

Zong Zheng (female, original name Guo Zhenyi) went to Yan'an in winter 1941 and studied at the Central Research Institute.

Pan Fang (original name Pan Huitian) went to Yan'an in winter 1941 and was involved in translation work.

Wang Shiwei was involved in translating Marx and Lenin's works both at the Lu Xun Arts Academy and the Central Research Institute.

The relationship between the five people:

a. My tuberculosis recurred in 1941 when I was working at the

Women's Affairs Committee of the Central Committee. So I stayed at my unit to be cured. In the winter of the same year, my classmate at Fudan University [in Shanghai], Zong Zheng, visited me together with her husband Pan Fang. In actuality, I had not been well acquainted with Zong Zheng at Fudan. I only got to know her because, seeing that she was sitting on the stage at the meeting commemorating March 8 International Women's Day in 1933, I considered her as somebody with progressive ideas. I was not acquainted with Pan Fang at all. He had gone to study in Germany and joined the CCP much earlier.

b. In the fall 1935, I was a middle school teacher in Jinan. In the same year, the December Twelfth [sic Ninth?] Movement broke out in Beijing. Cheng Quan and I were living in Jinan that was under the control of the warlord Han Fuqu. This was a very unsettled place politically. In early 1936 in Nanjing, my aunt Cao Mengjun (a progressive scholar) recommended Wang Shiwei to us as someone with progressive ideas. In April 1936, we went to visit Wang Shiwei accompanied by an old classmate of mine from Fudan. We merely had a chat, nothing significant. In May 1936, Ding Zuzhen was arrested. To find out about Ding, I visited Wang Shiwei twice. I had no further contact with Wang because he did not leave a good impression on me.

2. Why was I dissatisfied with Wang Ming and Meng Qingshu?

In the spring of 1940, I started working at the Central Women's Affairs Committee. At that time, Wang Ming was the acting party secretary. Wang Ming's wife, Meng Qingshu, was a member of the Women's Committee and ran most daily affairs there.

Around May, not long after I began working there, Wu Ping, the secretary in chief of the Women's Committee was sent to study at the Academy for Marxist-Leninist Studies. At the meeting for making an appraisal of Wu, Meng cursed Wu bitterly. Meng's rude work style left a very bad impression on me. I once discussed this with a colleague of mine at the committee named Zhao Shilan (she was persecuted to death during the Cultural Revolution) as to why Meng relied on her powerful connections in order to repress Wu Ping at the small group party meeting.

Wang Ming was also very tough and rude to cadres whenever he lost his temper. I heard about it when working at the Women's Committee. In 1941, the CCP committee decided to stop the publication of the journals of workers, youth, and women due to the lack of paper in Yan'an. Showing his disagreement with the termination of *China*

Women, Wang Ming ordered the editor, Zhang Yasu, to write in the last issue of the journal something like this: "Women's liberation is a symbol of the development of the revolutionary movement. Since women's journals are so important we should immediately reverse this decision halting the publication of *China Women!*" Wang Ming thus opposed the Central Committee's decision. After that, I heard that when Wang Ming was criticized by the Central Committee (there might be other reasons why he was criticized) he then claimed to be too ill to work. I really resented Wang Ming for that kind of behavior.

3. The process of communicating among the five people in Yan'an.

Zong Zheng and Pan Fang often came to see me in winter 1941 when I was recuperating at the Central Women's Affairs Committee. As we saw each other more often, we started to become friendly. The fact that we were both former classmates and revolutionary comrades made our conversations very casual. I mentioned to them how rude Meng Qingshu had been at the small group party committee meeting and how Wang Ming counteracted the CCP's decision and pretended to be sick just to get out of work. The assessment I made of Wang was that he suffered from a political disease. Hearing that, Zong Zheng said that it was a vivid description.

At about the end of the fall and beginning of winter 1941, Cheng Quan was transferred to the Central Political Research Office. I followed him to continue my recuperation. Cheng accompanied me every month to the outpatient service department of the Central Committee hospital. The outpatient service department was near the Central Research Institute. Zong Zheng suggested that, after seeing the doctor, we go to rest for a while at her place and return after lunch. My husband and I went to see Zong and Pan twice or three times. Soon after we arrived for our first visit to their place, Wang Shiwei suddenly appeared (Zong Zheng never talked about Wang). It would have been too impolite not to talk to Wang though in the past he had not left a good impression on me. I asked what he was doing and where he was living. Wang replied that he was translating Marx and Engels's works at the Central Research Institute and that he was living in the cave next door.

We did not meet Wang each time we went to Zong Zheng's place. The following were the topics of our discussion:

a. Zong Zheng asked me to repeat my comment on Wang Ming and Meng Qingshu (Wang Shiwei did not say anything).

b. Cheng Quan, after hearing Chairman Mao's report on the rectification of the three work styles, wrote a letter to Mao titled "Rectification of the Human Style" (*zhengdun renfeng*). The letter mentioned things such as the existence of the three classes of foods and clothes, and that some people walked on foot while others rode on horses. . . . Cheng appeared to be really enjoying himself while telling this to Zong and the others. None of us commented on it.

c. Wang Shiwei also enjoyed describing "Wild Lilies." He said, nowadays people are so egocentric that they are not even as good as cocks who once they find some food, will give some to the hen. The rest of us refused comment.

d. Wang Shiwei also mentioned off and on Chairman Mao's suggestion that literary and artistic works should be of the kind appreciated by the masses. Wang also said something like "success is based on thousands of bones." [This can be interpreted in one of two ways: That either self-sacrifice is necessary or, more critically, that lives will be uselessly sacrificed by their leaders—Eds.]. (Nobody commented on that line.)

e. Prior to the Spring Festival of 1942, Cheng and I invited Zong, Pan, and Wang to have a spring festival eve dinner. Since they didn't arrive too early and being busy with the preparation of food, we didn't have a chance to talk to them. After the dinner, Wang Shiwei said: "How about us forming a research group?" Cheng Quan replied that groups are not allowed in the party. After that, everybody became silent.

4. How the idea of "Five Member Anti-Party Gang" was proposed:

In May 1942, Wang was labeled as a Trotskyite and his "Wild Lilies" as "antiparty" at the meeting to criticize Wang held by the Central Research Institute (Wang himself was not present at the meeting). During July and August 1942, we were examined and criticized for our relationship with Wang Shiwei at the party meeting of the Central Political Research Office held by the Study Committee (members of the committee were Zhou Taihe, Deng Liqun, and Peng Lianzhang) of the Central Political Research Office. We told the truth.

In a large meeting called in September 1942 by the Central Research Institute, the relationship between we five was labeled as the "Five Member Anti-Party Gang." Major accusations were as follows:

a. The relationship between the five is a Trotskyite one because Wang Shiwei is a Trotskyite.

b. The contacts the five people had were labeled as Trotskyite activities. The few times we saw each other were labeled as "having meetings." The Spring Festival eve dinner we had in 1941 was labeled as the "Meeting on the Eve."

The chats between the five people were labeled as antiparty activities with an organization, an agenda, and guiding principles. My comment on Wang Ming and Meng Qingshu was labeled as "opposing Central Committee officials." Cheng Quan's letter on "Rectification of the Human Style" addressed to Chairman Mao was also labeled as a serious antiparty crime.

c. I was accused of providing information for Wang Shiwei's "Wild Lilies."

d. The prominent point was that Wang Kunlun was considered a spy. Thus the relationship between Cheng Quan, Wang Kunlun, and me was examined.

I was criticized most heavily at the meeting, accused of being the "leader" of Cheng Quan's group. That is because I did not buy the subjective conjectures raised at the criticism meeting. Even the fact that I did not cry at the meeting became an important factor prompting people to express a great deal of hatred for me.

That meeting was later on labeled as the Seventy-two-day Meeting. The above-mentioned information is what was examined and criticized. It also reflects my personal attitude.

B. The conclusion of the inspection:

In May 1945, the Study Committee of the Central Political Research Office sent me the conclusion of its inspection titled the "Five Member Anti-Party Gang." Its main point was that I had no organizational relationship with Wang Shiwei though I was used by Wang ideologically (the conclusion on Cheng Quan was the same).

The process of drawing up the conclusion took from 1942 to 1945. After all those years of criticisms and inspection, the result was still that we were labeled as ideological criminals.

I met Chairman Mao at Zao Yuan in June 1945. Mao said to me that the trouble brought to Cheng Quan and me was like hurting our comrades by mistake in a bayonet fight at night. Obviously, Chairman Mao's view was fundamentally different from the conclusion drawn by the Study Committee of the Central Political Research Office. It's a pity that those at the department did not act according to Mao's personal views.

C. The consequences:

The impact on Cheng Quan and me due to the "Five Member Anti-Party Gang" accusation:

1. During the Rescue Movement (*qiangjiu yundong*) in 1943, Cheng Quan was forced into a false confession by high pressure tactics. That hurt him a great deal psychologically. At the beginning of the ten-year disaster [i.e., the Cultural Revolution], Cheng recalled the events of 1943 and felt deeply depressed [over their impending repetition]. That's why he committed suicide.

2. I was criticized for three years in Yan'an and was labeled "anti-party." The whole thing destroyed me both physically and psychologically. During the ten-year disaster, I was once again labeled a spy working for Wang Kunlun. I was "segregated and inspected" by the rebel faction (*zaofan pai*) at the Shanghai Foreign Languages College based on the existence of one telegram taken from the files of the Wang Kunlun Case Group of the Central Committee. The judgment of my innocence was not issued until ten years later. I was tortured a great deal while my family was destroyed. I am the only one left alive.

D. My personal view:

The reason why the "Five Member Anti-Party Gang" appeared in Yan'an in 1942 was due to the following reasons:

1. It served Kang Sheng's political goal of gaining power over the inspection of cadres so that he could eventually win control of the entire party. He tried to find fault with everybody so that he would be able to appear to be "the only leftist and true revolutionary."

2. In order to point arrows at Comrade Zhou Enlai,* Kang deliberately included Cheng Quan and me in the "Five Member Anti-Party Gang," though it was clear that Comrade Wang Kunlun had done considerable work for the party in the rear areas [controlled by the KMT]. We can say that Kang Sheng's ability of "finding fault and fabricating crimes to make false charges against our comrades by frequently abusing his power" was no accident.

(*Note*: I [Wang Ruqi] visited Comrade Zhou Taihe during the na-

---

*Later purges and ideological movements, such as the Gao Gang affair in the early 1950s and the Anti-Confucian Campaign in the 1970s, were also directed at Zhou Enlai indicating that Zhou's position was an enduring source of conflict in the CCP top hierarchy, along with Liu Shaoqi's. See Frederick C. Teiwes, *Politics at Mao's Court: Gao Gang and Party Factionalism in the Early 1950s* (Armonk, NY: M.E. Sharpe, 1990), p. 37.

tional holiday [October 1] in Beijing in 1978. Comrade Zhou still remembers that he himself suspected that Cheng Quan and I were spies sent to Yan'an by Wang Kunlun. Later on, Comrade Zhou Enlai explained to Zhou Taihe and some other comrades Wang Kunlun's true political character [i.e., that he was not a spy, but a secret member of the CCP]. Zhou Enlai also said that if you people did not believe what I said, that they should go see Dong Biwu. Comrade Dong's four-hour explanation on Wang Kunlun finally dissipated their suspicions.)

3. Kang used every available means to attack intellectuals who dared to speak out.

Document 4.4

Comrade Liu Ying's Appeal, August 15, 1981*

I am from a property owner's family† in Changsha, Hunan. In September 1922, I entered the Women's Middle School in Zhounan. It had already been a year since the establishment of the [communist] party. In our province Chairman Mao and Comrade Guo Liang were leading the anti-Japanese struggle. The president of the Zhounan school, Zhu Jianfan (who after 1949 became president of Beida) actively participated with the students in the struggle. The local despot tried to pressure us and made false charges against President Zhu who then fled to Guangzhou in 1923 where he took part in the National Revolution. Afterward, Zhounan students carried on their struggle that expanded my political consciousness a great deal.

In the summer of 1926, after graduating from Zhounan, I passed the entrance examination for Beida and joined the party in October 1926 on the recommendation of my classmate, Li Fen (two years my senior). She was sincere and cordial to her classmates (who respected her), worked hard for the revolution, and was strict on herself. As I developed a deep friendship with Li Fen, she recounted to me the story of her marriage at an early age, her husband's sudden death, and the ill-treatment she received at the hands of her in-laws. . . . She also told me of her determination to devote her life to communism and never marry again.

One day in early summer 1927, Li Fen showed me a letter from Wang Shiwei in which he expressed his attraction for Li's sincere devotion to their common cause and thanked her for the help she

---

*This document contains extensive details of Wang Shiwei's life and his marriage to Liu Ying, much of which is seemingly innocuous and apolitical. Yet since the accusations against Wang had, as with most political enemies in China, portrayed him as a thoroughly evil character, Liu Ying's appeal for her husband's "rehabilitation" (*pingfan*) required a total review of Wang's personal life and entire career.

†Liu Ying's "class label" (*jieji laoyin*).

provided him. Wang also wanted to see Li more frequently. When I asked Li about her impression of Wang, she noted that Wang was a very able writer from Henan. Li also noted that after graduating from middle school Wang had studied for a year in the Preparatory School for Study in the United States After it closed down and since his family was unable to support his university study, Wang worked for a year in a post office to earn tuition money. In 1925, he passed the entrance examination to Beida and in spring 1926, he joined the CCP.

Li Fen joined the party as a student at the Teacher's School. After entering Beida, she saw Wang on several occasions and felt that he was sincere and industrious in working for the revolution. His defect was his enjoyment in ridiculing other people. While Li told Wang that he was a good comrade, she also let him know about her views of his personal flaw. Li did not expect Wang to write her that letter. Because she had decided never again to marry and was cautious in dealing with male comrades, she wanted to avoid trouble by not writing a return letter. . . . Half a month later, Li showed me another one of Wang's letters where he described his daily disappointment over not receiving a return letter from Li. Wang also said that since he had sisters Li should not be suspicious about his sincerity. . . . I asked Li Fen if she planned to write back and she said no. She also said that she was thinking about passing the letter on to the party branch secretary, Duan Chun, a fellow provincial familiar with her past. She thought about asking Duan to return the letter to Wang and to tell him that considering she already had a husband and children Wang should put a stop to the whole affair. She asked me to accompany her to see Duan which I did.

Right after hearing all of this, Duan Chun sent somebody to fetch Wang Shiwei. Li Fen and I left in a hurry. Afterward, we heard that an argument had broken out between the two when Duan failed to explain Li's situation to Wang patiently. Duan severely criticized Wang and ordered him to stop bothering her. Wang talked back and then Duan blamed Wang for his lack of organizational discipline and weak sense of party principles and his unwillingness to accept the party's criticisms. Duan even threatened to dismiss Wang from the party. Wang grew even more irritated with Duan, and replied cynically: "Of course you can dismiss me from the party organizationally by using your power, but you can't get rid of my communist ideas." Wang then left. Actually, though Duan didn't plan to dismiss Wang from the party, he eventually did because of Wang's comments during their argument.

Hearing that, Li Fen told me: "Duan blew the whole thing up. This is a loss to the party's work."

Later on, while we were in the midst of preparing for final exams at Beida, Wang returned to his hometown in Henan.

The above describes the situation involving Wang Shiwei from summer 1925 to summer 1927 at Beida. During those two years, there was no Trotskyite faction inside the party except that Chen Duxiu was still a party member. Therefore, it was impossible for Wang Shiwei to be a Trotskyite, nor could he have been a spy since Wang never tried to destroy Duan who had kicked him out of the party. Moreover, none of the party members in the Beida party branch were ever hurt or captured.

At the beginning of July 1927, Li Fen was transferred to work as a copy clerk at the party branch in Tianjin, while I became involved in the Tianjin's [communist] Youth League Committee. In early September 1927, I was transferred to work at the Northern Bureau of the Beijing [Youth] League as a copy clerk charged with managing some party documents. Half a month later, the enemy discovered the offices of the Beijing Party Committee and Youth League due to the betrayal of the municipal party secretary, Li Bohai. I accompanied Comrade Yang Shannan, secretary of the Northern Bureau of the Youth League, to Tianjin to discuss procedures with the Youth League Committee for restoring the work of the Beijing League.

In Tianjin, I ran into Li Fen who, as usual, was working wholeheartedly for the party, though she felt her work as a copy clerk was insufficiently intense. She really missed the fiery struggles at Beida. But she was as cordial to me as always and warned me to approach my work cautiously. I never expected that this would be the last time I would see her.

In the discussion between Yang Shannan and the Youth League Committee, they decided I would reestablish the work of the Youth League in Beijing. Returning to the capital, we were all arrested on the first day since the [warlord] enemy had discovered the location of the Northern Bureau office. More than ten days later, Xu Wanru, Yin Caiyi's wife and a member of the propaganda committee, was also arrested. Xu angrily told me in prison: "Mu Bingheng is the only one who knew the office address of the committee. He must be the traitor who owned up the information that led to the arrest of Yang Shannan and Li Yanrui. The only one not arrested was Yin Caiyi who happened to be out of the office on business."

Later on, we were transferred from the enemy's investigation office to the Police Department. Xu was not released until four months later while I was released on bail on New Year's eve with the help of my uncle. I immediately went to the Teacher's College and discovered that, except for Yang Shannan and Li Yanrui who had both received an eight-year sentence in an army prison, Mu Bingheng and the others had already been released. A few days later, Comrade Zhao Lianfang and I visited Yang and Li at the prison where Yang indicated that if I could raise some money and send it to the prison office, they would both be released. I immediately thought about the 1,000 yuan my grandfather left me to use as tuition and Yang agreed to use it. In March 1929, I returned to Hunan to ask my father for the money, but was refused which led to constant arguments between us. Each time I received Yang's letter requesting the money, I became very anxious. I did not manage to get it until July or August of that year.

One day when I was at home feeling frustrated, a letter from Yang arrived from Shanghai informing me of his release as part of a general amnesty for all political prisoners following the capture of Beijing by Chiang Kai-Shek's army [in the Northern Expedition]. Yang then became a leader in the Zhejiang Provincial Committee and married Chen Weizhen. He asked that I seek out the party organization in Shanghai immediately. Chen Weizhen, a student at the Obstetrical Department of Tongde School in Shanghai, was in charge of transferring mail. Happy as I was after reading the letter, I was still worried about how to acquire the funds to pay for my trip to Shanghai. I asked my father to support my schooling in the city, but was again refused. At the end of 1928, however, I was finally able to get 180 yuan indirectly from him and left for Shanghai in February 1929.

One thing must be mentioned here. Around September 1928, I bumped into one of my former middle school classmates, Deng Dechun, on a street in Changsha. Deng was a fellow provincial of Li Fen's and she told me some very sad news—Li Fen had died fighting for the party's cause. After returning to her hometown of Baoqing, Hunan to attend a funeral for one of her relatives, Li Fen had remained there and become the principal of the Sanmin Elementary School (established by her father). During the white terror [beginning in April, 1927] she continued to do underground work for the party by using her position as principal as a cover. Yet, she was ultimately discovered by the enemy who surrounded the school, though at the time Li fortunately happened to be away. Later on, however, she was sold out by her uncle. She was very calm before being executed at the age of twenty-four. She was a truly brave revolutionary.

In February 1929, I left Hunan for Shanghai hoping to contact the party organization so as to continue my fight against the enemy. Stopping over in Nanjing, I went to see my good friend Cao Mengjun (later secretary in chief of the All-China Women's Association before the Cultural Revolution) and Zuo Gong (later director of the National Library also before the Cultural Revolution). I also met Wang Shiwei at their home. Before the meeting with Wang, Cao said: "Wang is still pro-CCP despite the fact he was attacked by Duan Chun at Beida." She also said that Wang was very saddened on hearing of Li Fen's death. He hated the KMT from the bottom of his heart; he was a good young man with a sense of justice.

Cao also asked if I wanted to see Wang and I agreed. Our first meeting was at Cao's house where Wang told me how he could not wait to find the party and start work for the revolution so as to avenge the martyr [Li Fen]. He also revealed the personal conflict he was having over his desire before joining the party to fulfill his filial obligation by making some money to give to his father. Then he could work for the party wholeheartedly. I tried to encourage him to join the party as soon as possible. (I need to mention here that if he had been a spy, he would have tried every means to join the party as early as possible.)

In mid February 1929, I applied to the Tongde Obstetrical School in Shanghai. At that time, Zhang Xiaoyu (the daughter of the prominent anti-Japanese leader, Zhang Nanxian) was also residing in the school's student dormitory. Zhang was attending both the Obstetrical School and Nanyang Medical College nearby. Zhang and I agreed on various problems (including some of the women traitors' losing their virginity and integrity) and it turned out that Zhang was a party member. Through her I finally got in touch with the organization and attended party meetings of the branch party committee at Nanyang Medical University. That's why I did not search further for Yang Shannan.

In spring 1929 Wang Shiwei also came to Shanghai where he rented an apartment and planned to get involved in translating books for the commercial China Book Bureau. I saw him frequently because I wanted him to rejoin the party. During our contacts, I got to know more about his thoughts and his personality, and started to consider him as an honest young man with abundant revolutionary spirit.

I also came to know about his experiences after leaving Beida. With his family unable to support him in school, he had returned in summer 1927 to his hometown in Henan where his plan to become a teacher had failed since the semester had already started. His father wrote a letter to a former student in Nanjing (Wang's father was a teacher before retirement) asking him to help Wang find a job. (I can't remember the student's name since it was many years ago). After much haggling, he became a general clerk at the KMT Central Committee Office. (However, Wang never actually joined the KMT. At the time, KMT members could not work for the [communist] party.) Wang's salary was very minimal and he frequently cursed [the KMT] as he really couldn't tolerate working there. During that period, he wrote more than ten short stories condemning the dark side of society. He also received some royalties from the China Book Bureau by translating books (they can still be found in libraries today). Although he put considerable effort into writing, he still sought any opportunity to leave Nanjing.

In 1928 (I can't remember the exact date. Cao Mengjun and Zhang Tianyi might know because they spent a lot of time together in Nanjing) Wang Shiwei finally got a chance to leave Nanjing for Tai'an, Shandong Province where he taught in a middle school. But after experiencing so many bad things in Tai'an (then under KMT control), he returned in winter 1928 to Nanjing where he finally gave up looking for a regular job in favor of making a living by translating books. Though, as I already mentioned, Wang wished to make some money for his father, he was still thinking about the revolution. From the winter vacation till the end of spring 1929, Wang lived at Cao Mengjun's place until he left Nanjing for Shanghai.

In January 1930, Wang Shiwei and I, reflecting the good feelings we had toward each other and our common views, were married. We lived a hard life in a small apartment on Caishi Road and since we relied solely on Wang Shiwei's previous royalties and my father's allowance, I was unable to continue studying at the Obstetrical School.

One day in May in 1930, Wang Shiwei bumped into one of his former Beida classmates, Wang Wenyuan [Wang Fanxi], who had been a CCP member in school. Wang told him: "My wife is Liu Ying" and so Wang Wenyuan came over to see me. Wang Wenyuan had apparently just returned from the Soviet Union. He told Wang Shiwei of his desire to earn some royalties as soon as possible so his wife could visit her parents in Anqing (where she planned to give birth to their child). He particularly wanted Wang Shiwei to help him translate a small part of a book (The number of pages is unclear; it took Wang Shiwei an entire day to complete it). I didn't know that the book was actually Trotsky's autobiography [*My Life*] until after Wang Wenyuan came to fetch the translation. Since I was already a party member, I knew of the intense struggle against the Trotskyites' liquidationist faction. After their meeting, I informed Wang Shiwei of this and so Wang never contacted Wenyuan again. Indeed, we never saw him again in our entire life.

What kind of person was Wang Wenyuan? Was he a Trotskyite? The Trotskyite organization name list or his dossier, are all under the control of party or state organs. It is also not difficult to determine if Wang Shiwei participated in a Trotskyite organization. Facts will show that Wang Shiwei was definitely not a Trotskyite. Actually, at that time Wang would not join any organization since he was fully engaged in making money for his old father that effectively prevented him from entering the CCP. How could he go about the task of joining yet another "party"?

Furthermore, Wang Shiwei was certainly not a KMT spy. If he had been, progressive people with whom Wang had close contact at that time, such as Cao Mengjun, Zuo Gong, Zhang Tianyi, etc., and party members like myself and Zhang Xiaoyu, would have been reported to the police. Yet all of us remained safe and sound. As a Trotskyite or a spy, he would have exposed some personal traits during our life together, yet, I never discovered any.

Next, I'd like to explain how I left the party. Summer vacation at the private Nanyang Medical University began in July 1930. While Zhang Xiaoyu went to a medical school in the Northeast to continue with her schooling, I fell ill and near the end of August, had a miscarriage. For quite a while I did not join in the party's organizational activities. Due to Li Lisan's leftist policy, party organizations in Shanghai were destroyed by the KMT one by one. In the midst of all this, I was unable to find the director of the party organization at Nanyang Medical University. Also, I disagreed with the party's policy and activities of demonstrating in the streets, etc., as blind action that would not advance the revolution.

Furthermore, the experience of some of the women party members' after being arrested really made me hesitate. The possibility of being killed during the period of the severe white terror did not shake my revolutionary will at all. But I was horrified in learning that after being arrested some women party members had lost their female purity. Some of my former classmates and party members, such as Xiong Zongyi, Yu Min, and Liu Zhongyi, even gave up their revolutionary will and willingly became concubines for the enemy. As a child, my grandmother and my aunt (both of them were widows and cared for me very much. I grew up at my grandmother's) taught me the importance of keeping my virginity. Thus I was most afraid of being raped by the enemy, for once raped, the spot in your soul can never be cleansed. With this thought in mind, I did not search out the party and thus lost touch with it. This indicates my weak will.

One fact I need to clarify (I don't mean to defend myself) is that, although a party member, I failed at that time to study the party's principles. I thought that it would be acceptable if I searched out the party after the [Li Lisan] period had passed. Thus, prior to Liberation, I joined the sixth department—the underground front organization (*waiwei dixiazu*)* of the Social Section of the Central China Bureau— where I was responsible for contact work. This made me think that I had finally gotten in touch with the party and was automatically reinstated as a party member. I did not realize until later that I had effectively withdrawn from the party in Shanghai.

In January, 1931, Wang and I responded to an advertisement in *Shenbao* [newspaper] for teachers in Zhuanghe County, Liaoning Province, and were both accepted. Wang became an English teacher at the County High School, and I taught mathematics and chemistry at Zhuanghe's Women's Normal College. But since I was pregnant we had to leave after the first semester, something we considered a real inconvenience. We returned to Shanghai in July, 1931 where Wang continued to make a living by translating books for the China Book Bureau. We lived on the second floor of a coal store on Huanlong Road. Cheng Shaozong (the nephew of Cheng Fangwu's who was also translating books and who once worked at the [literary] Creation Society) lived on the third floor. Our life then was somewhat better. On November 6, 1931, I gave birth to our first child (daughter Wang Jinfeng). We saw a lot of Zhang Tianyi, Cheng Shaozong, Xu Yiding,

---

*Less than trustworthy party members were placed in these organs.

and Xu Luyi (who later died in the Shangrao Concentration Camp during the anti-Japanese war).

In 1931, with finances totaling 450 yuan—200 yuan savings from the work in Northeast China, and the rest from my husband's translations —Wang decided to return to Henan to act on his promise to help his father. He was also determined to work for the party wholeheartedly by joining in the fight on the literature front against the enemy. To realize this plan, we decided to move to a new residence so as to avoid being bothered by acquaintances and so as not to bring any harm to our revolutionary work. I wrote a letter to one of my former middle school classmates, Tong Wenhuan, asking her to let us stay with them for a month or two. Her husband, Zhao Quemin, an assistant professor at Shanghai University, was always grateful to me for the medical care I had offered his wife when she was seriously ill. So we moved in with them.

Wang Shiwei left Shanghai for Henan and spent a month there with his father. He persuaded his parents to support his participation in the revolution and left most of the money to his father. (Wang arrived in Henan in early July 1932 and returned to Shanghai in early August 1932.) So we ended our stay at the old address in July 1932. After Wang returned, we moved to a two-story building near a park in the French quarter. Wang was happy on completing his trip. He planned to translate another book to earn enough royalties for us to live on. Afterward, he would immediately contact The League of Left-Wing Writers and participate wholeheartedly in the [anti-Japanese] National Salvation (*jiuwang*) Movement.

During the process of discussing with the China Book Bureau a project for translating another book, Wang had an argument with an editor named Qian over an incorrect alteration of an earlier translation by Wang. As a result of this conflict, the new translation project was gone. The inability to translate another book, Wang now believed, would make it impossible for him to support his family and would also destroy his plans to join the National Salvation Movement. Afterward, whenever he returned home, he was very anxious and quite unhappy to the point he spit up blood for two days.

We moved to a small apartment on Caishi road in order to make ends meet (the rent was 10 yuan less per month). But we still had great difficulties as our child needed milk and Wang was spitting up blood. After learning in early 1933 that Ding Ling was teaching in Shanghai, my former middle school classmate, Wei Ying, recommended that

Wang make some money by grading student compositions for Ding Ling. But due to his poor health Wang did it only a few times. During February or March 1933, unable to make a living in Shanghai, I took my child home to Changsha. My father gave me 30 yuan to give to Wang Shiwei who was in Hangzhou receiving a cure for his tuberculosis. (Just think, if Wang was really a spy, how could he have become so poor as to be unable to support his wife and daughter?*). After ten months, he improved. In spring 1934, Wang was recommended to become a third-degree clerk at the Department of Education in Shandong province through his former teacher who became the secretary in chief of the same department.

In August 1935, I went to Jinan from Changsha. There we contacted, among others, Xu Zhiyu and Qi Yufan. On July 27, 1935, I gave birth to a second child (our son Wang Xufeng). Denied enough milk, the child was weak and sick, while Wang became ill again and started to spit up blood. We would not have been able to live through that difficult period if my elder brother (a research fellow at a research institute) had not sent us 20 yuan every month.

At the end of 1935, I accompanied Wang to Kaifeng, Henan, where he had been recommended by his former classmate, Zheng Ruogu, to teach at the Provincial Women's School. Wang taught there up until the time he left for Yan'an. Following the 1937 July 7 [Marco Polo Bridge] incident, the anti-Japanese national salvation tide swept the entire country, so we decided to join the troop of patriots treking to Yan'an. But since two children were still small and I was pregnant again, we decided that Wang would go ahead to organize his students to join the revolution in Yan'an. (I personally thought that the anti-Japanese victory would come soon.) Meanwhile, I first returned to my hometown in Hunan, with plans to make it up to Yan'an later.

Wang and I were separated from each other but held a common revolutionary will. Soon, I received his letters from Yan'an describing the exciting atmosphere of anti-Japanese national salvation and was greatly encouraged. In July 1938, I moved from Changsha to Xiangxi and lost touch with the letter messenger [to Yan'an], Yu Shuyun. Yu thus returned Wang's letters to him and from then on, I lost complete touch with Wang Shiwei.

---

*Nikolai Bukharin's wife made similar arguments against her husband's prosecutors in Stalinist Russia but to no avail. Medvedev, *Nikolai Bukharin*, p. 146.

After our separation, I longed day and night for the victory of the party-led anti-Japanese struggle and the revolutionary cause. The children longed to see their father. Together, we made a living, relying on one another. After returning to Changsha from Kaifeng, I became a tutor. Then following the Japanese attacks on Wuhan and Changsha, we escaped to Chenxi in western Hunan. I taught mathematics at the Yuanfeng Middle School and at a village teacher's school in Chenxi, not returning to Changsha until the end of 1947 where I taught at the Sanfeng Middle School till 1948. Dependent solely on my earnings from teaching, the children led a hard life. I participated in some of the party's underground work in spring 1949 with responsibility for establishing contacts. In August 1949, the day we had longed for day and night, finally came—Changsha was liberated, along with most of the country.

The children were extremely happy, for they would soon be able to see their father. We tried to look for Wang, but in vain. At the end of 1949, I wrote a letter to the Central Organization Department inquiring about Wang's whereabouts. According to the return letter, when the [KMT] enemy had attacked Yan'an, Wang had voluntarily requested work in enemy-occupied regions, which had been approved. Since then, nothing had been heard from him. I took as true the information contained in the return letter, and figured that Wang had died in enemy-occupied territory. I was happy with the liberation, and determined to raise the children well, devoting our lives to the revolution.

In April 1950, I was recommended by the Twelfth Army Corps to teach mathematics at the Women's Middle School in Jilin for a salary of 176 work points per day that only covered board for my children and me. My son was seriously ill; therefore, my daughter had to start work (without attending college) at the Jilin Library, where she is still employed. In the summer of 1953, I just happened to comment on where Wang Shiwei would probably stand in the then-current ideological reform movement. The school party organization gave me a book titled *Ideological Instructions* containing Chen Boda's article criticizing Wang Shiwei's "Wild Lilies." I couldn't bear to read the entire piece for I now knew that Wang had "committed mistakes."

Later, my daughter wrote to Lu Dingyi [former editor of *Liberation Daily* in Yan'an]. The return letter from the Central Organization Department said: "Wang Shiwei went to Taiwan." I thought he had gone to Taiwan to do underground work. I was so shocked as if struck by a lighting in fine weather when I heard that Wang was already considered a "counterrevolutionary" and that my family had thus become counterrevolutionary. My whole body trembled. We could not accept it. Where was the truth? Thinking about the effects on the children and the spiritual suffering we three have experienced in the past years, my only wish is that the party reexamine the entire case based on the principle of seeking truth from facts* and to clear Wang's name as soon as possible. I cannot tolerate letting a third generation [of my family] suffer and be humiliated by this. Of course, I also understand the significance of clearing his name in terms of the future course and direction of the party. Is it acceptable to scold or kill party members with different views? This is a matter of fundamental principle. Now I know that the iron hat of being a Trotskyite and a spy was forced on Wang by the killer Kang Sheng. Who knows how many people were attacked during the Cultural Revolution by that big stick who had also attacked Wang Shiwei. I believe that the party Central Committee will conscientiously "clear the poison" and create an environment that will prevent any recurrence of this kind of tragedy.†

---

*In the aftermath of the political liberalization led by Deng Xiaoping and Hu Yaobang begun in late 1978, "seeking truth from facts"—a phrase used to condemn Wang Shiwei in the 1940s—was now invoked, as in many other cases of political rehabilitation, by Liu Ying to clear Wang's name.

†See Liu Ying's reaction to Wang's "rehabilitation" (*pingfan*) in the afterword.

Document 4.5

A Few Aspects of Wang Shiwei's Chairing of the Yan'an Beida [Peking University] Alumni Association and His Conversation with Yang Xikun

An Interview with Comrade Wu Wentao,
December 7, 1986

The Academy for Marxist-Leninist Studies established in Yan'an in May 1938 had a Translation Department specializing in translating works by Marx and Lenin. As I recall, Ke Bainian, He Xilin, and Wang Shiwei, among others, were translators. I first met Wang Shiwei in fall 1938 after the completion of the first program at the college. In January 1939, I was transferred to work in the Propaganda Department. I asked Ke Bonian and Wang Shiwei to copy edit some of the translated articles needed by the organization. Thus I had some contact with them. In the fall of 1941, I left the Propaganda Department and never saw Wang Shiwei again.

There was one incident that left a deep impression on me.

From May to July, 1944, a delegation of Chinese and foreign journalists visited Yan'an. Those in the delegation, besides the leader Xie Baojiao and deputy leader Deng Youde, were staff members working for the KMT's Propaganda Department, including my former Beida classmate Yang Xikun.

At that time, in order to win over more KMT personnel [to the communist cause] the Committee of the Beida Alumni Association was established with Fan Wenlan as the chairman and myself as secretary. Yang Xikun was invited to join the meeting. Wang Shiwei was a Beida graduate, so he was also invited. During the criticism of Wang Shiwei in Yan'an, the KMT was actively spreading the rumor that Wang Shiwei, together with ten or so other party members, had been persecuted to death. The KMT also held a Memorial Service' for those people. Wang Shiwei's presence at the conference would prove the KMT rumor untrue.

As I remember it, about twenty Beida graduates participated in the meeting. He Xilin and Ji Jianbo may have also participated. When Wang Shiwei was introduced at the conference to Yang Xikun, he was greatly shocked. In Wang's impromptu speech he said: "I made some mistakes in Yan'an but I am leading a good life. Xi'an claims that I have been persecuted to death. Everyone has a family! If my family members heard of this, imagine their anxiety. Due to your [KMT] blockade, I cannot make contact with my family. Thus, I would be very grateful if my schoolmate Yang would upon his return inform my family of the truth. I shall be very grateful."

Yang could do nothing but mumble something to get through the embarrassing situation.

Document 4.6

Translations from the Academy for Marxist-Leninist Studies and Wang Shiwei

An Interview with Comrade He Xilin, October 9, 1986

May 5, 1938, was the hundredth anniversary of Marx's birthday. On that day, the Academy for Marxist-Leninist Studies was established. Its main task was to train cadres. To meet educational needs, several research departments were set up: Marxism, Problems in China, Philosophy, Political Economy, etc. In addition, a Translation Department specializing in translating and compiling works by Marx and Lenin was also established. The director of the translation department was concurrently held by Luo Fu (Zhang Wentian) who paid great attention to the translation of Marx's and Lenin's writings. This department, with only a few members, was directly led by him, though there were some changes in personnel. But it was the first organ in our party's history specializing in translating works by Marx and Lenin.

The main task of the department was to translate and compile the Marx-Engels Series and the *Selected Works of Lenin*. The translation and compilation work was very heavy. The rule was that each person would translate a thousand words per day, 360,000 words per year. At that time, working conditions were extremely bad: There were neither necessary reference materials nor useful dictionaries. We could only rely on my *Comprehensive English-Chinese Dictionary* published by the Commercial Press. Those comrades working in German had more difficulties as it was harder to find German-Chinese dictionaries. But in spite of the hardships, everybody worked diligently. In total we published ten titles in the Marx-Engels Series:

The Development of Socialism—From Utopian to Scientific Thought, vol. 3 (Liberation Publishing House, June 1938);

The Communist Manifesto, vol. 4 (Liberation Publishing House, August 1938);

The Civil War in France, vol. 5 (Liberation Publishing House, November 1938);

Essays on Political Economy, vol. 6 (Liberation Publishing House, March 1939);

Selected Letters Between Marx and Engels, vol. 7 (Liberation Publishing House, June 1939);

Revolution and Counterrevolution in Germany, vol. 8 (Liberation Publishing House, April 1939);

Outline of Das Kapital, vol. 9 (Liberation Publishing House, November 1939);

Critique of the Gotha Program, vol. 10 (Liberation Publishing House, December 1939);

The Eighteenth Brumaire of Louis Bonaparte, vol. 11 (Liberation Publishing House, August 1940);

The Class Struggles in France, vol. 12 (Liberation Publishing House, July 1942).

We did not finish the publication of *Selected Works of Lenin* until 1947 after the withdrawal from Yan'an. Most of the translations were done by the Translation and Compilation Department. The rest were copied from the Chinese translations published in Moscow.

Publication of those works advanced enormously the theoretical study of Marxist and Leninist works by the entire party and in all the anti-Japanese bases. It played a significant role in improving the proficiency of Marxist-Leninist theory for the entire party. Most of the selections in the Marx-Engels Series and *Selected Works of Lenin* were republished by the Xinhua [New China News Agency] Newspaper (located in the KMT-controlled region), by Life Bookstore, China Publishing House, and by some other publishing houses in the anti-Japanese Democratic Base areas.

I came to Yan'an in spring 1938. I was the first to work in the Translation and Compilation Department soon after it was established at the Academy for Marxist-Leninist Studies. Ke Bainian (Li Chunfan) arrived after me, and Wang Shiwei was the third. There were very short intervals in between. We three were the only people at the department at the beginning. Later on, Wang Xuewen (vice president), Zhang Zhongshi, Jing Lin, Zhao Feike, Chen Boda (later the director of the department), Zhu Zhongzang, Chen Xie, and another person whose name I can't remember, were also recruited. Altogether there were about ten people in the department. Later, the Department set up a

"Compilation Group on the General History of China" composed of a fewer number.

During those days, Wang Shiwei lived to the right of my cave while Wang Xuewen and his wife were on my left. I stopped seeing Wang Shiwei in May 1941 when the Academy for Marxist-Leninist Studies was changed to the Central Research Institute. The department was removed and I was transferred to work at the Central Political Research Office.

Wang Shiwei was involved in the translation of the Marx-Engels Series and *Selected Works of Lenin. Essays on Political Economy* (volume six) was actually translated jointly by Wang Shiwei and me though he only translated Marx's essay titled "Value, Price, and Profit." I translated "Employment, Labor, and Capital" and some other short articles by Marx and Engels. The book was published by Liberation Publishing House in Yan'an in March 1939. Wang Xuewen's name was also on the book because he was the copy editor. That book was later republished many times in the KMT controlled regions and the anti-Japanese base areas. It was also republished during the Liberation War era and after 1949. Wang Shiwei and Ke Bainian jointly translated Marx's *Revolution and Counterrevolution in Germany* (Marx-Engels Series, volume eight) to which Wang contributed more than Ke. Wang also translated part of the *Selected Works of Lenin.*

Wang Shiwei was an eccentric person in Yan'an famous for his bad temperament. He didn't get along with others and was arrogant. He ignored other people's criticisms and was very argumentative. He tended to go to extremes in viewing things. He neither admitted his own mistakes nor intended to examine them. His specialty was the humanities; therefore, he did not quite understand some of the special terms in Marxism and Leninism. In fact, he had some technical problems in translating some of Marx's works on political economy. Whenever some comrades pointed out some of his incorrect translations, he became so stubborn that he did not allow anyone to alter his version.

Our work at the department was well-paid. Our wages were 4.50 yuan per month, just slightly lower than the 5 yuan per month received by high-level cadres. We got additional pay for translation work—one yuan per thousand words or sometimes 0.50 yuan per thousand words. Part of our royalties received from publishing houses in Chongqing and other places were voluntarily handed over to Liberation Publishing House. The rest went to the Academy for Marxist-Leninist Studies to subsidize other publications.

Afterword: The Rehabilitation of Wang Shiwei*

After the Public Security Department publicized last year the document "Concerning the Decision to Reinvestigate the Trotskyite Problem of Wang Shiwei," having been wrongly accused forty-nine years ago, Wang Shiwei was finally rehabilitated.

Wang Shiwei, original name Shu Han, began as a translator and writer in 1930. In 1937, he traveled to Yan'an and became involved in translating Marx and Lenin's works as well as writing critical essays. During the Yan'an rectification he published a series of critical essays titled "Wild Lilies." In 1942, Wang Shiwei was wrongly accused of three crimes: "counterrevolutionary," "Trotskyite spy," "hidden KMT spy," and "member of the Five Member Anti-Party Gang." Afterward, he was wrongly executed.

Following the [1978] Third Plenum, the CCP Organization Department rendered a decision in February 1982 that denied the existence of the so-called Five Member Anti-Party Gang. The August 1986 version of the *Mao Zedong Reader* publicly acknowledged that regarding the [original] footnote on Wang Shiwei, "the accusation that Wang Shiwei was a hidden KMT spy was untrue." The document issued on February 7, 1991, "Concerning the Decision to Reinvestigate the Trotskyite Problem of Wang Shiwei," stated: "Upon reinvestigation, it is clear that Comrade Wang Shiwei accepted and sympathized with some Trotskyite views and helped translate some of Trotsky's works as the result of his contact with former Beida schoolmates Wang Fanxi and Chen Qingchen (both were Trotskyites) and during his stay in Shanghai.

---

*From the *Literary Journal* (Wenxue bao), February 20, 1992, reproduced in *Literary Digest* (Wenzhai bao), no. 908, weekly supplement to *People's Daily*, March 1, 1992.

In some of the materials containing Wang Shiwei's confession, Wang kept changing his story regarding whether he had participated in the Trotskyite organization. No evidence turned up during the reinvestigation proved that Wang Shiwei was ever involved with the Trotskyite organization. Thus, the conclusion against Wang Shiwei as a counter-revolutionary spy should be rectified and therefore Wang, who was wrongly executed during the [civil] war, should be rehabilitated."

Wang Shiwei's wife, comrade Liu Ying, is now eighty-five years old. Two comrades from the Public Security Department delivered this decision on Wang Shiwei to her, together with 10,000 yuan as consolation money (*weiwen jin*). Upon reading the decision restoring the appellation "comrade" to Wang Shiwei, tears streamed down Liu Ying's face. However, she absolutely refused to accept the money. Later, to memorialize Wang Shiwei, she decided to contribute the funds to the literary and artistic association in her resident town (Shiyan, Hubei Province) as part of its award to young writers.

A Few Words on the Commemoration of Shiwei

LIU YING

Wang Shiwei, as with many intellectuals in his time, explored all sorts of ways and struggled bravely to rescue the country and to achieve socialism! Shiwei was an intellectual with acute and sharp insight on society. He had his own idiosyncratic view of the various facets of human nature. From his perspective, human nature had a glorious aspect, but also an ugly side. Although internal factors have a great impact on the development of human nature, he believed the role of external factors in shaping and guarding the human condition cannot be ignored. He also thought that socialism was the best system for controlling this ugly and vicious side of human beings. In the past during many conversations, he frequently used his views on human nature to explain human behavior and various social phenomena. However, the kind of socialism that was bent and twisted by the leftist trend in Eastern Europe and the former Soviet Union fostered the ugly and vicious side of the human condition. Shiwei never realized the cause and effect relationship between the leftist poison and this ugly and vicious side of human nature, though he did warn against the dangers of corruption.

Recently, Mr. Deng [Xiaoping's] "Speech during the Inspection Tour in the South" has advanced the antileftist trend in the entire country. The speech is also a special contribution to the spiritual development of China. I sincerely hope that in its new twist the original glorious image of socialism will finally be revealed.

November 13, 1992

Appendix A: Namelist*

—Chen Qingchen (?–1937), former name Chen Qichang; joined the CCP at an early age, later became a Trotskyite and member of the Proletarian Society.

—He Xilin (1914–), translator of Marx-Lenin works, secretary of the party committee of Beijing Normal University, and consultant to the Bureau of Compilation and Translation after 1949.

—Jin Ziguang (1917–), contemporary drama writer, musician, deputy director of Beijing People's Drama House, deputy director of the North Kun Opera House in Northern China, and deputy director of the National Historic Relics Commission after 1949.

—Kai Feng (1906–1955), original name He Kaifeng. At one time the vice minister (*fubu zhang*) of the CCP's Propaganda Department.

—Ke Bainian (1904–1985), senior translator of Marx-Engels works, director of the United States-Australia Section of the Foreign Affairs Ministry, ambassador to Romania and Denmark, deputy director of the Institute of International Relations, and vice chairman of the China Political-Legal Association.

—Li Yan (?–1984), after 1949 Standing Deputy Director and party secretary of the Department of Law, CASS, and representative to the Third and Fifth National People's Congress.

—Liu Xuewei (1912–), art theorist and, presently, consultant to China Encyclopedia Publishing House.

—Rong Mengyuan (1913–1985), famous historian, researcher at the Institute of Modern History of CASS.

—Wang Duqing (1898–1940), literary figure, former provost of the Shanghai Art University [before 1949], member of the "Creation Society," editor in chief of *Creation Monthly* (Chuangzao yuekan); became a Trotskyite later on and was dismissed from the Creation Society.

---

*The information in this appendix was provided by Yong Guiliang of the Chinese Communist Party School library.

—Wang Fanxi, real name Wang Wenyuan, Trotskyite, and member of the October Society.

—Wen Jize (1915–), former president of the Graduate School of CASS.

—Yin Bai (1918–), pen name of Zhang Jingqiu, contemporary writer.

—Zhang Ruxin (1908–1976), famous philosopher, member of CASS. Previously, president of Northeast University and Northeast Normal University, and also director of the party History Department of the Central Committee's Central Party School.

—Zheng Chaolin (1900–), joined the CCP as a youth, later on became a Trotskyite, member of the Proletarian Society, and presently a member of the Shanghai Political Consultative Conference.

Appendix B: Research Materials on the Wang Shiwei Question, Selected Documents (Complete List)*

Section One: Wang Shiwei's Works

Introduction (*Shuoming*).
•"Preface to 'Education and Cultivation of Youth' "
(Lenin) (September 20, 1938) [Document 1.1].
"Old Mistakes and New Tendencies in National Forms of Litera-ture" (*Zhongguo wenhua*, vol. 2, no. 6, April 22, 1941).
•"Wild Lilies" [Book text].
•"Politicians, Artists" [Document 1.2].
•"My Criticisms of Luo Mai's Speech at the Mobilization Meeting for Rectification and Examination of Work" [Document 1.3].
•"Two Random Thoughts" (March 23, 1942) [Document 1.4].
•"Response to Comrades Li Yuchao [and Mei Luo]" [Document 1.5].

Section Two: Yan'an Period Criticism of Wang Shiwei

•Introduction.
Mao Zedong, "Talk at the forum on changing the format of *Libera-tion Daily*" (March 31, 1942) (see *Selected Writings of Mao Zedong on Journalism*).
Qi Su, "Thoughts After Reading 'Wild Lilies' " (April 7, 1942).

---

*Below is a translation of the full table of contents for the documents and interview transcripts compiled by Song Jinshou in 1986 for the study of Wang Shiwei. The collection is part of the manuscript Dai Qing gave Professor David Apter in 1988, but unlike the main text it has not been published. Copies of these documents and interviews are on file at the Fairbank Center Library, Harvard University, and will be available through the Center for Chinese Research Materi-als (Oakton, Virginia). Documents translated in the present volume are marked by bullets (•).—Eds.

Jin Canran, "After Reading Comrade Wang Shiwei's 'Politicians, Artists' " (May 17, 1942).

Mao Zedong, "Talks at the Yan'an Forum on Literature and Art" (May 23, 1942) (see *Selected Works of Mao Zedong*).

[Li] Bozhao, "Additional Thoughts on 'Some Feelings After Reading Wild Lilies' " (May 23, 1942).

Fan Wenlan, "On Comrade Wang Shiwei's Ideological Consciousness" (June 9, 1942).

Chen Boda, "Concerning Wang Shiwei's Speech at the Central Research Institute Forum" (June 9, 1942).

Zhang Ruxin, "Thoroughly Smash Wang Shiwei's Trotskyite Theories and Anti-Party Activities—Speech at the Central Research Institute Struggle Meeting" (June 10, 1942).

Ding Ling, "The Literary and Art Circle's Correct Attitude and Their Self-Examination Regarding Wang Shiwei—Speech at the Central Research Institute Struggle Meeting" (June 11, 1942) .

Luo Mai, "On the Ideological Debate in the Central Research Institute —From the Mobilization Meetings to the Forum" (June 11, 1942).

Fan Wenlan, "Speech at the Central Research Institute Forum" (June 11, 1942).

Zhou Wen, "From Lu Xun's Critical Essays to a Discussion of [Wang] Shiwei" (June 12, 1942).

•Wen Jize, "Diary of a Struggle" (June 1942) [Document 2.1].

Ai Qing, "Reality Does Not Permit Distortion" (June 16, 1942).

•"Resolution of the Yan'an Literature and Art Circles Forum on the Trotskyite Wang Shiwei" (June 18, 1942) [Document 2.2].

Chen Boda, "Writing After Reading Comrade Wang Shiwei's 'A Short Discussion on National Forms of Literature' " (dated January 7, 1941; first printed July 1942).

Zhou Yang, "Wang Shiwei's Literary Views and Ours" (July 28, 1942).

•Zhang Ruxin, "General Summary of Ideological Remolding in the Central Research Institute Since the Start of Rectification—Report on Party Rectification in the Central Research Institute" (September 1942) [Document 2.3].

Ai Siqi, "How to Reform Our Study—Report at the Conclusion of Study at the Central Research Institute" (September 1942).

•Yang Shangkun, "Activities of the Trotskyite Wang Shiwei and Liberalism in the Party" (October 31, 1942) [Document 2.4].

•"Abstract of Kang Sheng's Report to a Training Class" (August 1943) [Document 2.5].

Section Three: Use of the Wang Shiwei Question by KMT Diehards to Fabricate Rumors

Introduction.

"Preface to "Wild Lilies and Others" (selections).

Gu You, "Introducing Wild Lilies—The Most Popular Recent Short Story" (August 28, 1942).

"Notice Commemorating the Cruel Death of a Close Friend in Yan'an" (March 27, 1944).

"Memorial Meeting for the Yan'an Martyr Opens Yesterday" (March 30, 1944).

"Notice of Formal Thanks from the Preparatory Meeting for Commemorating the Cruel Death of a Close Friend in Yan'an" (April 1, 1944).

Section Four: Records of Investigations and Interviews on the Wang Shiwei Question

•Introduction.

•"Conversation with Li Yan on the Question of Wang Shiwei as a Trotskyite" (May 9, 1980) [Document 4.1].

•"Wen Jize on a Few Limitations of the Wang Shiwei Case" (June 9, 1980) [Document 4.2].

"On the Circumstances of Wang Shiwei—Interview with Comrade Pan Fang" (December 10, 1980).

•"On the Circumstances of Yan'an's 'Five Member Anti-Party Gang'—Interview with Comrade Wang Ruqi" (January 7, 1981) [Document 4.3].

•"Comrade Liu Ying's Appeal" (August 15, 1981) [Document 4.4].

"Resolution of Rehabilitation Concerning the Four Comrades Pan Fang, Zong Zheng, Chen Chuangang, and Wang Ruqi and the So-Called 'Five Member Anti-Party Gang' " (February 2, 1982).

Song Shu, "On the Wang Shiwei Issue" (*Party History News*) (August 1984).

Wang Fanxi, "Wang Shiwei and the 'Wang Shiwei Problem' " (February 10, 1985) [*The Nineties*], Hong Kong, May 1985.

•"A Few Aspects of Wang Shiwei's Chairing of the Yan'an Beida Alumni Association [Meeting] and His Conversation with Yang Xikun: An Interview with Comrade Wu Wentao" (December 7, 1986) [Document 4.5].

•"Translations from the Academy for Marxist-Leninist Studies and Wang Shiwei—Interview with Comrade He Xilin" (October 9, 1986) [Document 4.6].

"Extract of a Letter from Zheng Chaolin" (October 23, 1986).

"Wang Shiwei's Early Years," compiled by Wang Lizhi.

Index

Academy for Marxist-Leninist
Studies, 11, 183–84, 185–87
see also Central Research Institute
"Activities of the Trotskyite Wang
Shiwei and Liberalism in the
Party" (Yang), 135–45
Ai Qing, 110
Ai Siqi, xxx*n.6*, 41, 49, 103, 105,
106–7
Anti-Confucian Campaign, 169*n*
"April 12" massacre, 23
Arrow and Target (wall newspaper),
xxiii, 20–21, 37, 41, 146
Art, 45, 52–53, 76*n.29*, 79
Autobiography. *See* Ideological
autobiography

Beida Alumni Association, 183–84
Bo Gu, 74*n.11*
Bukharin, Nikolai, 180*n*

Cadre uniform, 20*n*
Camel Bell, 146
Cao Mengjun, 26, 165, 175
Cao Yiou, 74*n.11*
CASS. *See* Chinese Academy of
Social Sciences
CCP Organization Department, 159
Central Investigation Bureau, 158
Centralism, 117
see also Democratic-centralism
Central Propaganda Department, 52
Central Research Institute, 11–12,
140, 144, 149, 153
Central Social Department, 41, 54, 162
Changsha (China), 181

Chen Boda, xxi, 18*n*, 31, 33, 34–35,
49, 61–62, 108, 110, 136, 149,
152, 162, 186
Chen Dao, 21
Chen Duxiu, 44, 173
Chen Jie. *See* Chen Jusun
Chen Jusun, 34–35
Chen Qingchen, 22, 24, 54–56,
190
Chen Weizhen, 174
Chen Xie, 186
Chen Yi, 69*n*
Cheng Quan, 62–63, 80, 135–45, 146,
149–55, 162, 164–70
letter to Mao, 146–48
Cheng Shaozong, 178
China Women (journal), 165–66
Chinese Academy of Social Sciences
(CASS), 11
Clothing, xxii, 20, 36
Coercion, 122
Committee to Examine Rectification
Work, xxii, 14–16, 94
"Concerning the Decision to
Reinvestigate the Trotskyite
Problem of Wang Shiwei,"
189–90
Condemnation, 122
Criticism, 93
see also Self-criticism
Cultural Revolution, xxv, 106*n*,
182

Dai Li, 150
December Twelfth Movement, 165
Democracy, 117, 123, 148
see also Extreme democratization

Dai Qing, daughter of a revolutionary martyr, adopted by a famous marshal, trained at an elite military academy, employed first as a missile technician then as an agent for military intelligence, the columnist with the most devoted following in one of China's largest dailies, and, in 1989, prisoner in the infamous Qin-Cheng Prison. Ms. Dai wrote this story, which the Chinese Communist Party concealed for half a century.